The Development of American Petroleum Pipelines:

A Study in Private Enterprise and Public Policy,

1862-1906

Prepared and published under the direction of the American Historical Association from the income of the Albert J. Beveridge Memorial Fund.

The Development of

American Petroleum Pipelines:

A STUDY IN PRIVATE ENTERPRISE

AND PUBLIC POLICY, 1862–1906

By Arthur Menzies Johnson

DEPARTMENT OF ENGLISH, HISTORY, AND GOVERNMENT

UNITED STATES NAVAL ACADEMY

PUBLISHED FOR

The American Historical Association

CORNELL UNIVERSITY PRESS

ITHACA, NEW YORK

PRINTED IN THE UNITED STATES OF AMERICA BY THE

VAIL-BALLOU PRESS, INC., BINGHAMTON, NEW YORK

To my wife, Emily Wilford Johnson

Preface

WHY anyone not connected with the petroleum industry should choose to write about the history of pipelines is a question that I have been frequently asked. It is a question that the reader certainly has a right to raise and to which he deserves an answer.

This study began in a seminar at Vanderbilt University in 1951 as an investigation of the striking similarity between the charges made in the United States Industrial Commission hearings of 1899 against the practices of pipeline companies and those made in the Temporary National Economic Committee hearings more than forty years later. Although during the intervening period interstate petroleum pipelines had been declared common carriers and placed under federal supervision, the complaints made chiefly against the lines of a single company before the turn of the century were in effect repeated by a new generation of critics against a group of companies. It was this facet of the development of pipeline enterprises that first called my attention to the underground oil carriers.

Even limited investigation showed that the apparent conflict between private enterprise and public policy in this field was firmly rooted in the historical context of pipeline development. Research, conducted in Washington from 1951 to 1953, indicated that the role of pipelines in the formative period of the petroleum industry had never been assigned the importance that it deserved. Experience gained as historian of the development and use of new weapons in our current national defense effort taught me that the cumulative impact of decisions once made is not easily counteracted. Research on the decisions made in the early development of petroleum pipelines, which were competitive weapons in a new industry, showed that this observation was just as applicable to that field. I was, therefore, led to explore further the forces at work in the development of pipelines.

It proved impossible to separate an investigation of pipelines from a study of their relation to the other branches of the petroleum industry. It soon became apparent that the effort to sway public opinion and to influence public policy in the interests of the parties to an intra-industry contest for profits had obscured the true nature of the struggle and given rise to misconceptions that have persisted to the present. My purpose in this book, therefore, is to trace the relationship of private enterprise to public policy in connection with an obscure but important segment of the larger conflict. I selected the terminal date of 1906 because it coincides with the emergence of the pipeline problem as an issue of public policy on the national scene. By that time the framework of the problem was firmly molded by past decisions on public policy and private enterprise. Future changes would require a new process of historical evolution. I believe that in microcosm the development of pipelines is typical of what was happening throughout American industry in our post-Civil War age of enterprise.

Many people have contributed to whatever merit this work may have. I am grateful to Professor Frederick Merk of Harvard, who first introduced me to economic history and set standards to which I still aspire. Drs. William C. Binkley, Robert A. Lively, Henry L. Swint, and Dewey W. Grantham, Jr., guided this work through various stages as a dissertation at Vanderbilt University and were unfailing in their encouragement, assistance, and constructive criticism. Mrs. J. C. Swingley of the Vanderbilt History Department and Mrs. Carol McCarthy typed the manuscript through seemingly endless versions. Miss Rosabelle Kelp prepared the index.

I am happy to acknowledge the co-operation of the Library of Congress in providing the maps and the photograph of Henry

Harley. The Drake Well Museum, Titusville, Pennsylvania, kindly provided the remaining illustrations.

I am deeply indebted to the Beveridge Award Committee of the American Historical Association for the honor they have done me in selecting my manuscript for publication. Dr. Ralph W. Hidy, who supervised revision of the manuscript, gave generously of his expert knowledge and has saved me from many errors. Those that remain are entirely my own.

ARTHUR M. JOHNSON

Annapolis, Maryland
July 15, 1955

Contents

Illustrations and Maps

The Development of American Petroleum Pipelines:

A Study in Private Enterprise and Public Policy,

1862–1906

I

The Introduction and Early Development of Petroleum Pipelines, 1862-1872

THE role of pipelines in the development of the American petroleum industry provides the basis for an illuminating comparison between two instruments of economic development—private enterprise and public policy. Pipelines, the product of enterprise in oil transportation, became the weapons of enterprise for railroads, oil producers, and oil refiners. Efforts to offset the competitive advantages that they gave their owners made pipelines the subject of public policy proposals stemming from intra-industry conflict. Neither the public nor its elected representatives, state or national, appeared deeply concerned with the nature of pipeline ownership and operation. Even within the industry, proposals for public policy affecting these matters were sporadic and generally ineffective. A tremendous aggregation of pipeline power under unified control resulted. When national political policy threatened this power, virtually the entire petroleum industry raised its voice in protest. An explanation of this apparent paradox lies in the pattern of relationships between enterprise and public policy woven throughout the early development of American petroleum pipelines.

Pipelines were introduced to collect oil and to transport it over the rugged terrain of the Pennsylvania Oil Regions to railroad depots.[1] These so-called "gathering" pipelines offered the economy and efficiency which insured their triumph over the wagons that dominated this trade in the early days of the oil industry. They also offered their patrons the difference between subjection to the demands of a single railroad and the opportunity to invoke railroad competition. Eventually the economies of pipeline transportation resulted in "trunk" pipelines displacing the railroads as the main transporters of crude oil on long hauls. In short, pipelines developed from feeders into rivals of the railroads for the crude oil traffic. The process of this change and its results had significant repercussions throughout the petroleum industry. The first steps in this direction resulted from the fiercely competitive struggle for the rewards which lay in the torrent of oil that streamed from the mud farms of western Pennsylvania in the 1860's.

Early Methods of Crude Oil Transportation

Writing of his visit to the Pennsylvania oil fields in the fall of 1865, the British financier, Sir Samuel Morton Peto, declared, "The great difficulty which has hitherto attended the oil trade has been transport." [2] As he pointed out, the production of oil was easy compared with the difficulty and cost of transporting it to the consumer. Provided with an adequate railroad network, the Oil Regions could send its product throughout the nation, but to get the oil aboard the railroad cars in quantity safely and cheaply required a revolution in transportation. Even as Sir Samuel was traveling the mud-choked roads of the valley of oil, this revolution was in the making with the completion of the first successful crude oil pipeline.

When oil was discovered close to Oil Creek in Titusville, Pennsylvania in August, 1859, there were but two ways of moving it out of the area—boats and wagons. The fact that Oil Creek emptied into the Allegheny River made water transportation to Pittsburgh a natural avenue for the oil trade. Boats of all types were quickly pressed into use, ranging from the small "guiper" boats carrying 25 to 50 barrels of oil to "bulk" boats 120 feet in length and capable of carrying over 1,000 barrels.[3] The smaller craft were towed up Oil Creek and its tributaries; when they were loaded, arrangements were made with the local sawmills to release the water which the mills usually stored for floating logs downstream. On these freshets the oil boats floated down Oil Creek to Oil City, where their cargoes were transferred to larger boats for the voyage to Pittsburgh, 132 miles away. On a single freshet 10,000 to 20,000 barrels of oil could be brought out without serious mishap.[4]

The hazards of boating on the creek were many. In the rush of boats downstream on a freshet, an accident to one might mean the destruction of those following in its wake. Insufficient water in the freshet of May, 1863, resulted in the grounding of numerous boats and the loss of 1,500 barrels of oil.[5] The preceding December 150 boats and 30,000 barrels of oil were lost when an ice gorge broke loose on Oil Creek.[6] Fire in the closely packed oil fleet was another constant and deadly menace.

Despite these drawbacks, in the early days of the petroleum industry, boats provided the only link between the wells and the shipping and refining center of Pittsburgh. At the height of this traffic 1,000 boats were in use as well as 20 to 30 steamers, passenger boats, and towboats.[7]

Rising oil production stimulated railroad construction in the Oil Regions. North of the producing district, the only rail outlet for oil prior to May, 1861, was the Sunbury and Erie Railroad running between Warren and Erie, Pennsylvania.[8] Its closest station was at Corry, more than twenty miles from Titusville. The Atlantic and Great Western Railroad reached Corry in 1861 and by 1863 had been extended to Franklin, seven miles west of Oil City. In the same year the road also gained access to Cleveland, thus opening up a new market for oil as well as providing service to New York through its connections with the Erie Railroad. Meantime, the gap between Titusville and Corry had been closed by construction of the Oil Creek Railroad, which opened October 1, 1862. In the next two years it was extended to Shaffer Farm, seven miles below Titusville. In the summer of 1864 Thomas A. Scott, vice-president of the Pennsylvania Railroad, and Dean Richmond, president of the New York Central Railroad, purchased control of the line.[9] The Pennsylvania had already secured control of the Sunbury and Erie, whose name had been changed to the Philadelphia and Erie, and was thus in a position to compete with the Atlantic and Great Western for crude oil shipments eastward.

Improvements in the bulk transportation of oil by the railroads were quickly made. The first railway "tank car" consisted of two wooden tanks, each of approximately 40 barrels' capacity, mounted on a flatcar. This arrangement was widely adopted, but by 1869 it was replaced by the iron-boiler tank car. Long lines of these cars, waiting to be loaded from the storage tanks at the various depots throughout the Regions, became a familiar sight.[10]

Oil had to be brought from the wells to the railroads, and initially the only means at hand was the horse-drawn wagon. This method of oil transportation at its peak employed six thousand two-horse teams.[11] A correspondent of the Philadelphia *Press* in 1863 found 1,800 such vehicles serving Titusville from the oil wells. In July, 1865, two thousand teams were counted passing over the Franklin Street Bridge in Titusville in one day.[12] The cost in horses, lost oil, and profanity, as these teams, loaded with five to seven barrels weighing 360 pounds each, lumbered through the mud of the oil farms, was staggering.

The teamster was well repaid for his trouble. He reportedly charged extra for each mud hole in which he got stuck and double if the wheels sank to the hub. A driver employed by Barney Bosch of Titusville, working steadily for nine weeks, made $1,900. Small wonder that men who had witnessed such rewards for crude oil transportation wrote: "Rich, indeed, was the golden harvest reaped by teamsters and boatmen in those days. They made their own terms, regardless of the ruling prices of the product, never failing to take advantage of the necessities of the shipper." [13] Small wonder that Sir Samuel Peto was moved to write of the "very excessive charges for the carriage of the oil" occasioned by the fact that "everything has to be hauled through an immense slough." [14]

The Introduction of Pipelines

Clearly there was a pressing need for a more efficient and less costly method of moving crude oil from the wells than by wagons. The idea of using pipes to perform this carrying function had appeared as early as 1860, but the commercial success of gathering pipelines awaited five years of experimentation and development. The final result had not yet proved itself when Sir Samuel visited the Oil Regions. Consequently, he failed to report on a development that

was soon to make the "execrable roads" of the Oil Regions no obstacle to the rapid local transportation of oil.

Apparently the first proposal to construct a gathering pipeline
was made by Samuel Duncan Karns in November, 1860. He proposed building one to transport oil from a well at Burning Springs,
Virginia, to the Ohio River, but the outbreak of the Civil War in-
terfered with this project.[15] Young Karns joined the Union Army,
from which he returned to make a successful career in the oil business.

In November, 1861, Heman Janes, one of the producers on the
Tarr Farm, five and one-half miles above Oil City, proposed construction of a wooden pipeline to connect the producing area with
that shipping point. He was advised, however, to postpone the
undertaking pending legislative action on a general pipeline charter.
With the votes of four thousand teamsters in the balance, the legislature failed to act and Janes's line was not built.[16]

The same legislature, on the other hand, did not hesitate to grant
the Oil Creek Transportation Company the exclusive privilege of
transporting oil by pipes or tubes from any point on Oil Creek to the
mouth of the creek or to the Philadelphia and Erie Railroad.[17] Such
legislative favors were not uncommon, and, although this favor was
not put to immediate use, the rights it conveyed later made the charter of this company the cornerstone of the first great pipeline corporation.

The first demonstration of the potentialities of pipelines was made
on a limited scale by James L. Hutchings, a New York inventor and
engineer. In the fall of 1862 he constructed a successful pipeline for
Barrows and Company of Tarr Farm, connecting one of their wells
with a refinery one thousand feet away. Although the line operated
on the siphon principle, which was not practical for great distances,
Hutchings was confident that a rotary pump which he had invented
would overcome this problem. With the backing of the producers at
Tarr Farm and Foster Farm, he constructed two pipelines in 1863.
The first was a two-inch, cast-iron pipe from the Tarr Farm to the
Humboldt refinery below Plumer, a distance of two and one-half
miles.[18] A pump at Tarr Farm and two others along the route were
utilized to force the oil over an elevation four hundred feet above
Oil Creek, but neither the pumps nor the cast-iron pipe proved

adequate for the job.[19] This failure did not deter Hutchings from another effort, and in the winter of 1863–1864 he constructed a line from the Sherman well to the Oil Creek Railroad station at Miller Farm, a distance of three miles. With its protruding pumps, which resembled ornamental fence posts, the long line of pipe excited considerable curiosity. This second undertaking suffered the same fate as its predecessor, however, and teamsters finished the project by tearing up the pipes.[20]

That same winter the Warren refinery at Plumer, avoiding Hutchings' mistake, used wrought-iron pipes in the construction of a successful line to transport refined oil.[21] But, an ill-starred five-inch line of cast iron constructed between the Noble well and the Shaffer Farm station of the Oil Creek Railroad leaked "like a fifty-cent umbrella." [22]

A slackening of production, coupled with an enlarging market and an advance in the value of gold, early in 1864 had touched off an oil boom, which brought large profits to all branches of the industry.[23] Samuel Van Syckel, a pioneer in the production of kerosene, who came to Titusville in the fall of 1864, later recalled: "I saw, when I reached Titusville, that the most money was to be made in shipping oil. I made a dollar a barrel, and in six months I was $100,000 in pocket. The land speculation I wouldn't touch. It was wild. It scared me to see men sitting around on logs, and trading off little pieces of land for hundreds of thousands of dollars." [24]

Reaping their share of this golden flood, the teamsters attempted to protect their profitable enterprise. In 1864, for example, they successfully blocked a scheme for laying a pipeline down the Allegheny River to Pittsburgh.[25]

An analysis of the costs involved in the shipment of a barrel of oil in the fall of 1864, however, shows why the teamsters could not much longer bar the march of progress in oil transportation. In October, 1864, oil was selling at the well for $7.00 a barrel, and it was bringing $15.58 in New York. It cost $1.50 to haul it to the railroad station at Titusville or Franklin, and the rail charges from there to New York were $3.60. The barrel itself cost $3.25 new and had a resale value of $2.50. If the shipper retained the barrel, his gross profit was only 23 cents. If he sold it, the figure rose to $2.73.[26] The cost of the container necessary for transportation of the oil and the charge for moving it by team thus represented the difference between a wide or narrow profit margin for the shipper. Pipelines, which would eliminate the cumbersome and expensive barrel and its horse-drawn conveyance, offered the prospect of large dividends to those who could choose a method of money-making so pedestrian in comparison with land speculation.

By the spring of 1865 conditions invited pipeline development. During the winter the Atlantic and Great Western Railroad had extended its tracks into Oil City, relieving the Oil Creek Railroad, whose facilities had been severely taxed by the flow of oil and the Atlantic and Great Western's inability to provide cars at Corry.[27] A new boom in oil production had commenced with the discovery of flowing wells along Pithole Creek, which emptied into the Allegheny eight miles above Oil City. A frenzy of oil speculation hit the Regions. The Holmden farm, on which the Frazier well started flowing at the rate of 250 barrels a day in January, 1865, sold for $25,000. In September of the same year it was resold for $2,000,000.[28] The rise of Pithole City was just as meteoric. The town plot was laid out in May, 1865, and within six months it boasted between four hundred and five hundred houses as well as fifty hotels.[29]

The Pithole boom offered a challenge to transportation. David Kirk, later a prominent figure in pipeline activities, succeeded in teaming the first oil out of the Pithole area. Over three thousand teamsters were soon engaged in transporting oil to the river and railroad depots.[30] Samuel Van Syckel arrived on the scene as an oil buyer and soon had visions of becoming the only buyer by cornering the supply of barrels. Even had he obtained control of the oil containers, he would still have had to reckon with the teamsters. With a pipeline, however, he would need neither barrels nor teamsters. Accordingly, with $30,000 borrowed from the First National Bank of Titusville, Van Syckel and his partners commenced construction of a pipeline between Pithole and the Miller Farm station of the Oil Creek Railroad.

The pipeline project met with little encouragement from Van Syckel's friends and with active opposition from the teamsters. To avoid the ridicule of even his close friends, whose favorite jibe was, "Do you expect to put a girdle around the earth?" Van Syckel reportedly took to eating alone at his hotel. The hostility of the teamsters was a far more serious matter. They had wrecked previous efforts at pipeline construction, and they threatened this one. Along the route of the pipeline placards appeared denouncing it. One of Van Syckel's employees, Alfred W. Smiley, later recalled: "All the officials of the company, including the writer, were threatened by the teamsters with transportation to a warmer climate." [31]

Despite ridicule and active opposition, work went ahead on laying the 32,000 feet of pipe, which came in fifteen-foot sections, whose joints were lap-welded. It was laid partly above ground and partly below ploughshare depth, and, although watchmen were employed to guard it, the teamsters attacked it with pickaxes and attempted to pull it apart with their teams.[32] The sheriff was called in as an added measure of protection while construction continued. Three Reed and Cogswell pumps were installed along the route to force the oil through the line at the rate of 80 barrels an hour; and a telegraph line, to relay information about oil shipments, was added. It was estimated that the line could do the work of three hundred teams working ten hours a day.[33] Moreover, the enthusiastic Pithole correspondent of the _Titusville Morning Herald_ declared: "These pipes will reduce the price of transportation about two dollars per barrel." [34]

Opened October 10, 1865, Van Syckel's pipeline proved an immediate success, and he quickly followed it with a second one from Pithole to Meredith on the Miller Farm. This gathering line was completed in early December, 1865, and was shortly carrying 2,000 barrels of oil a day.[35] Local comment, except by the teamsters, was most favorable. The first pipe was described as "one of the most wonderful of the many wonders produced at Pithole." [36] Charging one dollar a barrel, the lines proved very profitable. Shortly after the opening of the second pipe, the Titusville paper reported: "The two tubes yield a dividend to the owners of over two thousand dollars per day." [37] Here at last was the answer to the mud sloughs and exorbitant charges which had hampered transportation of oil from the wells, and investment in pipelines offered the profits that typically accompany technological innovation.

Although Van Syckel had been the first to complete a pipeline into Pithole, he did not dominate the field for long. Other companies were intent on reaping the rewards of innovation by laying pipes to the Allegheny River, where shipments could be made to Pittsburgh. The Warren Oil Company succeeded in reaching the river with a crude oil pipeline from Pithole to Henry's Bend on the Allegheny. The Pennsylvania Tubing Transportation Company completed a pipeline from Pithole to Oleopolis on the Allegheny in December, 1865. Using gravitation feed, it was capable of delivering 7,500 barrels per day.[38] To store this oil the company erected iron tanks, each capable of holding 15,000 barrels.[39] The projectors of the pipeline were not confident of success, however, for they had graded the route as befitted a railroad and feared that the effect of friction might render it unsatisfactory. Before the job was finished, the company ran into trouble, and David Kirk, who had agreed to provide tankage for the first 30,000 barrels through the pipe, completed it. The initial run of 10,000 barrels in December, 1865, not only paid for the tankage but also provided a reported additional profit of $20,000.[40]

Meanwhile, Titusville shippers had recognized the advantages of gathering oil by pipeline. In November, 1865, they commenced construction of parallel lines connecting Pithole and Titusville. The two-inch, wrought-iron pipes, laid in the same trench but independent of one another, had a daily capacity of 1,000 barrels each. The cost of constructing such a line varied with the conditions encountered. At that time lap-welded, two-inch pipe cost about 45 cents a foot, delivered. Under good circumstances, it cost about $1,000 a mile to dig a trench and lay the pipe to a depth of thirty inches. A force pump and steam engine cost about $800, while a steam boiler for two pumps cost about $2,000.[41] When the Titusville line was opened in March, 1866, it was estimated to represent an investment of $150,000. The cost of operation, provided a constant supply of oil was available, was estimated to be five cents a barrel per pumping station.[42] Charging just enough less than the teamsters in order to displace them, the pipelines offered handsome profits.

The teamsters did not propose to surrender their hold on local crude oil transportation without a struggle. Henry Harley, who laid two pipes between Bennehoff Run, a tributary of Oil Creek, and Shaffer Farm on the Oil Creek Railroad, felt the full impact of the teamsters' wrath. The completion of his line in early March, 1866, destroyed the livelihood of four hundred drivers.[43] Anger against the new pipes mounted steadily and at 3:00 A.M. on the morning of April 18, 1866, an "incendiary mob" of teamsters set fire to Harley's oil tanks at Shaffer. In the resulting conflagration four Oil Creek Railroad cars, each fully loaded with oil, as well as loading platforms, pipes, and about 1,000 barrels of oil, were burned.[44] The loss to Harley and Company was set at $10,000. The fact that one teamster had fallen victim to a guard's bullet did not deter a new attack two days later. This time the damage was placed at $8,000.[45] Harley, far from intimidated, rose to the challenge and proved himself more than a match for his opponents. The damage caused by their vandalism was repaired, and detectives were hired to act as teamsters in an effort to identify the ringleaders. Through their efforts more than twenty teamsters were arrested, and the attacks on the pipeline were ended.[46]

Harley's achievement in overcoming the teamsters was recognized as an important step forward in the introduction of the new form of crude oil transportation. The *Titusville Morning Herald*, reporting the attacks on the line, declared: "This process of moving oil has entirely superseded the old method of hauling oil in barrels from Bennehof[f] to Shaffer." [47] A visitor to Oil Creek informed readers of the *Scientific American* in September, 1866: "Through these pipes the oil flows almost literally out of the wells aboard of the railroad car. The propelling agent is, of course, the steam pump. Thus oil, 600 feet below the surface of the earth at Oil Creek, reaches Jersey City, a distance of over 400 miles, without having been touched by the hand of man." [48]

By January, 1867, the pipeline gathering charge had dropped to 50 cents a barrel.[49] Profits even at this level encouraged pipeline construction and speeded the disappearance of oil-freighting teamsters. The *Titusville Morning Herald* observed that "in the past year or two there has been a complete revolution in the manner of transporting oil, and that instead of piles of barrels and many teams employed, one sees miles of pipe lines and great numbers of tank cars." [50]

Like all innovations, pipelines went through successive stages of development. On the one hand, improvements were made to increase operational efficiency and, on the other, standardized practices and procedures were adopted to facilitate the handling of oil shipments.

None of the early lines connected directly with the wells. This refinement was introduced by Alfred W. Smiley, Van Syckel's buyer at Pithole, and George E. Coutant of New York. They built the Accommodation Pipe Line across the flats of Pithole Creek to connect the tanks at the wells with the dump tanks of the pipelines. Their outfit consisted of one 20-horsepower boiler, one 12x8-inch pump, two 250-barrel tanks, and about four miles of two-inch pipe with fittings. Charging 25 cents a barrel for their service, they quickly displaced the teamsters who charged 50 cents to one dollar. This extension of gathering pipelines to field storage tanks was so successful that it was rapidly adopted by the established pipelines.[51]

The problem of accounting to the producer for the amount of oil drawn off by the pipeline was met by the introduction of the run ticket, which Smiley claimed was first used by the Accommodation Pipe Line in the summer of 1866.[52] Prepared in duplicate, it provided the producer and the pipeline with a record of the amount of oil drawn off by the pipeline as determined by gauging the producer's tanks before and after the pipeline run.

Since the run ticket did not represent ownership of oil, it did not protect the pipeline against producers who sold by transfer oil which they did not actually have in the line. To deal with this problem, certificates for credit balances of oil in the possession of pipelines were introduced in 1868. Usually representing 1,000 barrels of oil credited by the pipeline to the producer, the certificates were fully negotiable and provided a much-needed flexibility in the sale of oil. Credit for introduction of the certificate for credit balances of oil and the run ticket was claimed by Charles P. Hatch, who had entered the business as agent for the Empire Transportation Company at Shaffer Farm in June, 1865.

The early pipeline companies also began the practice of providing storage for oil. A slump in oil prices in 1867 forced rapid expansion of this service as a means of relieving producers of their oil without dumping it on a depressed market. Iron tankage was provided by the pipelines in increasing quantity, and by 1870 storage capacity in the Oil Regions was over 1,000,000 barrels.[53] With facilities for storing as well as transporting oil, the pipeline companies themselves also engaged in purchasing and selling the certificates promising delivery.[54]

Charles Hatch claimed credit not only for introducing run tickets and oil certificates but also for other practices which became standard with pipeline companies. Among these was the deduction of 2 to 3 per cent of each run to cover leakage and evaporation. Prior to the introduction of gauging, oil had been delivered by the pipelines, barrel for barrel. Some loss was, however, inevitable in transit and storage, and the presence of water in the storage tanks had to be taken into account. The deduction was made to cover these items. Since no insurance company would cover losses due to pipeline fires, Hatch, borrowing from the insurance companies the idea of the average assessment, introduced the practice of assessing for such losses all producers with oil in the line.[55]

In a few short years, then, gathering pipelines became an integral part of crude oil transportation. They quickly displaced teams as a means of moving oil from the wells to railroad depots. The storage of oil became an important function of pipeline companies, and oil certificates became the "legal tender" of the oil trade.

The Pipelines and the Railroads

The growing importance of pipelines as feeders made them factors in railroad competition for the oil traffic. Hatch, in fact, made his contributions as superintendent of a pipeline belonging to the Pennsylvania Railroad's fast-freight affiliate, the Empire Transportation Company. Although the Pennsylvania had monopolized oil shipments from Pittsburgh by rail, the entry of the Atlantic and Great Western Railroad into Oil City in early 1865 brought a dangerous competitor into the heart of the Oil Regions. The completion of the Philadelphia and Erie to Philadelphia and the creation of the Empire Line, which was given the exclusive privilege of transporting oil over the Pennsylvania's lines to New York, were the reply of the Pennsylvania's vice-president, Tom Scott.

The Empire's venture into the pipeline field was apparently inspired by a report that the Erie Railroad was seeking to purchase pipelines with which to cut off the Empire's oil supply. In early 1866, Colonel Joseph Potts of the Empire Transportation Company instructed Hatch to obtain an option for purchase of Van Syckel's Miller Farm line. While Hatch was negotiating for the option, the Atlantic and Great Western was in the process of gaining direct rail access to Pithole. Presumably to counter this threat, the Empire Line purchased the brand-new Pithole-Titusville pipeline rather than Van Syckel's.[56] By then, however, the Pithole field was on the decline, and in April, 1866, the combined capacity of the four pipelines serving it was over 12,000 barrels a day, while production did not exceed 2,000 barrels.[57] Although the Empire's new feeder operated for months at a deficit, the acquisition of the pipeline by the fast-freight company finally permitted the through shipment of oil. In July, 1866, arrangements were perfected for shipping oil directly to New York via the Empire Line, using the pipeline bill of lading for the whole distance.[58]

Meantime, Henry Harley was planning a pipeline combination. He and William H. Abbott joined forces for this purpose in early 1867. Their first purchase was Van Syckel's line, which had fallen into financial difficulties and had passed into the hands of the First National Bank of Titusville and then to one of its creditors.[59] This move placed Abbott and Harley in control of two pipeline systems —Harley's Bennehoff Run line and Van Syckel's Miller Farm line— and they next turned to seeking a charter which would allow further expansion. They found it in the previously mentioned charter of the Oil Creek Transportation Company. In 1862 the company had received the exclusive privilege of connecting the oil wells with the Philadelphia and Erie Railroad, and to this legislative favor the right of eminent domain had been added in 1863. Although the sequence of events is not clear, it seems that these privileges were subsequently transferred to the Western Transportation Company.

Apparently in anticipation of Harley's plans, the Pennsylvania legislature in February, 1867, in effect revoked the exclusive privileges granted the Western [Oil Creek] Transportation Company, at the same time changing its name to the Allegheny Transportation Company.[60] This action did not prevent Abbott and Harley from acquiring control of the company by the fall of 1867.[61] Shortly thereafter the legislature obliged the firm by repealing the act of the preceding February and thus restored the rights which it had then removed.[62]

The pipeline firm cemented an alliance with the Erie and the Atlantic and Great Western in the spring of 1868. The terms of these contracts, by which the Allegheny Transportation Company agreed not to extend its pipelines to Franklin or Oil City, were apparently aimed at diverting oil shipments from the Pennsylvania Railroad. A few weeks later three Cleveland refining firms, including that of John D. Rockefeller, Samuel Andrews, and Henry M. Flagler, were given a one-fourth interest in the Allegheny Transportation Company, which thus served as the medium for payment of drawbacks by the Atlantic and Great Western to these concerns.[63] About this time Jay Gould of the Erie bought control of the pipeline company, and it became a weapon in the Erie's competition with the Pennsylvania Railroad for the oil traffic.

These developments undoubtedly alarmed Tom Scott of the Pennsylvania Railroad, which had an admirable network of rails through the Oil Regions. From Pittsburgh the Allegheny Valley Railroad arched northward to Oil City. A route eastward from the Regions was provided by the Philadelphia and Erie and the Empire Line. In 1868 several small lines which served as oil feeders had been merged with the Oil Creek Railroad to form the Oil Creek and Allegheny River Railroad, and control of this road was purchased by the Philadelphia and Erie in early 1869. With these facilities at hand, Scott was in a position to make a real contest for oil traffic. The struggle became one between rival refining centers, each with its railroad allies.

The Railroads and the Refiners

Refineries had first sprung up in the Oil Regions, but new plants soon dotted the landscape of many cities. The Atlantic and Great Western's connection with Cleveland in 1863 had aided the city's development as a petroleum refining center. By the end of 1866 it boasted over fifty refineries.[64] In the same year Pittsburgh had fifty-eight refineries.[65] Others were located along the Atlantic seaboard from Portland, Maine, to Baltimore, Maryland, and there were scattered refining operations west of the oil fields to the Mississippi River. Although the domestic market expanded rapidly, much of the refined oil transported to tidewater was destined for export through the ports of New York and Philadelphia, which also sent oil to coastal points by water. Understandably there was keen competition for business among the major oil refining and export centers.

Railroad competition sharpened especially the rivalry between refiners in Cleveland and Pittsburgh. Situated on water and rail routes, both cities enjoyed privileged positions in certain western markets. Cleveland had all the advantages of Pittsburgh except proximity to the wells. Pittsburgh, which was at the mercy of the Pennsylvania Railroad, lacked Cleveland's advantage of access to lake and canal transportation eastward.

In its efforts to generate traffic west of Pittsburgh, the Pennsylvania Railroad discriminated against the Iron City, whose rail outlets it monopolized. Testimony before a committee of the Pennsylvania State Senate in 1867 revealed that the railroad was charging the same rate for hauling crude oil from Oil City to Philadelphia as from Pittsburgh to Philadelphia, though the latter run was nearly a hundred miles shorter. Moreover, it was charging more for transporting refined oil between the latter points than the Atlantic and Great Western's rate for transporting it from Cleveland to New York, a distance 274 miles longer.[66]

Testimony also revealed that railroad competition led to the granting of rate reductions to shippers whose volume of traffic warranted such consideration. The practice of negotiating rates, however, was already a familiar one when it came to be applied to the oil traffic. Deductions from "open" or "published" rates took the form of "rebates" or "drawbacks." Technically a "rebate" was a net charge less than the established rate, while a "drawback" was a deduction from gross charges to be repaid at a later date. The term "drawback" had been used at least since 1858 to denote any special rate resulting in a reduction from prepared rates, and although both terms were used interchangeably, "rebate" did not become popular until the seventies.[67]

A Cleveland firm, of which John D. Rockefeller was the guiding genius, proved adept at securing these railroad favors. Rockefeller, who had been interested in refining since 1862, had built up his concern, Rockefeller and Andrews, until it was the largest in the city. In 1867 Henry M. Flagler was brought into the partnership, and the job of negotiating freight rates was turned over to the new partner.

Flagler approached the Lake Shore Railroad, pointing out that his firm moved the largest amount of oil in and out of Cleveland and hence could effect economies for the railroad in return for favorable rates. The argument was sufficiently convincing to win for Rockefeller, Andrews, and Flagler a rebate, believed to have been 15 cents a barrel. Apparently this was followed by a comparable concession on the part of the Atlantic and Great Western.[68] Unquestionably other Cleveland firms also received rate reductions, and railroad competition helped Cleveland to outdistance Pittsburgh's crude oil receipts in 1869.[69]

A fierce trunk-line railroad rate war broke out in that year and threatened Cleveland's position. The Pennsylvania Railroad had to fight for oil traffic in the Regions. According to General James H. Devereux of the Lake Shore, the Pennsylvania's rate arrangements were such "that it was publicly proclaimed in the public print in Oil City, Titusville, and other places that Cleveland was to be wiped out as a refining center as with a sponge." [70] Devereux recalled that Cleveland refiners had expressed fears that they might have to move to the Oil Regions or lose their business to refiners benefiting by the Pennsylvania's new policy. The Lake Shore, however, had extended its Jamestown and Franklin branch into Oil City by 1870, and the firm of Rockefeller, Andrews, and Flagler, which became The Standard Oil Company (Ohio) in January, 1870, proposed to stand its ground with the aid of Devereux's road. By providing a guaranteed amount of freight and assuming all risks and losses connected with the shipments, Flagler obtained rates which were five cents less per barrel on crude and 60 cents less per barrel on refined than was currently being charged other shippers. In Devereux's judgment this arrangement marked the "turning-point which secured to Cleveland a considerable portion of the export trade." [71]

The Erie Railroad also made favorable arrangements with Cleveland refiners in addition to offering rates from Oil City to New York calculated to be as attractive as the Pennsylvania's.[72] Through its contracts with the Erie, the pipelines of the Allegheny Transportation Company paid large and frequent dividends, reimbursing Gould for his investment "*many times over.*" [73] Although Harley had sold his interest in the company to Gould, the pipeline pioneer remained a director and was elected president in 1869.[74] In addition, he was made general oil agent for the Atlantic and Great Western and the Erie.

This pipeline alliance of the Erie's inspired counteraction by the Pennsylvania Railroad's management. With the backing of the Oil Creek and Allegheny River Railroad, the Western Oil and Pipe Company and the Rural Dispatch, both chartered and organized in 1869, were combined under the Commonwealth Oil and Pipe Company in the following year.[75] Shortly thereafter Henry Harley engineered a merger of this company with the Allegheny Transportation Company. Gould of the Erie held about $450,000 worth of stock in the new combination, which had a paid-up capital of $1,700,000.[76] The consolidation, managed by Harley, appears to have united the pipeline interests of the Erie and the Pennsylvania, though control apparently rested with the latter.[77] In any event, this railroad-controlled pipeline network was the most extensive in the Regions.[78]

The First Pipeline Legislation

The railroads' efforts to dominate the pipelines, the feeders of their crude oil traffic, were paralleled by the oil producers' efforts to reach competing roads and water transportation by means of legislation granting pipelines the right of eminent domain. The first bill for this purpose was introduced in 1868 and failed.[79] Falling crude oil prices led to the organization of the Petroleum Producers' Association in February, 1869, but its efforts to secure a "free pipe bill" likewise failed. A delegation of thirty-five members of the Association, sent to Harrisburg in 1870, met no better success.[80] The influence of the Pennsylvania Railroad in the Pennsylvania legislature was not easily challenged, and the passage of a pipeline bill awaited an aroused public opinion whose wrath was more fearsome to the legislators than that of Tom Scott. Such an opportunity arrived in early 1872 with the unveiling of the South Improvement Company scheme.

By the end of 1871 overproduction of crude and refined oil, a disastrous price situation, and ruinous railroad competition for the oil trade had created conditions that demanded action. The *Pittsburgh Commercial* summed up the situation concisely, pointing out: "The entire petroleum business has been a losing one for the past year, not only for refiners and producers, but for the railroad companies who have transported the oil."

A vehicle for united action to combat this situation existed in the form of the charter of the South Improvement Company, obtained from the Pennsylvania legislature in 1870 by close associates of Tom Scott. The powers it granted were broad and included the right to hold stock in other companies. In short, it was well suited to the purpose for which the promoters of a railroad-refiners' combination acquired it in January, 1872. Their plans were developed in the strictest secrecy, each member pledging himself to reveal nothing about the workings or organization of the company. The president and only railroad representative among the stockholders was Peter H. Watson of the Lake Shore. The other stockholders represented refiners in Pittsburgh, Cleveland, and Philadelphia. Both John D. Rockefeller and Tom Scott were deep in the scheme, and both have been credited with developing it.

In essence it was a twofold plan. First, it was to create an "evener" for an oil traffic pool among the trunk railroads, whose task was to eliminate rate cutting by allocating to each a fixed share of the traffic. Second, by favoring member refineries in freight rates, it would increase their profits and force competitors to become allies or be eliminated. The South Improvement Company itself could be viewed as a commission agency for its members, buying and selling oil and negotiating railroad rates in return for a commission on petroleum shipments.[81]

Under the terms of the South Improvement Company's contracts with the railroads, the Pennsylvania was to receive 45 per cent of the oil traffic and the Erie and New York Central systems were each to have 27.5 per cent.[82] The published rates on crude oil shipments to Cleveland and Pittsburgh were to be doubled, but members of the combination were to receive rebates of 40 cents per barrel on these shipments and $1.06 on those to New York, Philadelphia, Boston, and Baltimore. Similar drawbacks on shipments of nonmembers were to be shared among the members of the South Improvement Company. Rates on refined oil were to be treated in a comparable manner.[83]

It was a clever plan, but it contained fatal flaws. Success depended on coercion, too few refiners were initially involved, and no provision was made for the producers. When an official of the Lake Shore's oil feeder put the new rates into effect prematurely, oilmen from Oil Creek to New York harbor exploded in indignation.

The reaction of the *Petroleum Centre Record* was typical of the anger in the Oil Regions. On February 20, 1872, the paper declared that if such a "scheme of robbery and swindling" were attempted, a half-dozen pipelines and the completion of half-built railways would be forthcoming in thirty to sixty days.[84]

These sentiments were echoed at a mass meeting of producers and refiners in Titusville a week later. The legislature was condemned for "putting chains on the people" by authorizing powers as broad as those granted the South Improvement Company. Construction of a pipeline to Erie, Pennsylvania, was proposed as a means of escaping the combination's grasp. This motion died, however, when it was pointed out that a pipeline could carry only one commodity and would leave the railroads with the power to starve the Regions into submission.[85] A more effective approach, it was suggested, would be a general shutdown of oil production and a canvass of the possibilities of building a railroad to compete with the combination.[86]

Meantime, Henry Harley, who was the Erie's oil agent as well as the head of the railroads' pipeline combination, hit on a scheme which he thought might prove more acceptable to the oilmen than the South Improvement Company. With John D. Archbold, a young man who was rising fast in the industry and was later to become Rockefeller's protégé, Harley hurried to Peter H. Watson for authoritative information on the South Improvement plan. Learning the details, the two men approached the Erie directors with an alternative, proposing that the Regions' producers and refiners provide the railroads with as much oil as the South Improvement Company could deliver. In effect, the Regions would act as an "evener" for the railroads. This proposal was rejected when Gould received a telegram stating that neither Harley nor Archbold was authorized to make such overtures.[87]

The mood of the more incendiary of the oilmen was shown at a mass meeting in Franklin on March 5. There a resolution was offered to the effect that no overtures or propositions should be accepted from the railroads or the South Improvement Company until the latter had used its influence to secure passage of a free pipeline bill by the legislature and its approval by the governor.[88] Calmer counsels prevailed, however, and the resolution was shelved as insulting to the state's governing body.

While boycotting the combination, preparing to handle their own oil, and requesting a congressional investigation, the oilmen also insisted on the passage of a pipeline bill granting them the right of eminent domain. In their view this measure would facilitate pipeline access to competing rail lines and water transportation. In addition, the bill offered its proponents an issue on which public opinion might be mobilized against the South Improvement Company. At a meeting in Oil City on March 8 a letter was read from J. D. McJunkin, of Venango County, who had introduced a free pipe bill in the current legislative session. He reported that progress had been blocked by a Philadelphian but that the bill would come up again shortly, and he would give its opponents "a lively time." [89] With mounting indications that the local oilmen would have the support of outside oil dealers and refiners, especially some from New York, the Oil City meeting referred to committee proposals to interview all candidates for governor as to their stand on the pipeline bill and to send a delegation of one thousand members to Harrisburg on behalf of the measure.[90]

The oilmen's primary weapon, however, was a boycott on the sale of crude to members of the South Improvement combination, and enforcement of the boycott inevitably involved the pipelines. Those accused of aiding the South Improvement Company by purchasing or transporting oil for its members felt the pressure of hostile public opinion. Among them was the New York Pipe Line, which was charged with offering 30 cents above the market price for oil in the Pleasantville region in an attempt to break the blockade.[91] The line's superintendent, A. B. Howland, in reply to the charges against his line, wrote:

Our position before the public is and has been simply that of a common carrier of oil; receiving it from the well owners, and delivering it to whoever presents a proper order for it, precisely as a bank cashier pays a certified check, if properly indorsed, no matter by whom presented. The ownership and ultimate destination of the oil is entirely in the hands of the producer from whom we receive it, and of the party who buys it, we not even knowing who owns it, from day to day, until called for at Garland.[92]

A similar charge and denial were made in the case of the Empire Transportation Company's Mutual Pipe Line, which served Armstrong and Clarion counties.

In the eyes of the Regions' oilmen there was no inconsistency in demanding legislation based on the public function of pipelines while at the same time advocating that pipelines refuse to carry for South Improvement Company members. A ninety-three-foot petition requesting passage of the free pipeline bill was sent to Harrisburg, and a committee was sent to wait on the Pennsylvania Railroad's Tom Scott, whose influence with the legislature on this matter was regarded as decisive. Acutely aware of the dangers to the Pennsylvania Railroad inherent in the public furor which was being carefully nurtured by oil producers, Scott was willing to see the bill passed—on his terms.

Among the group that waited on Scott in connection with the bill was Lewis Emery, Jr., an enterprising and volatile young man who became a leader in the independent oilmen's attack on the Standard Oil group in later years. Testifying on this particular episode many years after the event, Emery recalled:

I asked Mr. Scott, [vice-]president of the Pennsylvania Railroad, to permit this law to become general. He refused. He said that he would permit us to have a law for the eight counties named, but he would not permit us to have a law by which we could run our pipes to the city of Pittsburg. Our hope was to get a law by which we could reach competing lines of railroad and the Ohio River, so that we might transport our product by water. He said he would permit a law to pass for the eight counties named, but he would provide in the law that no pipe should go within a mile of the State line, nor within a mile of any railroad but the Pennsylvania.[93]

This startling commentary on the railroad's power over the Pennsylvania legislature is sustained by the events that followed.

Recognizing that Scott's restrictions were the price of any bill at all, the oilmen agreed to them, and the pipeline bill became law on March 12, 1872. Technically the new law extended to pipelines the rights conferred by an "act relating to corporations for mechanical,

manufacturing and quarrying purposes approved July 18, 1863." In
accordance with Scott's qualifications, it conferred the right of
eminent domain only in the oil-producing counties of Venango,
Warren, Forest, Armstrong, Clarion, Butler, Crawford, and Erie. It
was also provided that no pipeline should be constructed under the
provisions of the law within five miles of the state line for the purpose of taking oil out of the state. Furthermore, owners, producers,
and shippers of oil for New York, Baltimore, and Philadelphia using
such pipelines were to give preference to the railroad "traversing the
greatest distance in this state, at the same rates for transportation." [94]
These requirements were obviously calculated to help keep the
Pennsylvania's grasp on the oil trade, but the architects of the proviso failed to provide any penalty for noncompliance with it. Consequently, shippers were actually as free as before to choose their
transportation routes.

Despite this loophole in the law, the press of the Oil Regions was
outraged by the legislature's patent favoritism to the Pennsylvania
Railroad. The *Tidioute Commercial* of March 13, 1872, angrily declared: "Let's DEMAND from the Legislature a proper and un-
restricted bill, and let us also demand the repeal of the S. I. Co.'s
charter." The next day the *Titusville Morning Herald* fumed:

Not enough that we should bear all past discriminations, not enough that
the Southern Improvement Company is trying to absorb us, not enough
that we should make this State first in the Union in her material wealth,
but we must in the midst of it all bear this picayune indignity sent at us
through a two inch pipe.

With the Pennsylvania Company's special privileges endangered
by the rising clamor for repeal of the South Improvement Company's charter and with a congressional investigation in the making,
Scott must have viewed insistence on retention of the proviso as
dangerous. In any event McJunkin introduced a bill for repeal of
the Scott-inspired proviso, and it passed the lower house without
difficulty. In the Senate on March 18, 1872, it was announced that
the oilmen demanded repeal of the proviso.[95] With no railroad opposition, that was all that was required to insure passage of the repeal bill. Within a week the pressures brought against the South
Improvement Company plan had also brought about its collapse.

Elimination of the railroad proviso from the pipeline law did not represent a major victory for the oilmen, since the law still applied to only the eight oil-producing counties, and Allegheny County, in which Pittsburgh was located, was not included.[96] The Pennsylvania Railroad was still in a position to block any effort at constructing a local pipeline to serve Pittsburgh refiners, who otherwise might have found an outlet eastward via the Connellsville Railroad, which had been completed to Pittsburgh in 1871, and the Baltimore and Ohio.

Pipelines and the South Improvement Company Scheme

Control of pipelines would clearly have been essential to the success of the South Improvement Company scheme; otherwise access to crude oil supplies would have been precarious. This point did not escape a writer for the *New York Herald,* who interpreted the whole effort to gain control of the oil trade in terms of pipelines. Beginning with 1868, he traced various pipeline combinations, ending with the extravagant charge that the South Improvement Company had absorbed all pipelines, with one exception.[97] A dispatch from Titusville to the *Cleveland Leader* also suggested that the South Improvement Company plan rested on pipelines.[98]

Certainly this episode and its aftermath indicated the value of pipelines as competitive weapons. While the Pennsylvania producers had turned to pipelines and pipeline legislation as a partial answer to railroad discriminations, the collapse of the South Improvement Company also turned Cleveland's attention to pipelines as an answer to its problem of competing with Pittsburgh, Regions, and seaboard refineries. Cleveland parties had already attempted and failed to secure charter rights for a pipeline.[99] Now the need appeared urgent, for under the terms of an agreement signed by the railroads on March 25, 1872, both Cleveland and Pittsburgh refiners were to pay the same amount per barrel on oil shipped to the seaboard.[100] This situation placed Cleveland at a disadvantage, since its refiners had to pay an additional 50 cents a barrel to get crude from the Regions by rail.

The *Cleveland Leader* on March 30, 1872, viewed a trunk pipeline from Cleveland to the Regions as the answer to Pittsburgh's freight advantage on crude, created by the supposed end of railroad discriminations. It declared: "Such a line, capable of bringing forward

a requisite quantity of crude oil, could be built for a million dollars."
Charging 15 cents a barrel rather than the 50 cents agreed upon by
the railroads, a pipeline might furnish "the ultimate solution" of
Cleveland's refining problems. The *Leader* waxed enthusiastic over
the prospects. On April 2 the paper asserted that a pipeline to the oil
fields "will be the end of all monopolies, all warring with eastern
corporations for just rates and all danger of defeat at the hands of
our rivals."

In April the Ohio legislature granted a charter to a company
which proposed to construct a trunk pipeline from Cleveland to the
Regions.[101] The chances of success for such projects in the face of
railroad opposition would be improved by granting pipelines the
right of eminent domain, and the *Leader* came out strongly in favor
of such legislation.[102] On April 29, 1872, the Ohio legislature passed
an act amending a law of 1868 and granting pipelines organized
thereunder the right of eminent domain subject to their acting as
common carriers.[103] Since the agreement of March 25 had not spelled
the end of railroad discriminations, there was no immediate need
to put the new law to use to protect Cleveland refiners, who made
new agreements with the rail oil carriers.

The role of the railroad-controlled Pennsylvania Transportation
Company in the South Improvement plan is obscure. Although the
former's name had been adopted in August, 1871, the company's
major components, the Allegheny Transportation Company and the
Commonwealth Oil and Pipe Company, were operating under their
own names during the height of the excitement over the South Improvement Company. On March 18, 1872, a reporter for the New
York *Sun* sought out Henry Harley, president of the Pennsylvania
Transportation Company and the Erie's oil agent, for his comments
on the struggle in the Oil Regions. Harley declared that it had been
a mistake not to conciliate the producers, but he saw the possibility
of a compromise and argued that the South Improvement plan
would force exporters to pay what oil was worth, give the railroads
a fair freight, and bring producers a good price.

On the same day that he granted this interview, Harley telegraphed William H. Abbott that the Pennsylvania Transportation
Company was "in favor of a free and untrammeled pipe bill, and
will do nothing to oppose its passage." This willingness to see

Tom Scott's proviso repealed did not mean, however, that the pipe-line company was turning on the railroad, for Scott had already ac-quiesced in the change. Moreover, on that very day the legislature confirmed the title of the Pennsylvania Transportation Company.[104]

The following day, March 19, the public prints carried a notice that the Pennsylvania Transportation Company had succeeded to the business of the Commonwealth Oil and Pipe Company and the Allegheny Transportation Company. Thus the Pennsylvania legisla-ture confirmed title to the major railroad-affiliated pipeline company while making a gesture toward those who would challenge it.

The introduction of pipelines resulted not only in a revolution in local crude oil transportation but promised to affect the geographical struggle for control of the refining branch of the petroleum industry. The Pennsylvania and Erie railroads early became interested in pipelines, and contemporary accounts stressed the close connection between railroad discriminations and railroad-pipeline affiliations. While the exact nature of this relationship to Cleveland's rise as a refining center and to the South Improvement Company scheme is not clear, the available evidence suggests that it was an important one. Similarly it is significant that the producers and refiners of the Oil Regions, outraged by the South Improvement scheme, turned to pipeline legislation as one remedy. Threatened with the end of railroad favoritism, Cleveland refiners also took a preliminary step in this direction.

With pipeline access to Pittsburgh and the Baltimore and Ohio Railroad barred to producers by Tom Scott, the Regions' chances of successfully fighting railroad discriminations were greatly reduced. As the New York *Sun* pointed out, however, the struggle over the South Improvement Company was simply one over "who shall make the most money."[105] In this struggle pipeline legislation became merely one field for a test of strength or, as the *Cleveland Leader* put it, a piece of "grand strategy." Public policy toward pipelines was not the immediately decisive battleground, but the contest over it pointed up the fact that the possession of pipelines was be-coming indispensable to survival in the fiercely competitive petro-leum industry.

II

Pipeline Combination and
Public Policy, 1872-1875

DURING the years 1872–1875 a pattern of intra-industry conflict involving pipelines and public policy was established. The petroleum industry felt the full impact of the depression which then gripped the whole American economy, and pipelines became increasingly important as competitive weapons of producers, transporters, and refiners of crude oil. In the face of falling oil prices and relentless competitive tactics, pipelines grew in mileage and value and manifested the same trend toward consolidation that appeared in other sectors of the petroleum industry. The producers found themselves tightly squeezed between lower and lower oil prices and the pressures of powerful transportation and refining units. Unable to check oil production or to maintain a united front against other groups, the embattled producers turned again to the Pennsylvania legislature for aid. Encouraged by the precedent set in the free pipe law of 1872, they demanded laws which they believed would offset to some extent the power of the organized groups that confronted them. Although the attempt to extend the provisions of the 1872 act failed, the producers' proposals formed the basis of their legislative efforts for more than a decade to come. Their case was somewhat strengthened by the enactment in 1874 of one law which recognized pipeline and oil storage operations as a proper subject for public policy, albeit a relatively passive one.

Railroad Competition, Pipelines, and Standard Oil, 1872–1874

Railroad participation in the South Improvement Company plan had been inspired by the ruinous effects of railroad competition for the oil traffic. Peter H. Watson, testifying before a congressional committee investigating the company, declared that the railroads "had been transporting [oil] at a loss during the whole of 1871." [1] The collapse of the scheme had not ended the conditions which gave rise to it, and fierce railroad competition quickly broke out anew.

George H. Blanchard, who was appointed general freight agent of the Erie Railroad in October, 1872, found that his road was suffering in the new competition. He told a committee of the New York General Assembly in 1879 that he was convinced that the agreement of March, 1872, to end rate discriminations had lasted less than two weeks. "At that early date," Blanchard declared, "the Empire Line was receiving a large drawback or commission from the Pennsylvania Railroad, which was either being shared with its shippers or an additional amount was allowed to them, besides that which the Empire Line itself received from the Pennsylvania system; and as the Empire Line also owned the Union Pipe Line, its shippers had advantages which our company and its shippers did not even jointly possess." [2]

Although Blanchard charged the Pennsylvania with breaking the compact, that road was not alone in making new rate concessions. The Erie and the Great Western soon offered similar inducements to shippers. The Lake Shore on April 15, 1872, concluded an agreement which gave it a monopoly of Standard Oil's refined oil shipments from Cleveland to New York in return for favorable rates and a guaranteed minimum volume of traffic. [3] In December, 1872, Flagler called on William H. Vanderbilt to protect the oil concern against the Pennsylvania's drastic rate cuts. Vanderbilt reluctantly made a lower rate, but it was in effect for only one month. Standard Oil retaliated by reducing its shipments to the minimum specified in its contract with the road, and there they remained until a new contract was signed in April, 1873. [4] Meantime, the Erie and the Empire

Line engaged in a rate-cutting contest which was not concluded until the following November.[5]

In the seesaw battle between the northern trunk railroads and the Empire-Pennsylvania combination, pipelines assumed increasing importance. The Empire Transportation Company had long recognized the importance of pipeline ownership as an asset in the struggle for oil freights. Beginning in 1866 with its acquisition of the Titusville Pipe Line Company in a move to counter the Erie, the Empire had slowly but steadily built up its pipeline holdings. When the furor over the South Improvement Company broke, the fast-freight line had just acquired the Mutual Pipe Line, which by 1873 had nine branches, one hundred miles long. Challenged by increasingly competitive tactics, the Empire in the summer of 1873 purchased the Union Pipe Line, which stretched for 125 miles through the new, heavy-producing Butler County oil field.[6]

By this acquisition the Empire, with about 250 miles of pipe, became one of the three major pipeline interests. The others were the Pennsylvania Transportation Company, with over 400 miles of pipe, and Vandergrift and Forman, with upwards of 200.[7] In addition to the Empire's pipelines the Pennsylvania Railroad had an advantage over the northern trunk railroads because they were forced to use the Pennsylvania's Allegheny Valley Railroad between the oil fields below Oil City and that railroad terminus.

This situation probably prompted the New York Central and the Lake Shore to join in 1873 with Standard Oil in acquiring an interest in the Vandergrift and Forman pipelines which served the oil-producing districts both above and below Oil City. Standard Oil acquired a one-third share in this pipeline network by contributing an interest in a small line and paying $233,333.33 in cash.[8] William H. Vanderbilt of the New York Central and Amasa Stone of the Lake Shore each obtained a one-sixth interest, while Vandergrift and Forman retained the remaining third.[9] The motive of the railroad men in making this investment was explained by Vanderbilt in 1879 when he said: "I think the object of our getting an interest in it, was to establish tankage at a place to protect the Lake Shore. . . ."[10] As these words suggest, pipeline ownership had become a condition of successful railroad competition for the crude oil traffic. Standard

Oil's motives are not so clear, but undoubtedly they included a closer alliance with the northern roads against the Pennsylvania, closer ties with Vandergrift and Forman, one of the major firms in the Regions producing, transporting, and buying crude oil, and finally assurance of a supply of oil from the lower district.

The role of pipelines in cutting off Standard Oil's crude supply during the South Improvement Company episode certainly could not have been lost on the Cleveland firm's astute management. The aggressive Joseph Potts, head of the Empire, backed by the Pennsylvania and a fast-developing pipeline network, must have caused Standard Oil's leaders to assess the importance of pipelines to their own operations. The purchase of an interest in Vandergrift and Forman's pipelines was one result; the construction of a pipeline from Emlenton to the Clarion County oil fields in 1873 was another.[11]

The job of building the first pipeline in the interest of Standard Oil fell to Daniel O'Day of J. A. Bostwick and Company, Standard Oil's principal buyer. Although O'Day was only twenty-nine years old, he had already made an impressive record in the oil transportation business. In 1865 he had joined Empire Transportation and brought order out of the confusion which postwar demand for cars had created. Later he had been hired by Joseph Seep, Bostwick's agent at Titusville, to handle that firm's large shipments. He had been borrowed by Jay Gould to divert the Empire's oil traffic to the Erie, a task at which he proved adept. Throughout the South Improvement Company uproar both he and Seep had stood loyally by Bostwick, whose firm had been one of the first added to the Standard Oil alliance early in 1872. O'Day brought to the new field of pipeline construction both ability and wholehearted allegiance to the interests of his employers.[12]

In developing its counterpoise to the Empire Transportation Company's growing pipeline power, Standard Oil established the two cornerstones of what was to become a great pipeline empire—the American Transfer Company and United Pipe Lines. The Bostwick lines were originally organized under the charter of the Novelty Power Company, but this name was changed to the American Transfer Company at a meeting of stockholders on December 4, 1873.

Standard Oil acquired complete control of the company in November, 1874.[13] The Vandergrift and Forman lines, together with others, became the United Pipe Lines, a name which was adopted by mid-1874.

The possibility of profiting from railroad competition by the use of pipelines was demonstrated by an agreement between the American Transfer Company and the New York Central in the fall of 1874. Daniel O'Day had just completed a pipeline from the Parker District of Clarion County to Oil City, and Jabez Bostwick approached James H. Rutter, general freight agent of the New York Central, with a proposition that the railroad pay the American Transfer Company as much for transporting crude to Oil City by pipe as was being paid the Allegheny Valley Railroad. At first Rutter demurred, but he was faced with the possibility that if satisfactory arrangements were not worked out, Bostwick's profitable oil traffic might be switched to another line. Rutter recalled:

I undertook to make him do it for less, and he refused to do it, and in our competition with the other lines, I saw that it was an opportunity to meet their competition by allowing a shipper something in his own favor, and I made the arrangement, the charge and cost to us being the same as it had been before.[14]

Although the New York Central paid the same charge as before, a Standard-affiliated pipeline had diverted traffic from the Pennsylvania Railroad and profited by the traffic of another road. This balanced in part the traffic and dividends brought to the Pennsylvania by the Empire Transportation Company's pipelines. The lesson was not lost on Standard Oil.

By 1874 pipelines had become strategically important in the constantly shifting competition that characterized the petroleum industry. The Lake Shore and the New York Central entered the pipeline field in an effort to offset the advantages given the Pennsylvania by the Empire Transportation Company's pipelines. In this enterprise the northern trunk roads were partners with The Standard Oil Company (Ohio). Its interest in United Pipe Lines was equal to that of Vandergrift and Forman, the leading pipeline partnership in the Oil Regions, and to the combined holdings of the two railroads. Standard Oil also had the growing pipeline system of the American Transfer Company. Predominant in Cleveland and expanding in the New York area, Rockefeller and his associates seized upon ownership of gathering pipelines as a source of strength in the competitive struggle in the petroleum industry as well as a means of assuring a supply of crude oil for their refineries.

Competition in transportation and refining had produced this side of the picture. Overproduction and the producers' keen struggle for profits in the face of falling prices completed and complicated the picture.

Pipelines and the Producers, 1874

The early history of the petroleum industry is replete with examples of efforts to end economic distress resulting from unrestrained competition. The South Improvement Company plan was one such effort, but it failed because its methods were too gross, its membership too limited, and the opposition that it aroused too violent. A new effort, embodied in the so-called "Pittsburgh Plan," which proposed to improve profits through an organization open to all refiners, failed in mid-May, 1872, because of the Regions' suspicion of the plan's backers, former members of the South Improvement Company. Another attempt at organization in the summer of 1872 was successful, resulting in the establishment of the Petroleum Refiners' Association.

The refiners' efforts to organize were matched by those of the producers. By August, 1872, the Clarion and Butler fields were spewing out oil so rapidly that available tanks and pipeline terminals could not accommodate it.[15] The price of crude was down a dollar from the corresponding month the year before and was approaching three dollars a barrel, which the producers firmly believed was not a "living price." The Petroleum Producers' Association sought vainly to deal with the problem through a Producers' Agency which attempted to control production while contracting with the Refiners' Association for oil at five dollars a barrel during the fall of 1872.

The small producers did not prove amenable to regimentation, and they viewed the arrangements with the Refiners' Association as chiefly beneficial to the large producers. By mid-January, 1873, the effort to control production had collapsed completely. The *Oil City Derrick* declared:

It turned out that the pledge to drill no wells for six months had tended to increase development by persons who wished to take advantage of the idleness of others. So we come to the end of this short-lived combination. It was wrong in principle, impossible in practice, and inconsistent with the record of the oil producers of Pennsylvania.[16]

The individualism of the producers had its counterpart among the refiners, and within six months the Petroleum Refiners' Association followed the Producers' Association into oblivion.

Attempting to maximize income by increased drilling, the producers only added to their own distress. During 1873 production touched nearly 10,000,000 barrels, and the end of the year found over 1,300,000 barrels of it still in the tanks and pipes of the pipeline companies.[17] Whereas three-dollar oil was not considered a "living price" in 1872, in the Butler County field in 1874 the price of crude sank to a dollar and less per barrel.[18] Again a shutdown of production was proposed, but again repugnance to organized action resulted in failure.

The producers' predicament brought charges against Standard Oil, the railroads, and the pipeline companies. Standard Oil, which reportedly did not have large stocks on hand, was accused of deliberately "bearing" the market by refusing to purchase. John P. Zane, a Rouseville producer, in a letter to the *Titusville Courier* in March, 1874, claimed that the "Oil Ring" was purposely creating the impression of overproduction in order to keep down the price of oil.

According to Zane, the various pipeline companies either did not know or would not reveal how much oil they had on hand. He reported that the only way to arrive at a rough approximation of the oil in storage was to observe the height of moisture on the tanks in damp weather. From this rough index and his own calculations Zane estimated that there were in the Regions 1,400,000 barrels of empty iron tankage, which, he maintained, did not reflect any surplus of oil. In Zane's opinion the pipeline companies were "to a large extent speculators in oil, when in reality they should only be common carriers." As a partial remedy he recommended that state gaugers be appointed to measure the tanks and that the pipelines be forced to make monthly reports on their business.[19]

Zane undoubtedly expressed the sentiments of a large segment of the producers, and one of the measures that he advocated was soon before the Pennsylvania legislature. On April 14, 1874, Representative Allen of Warren introduced a bill calling for a detailed monthly report by pipelines on the amount of oil that they transported and stored. Two weeks later a companion bill, which also called for a quarterly report on petroleum transported by the railroads, was introduced in the Senate. The latter bill passed the Senate without incident, but the House regarded its provisions as "inquisitorial." The Regions was reported to be opposed—for some unexplained reason—to making railroads provide the same type of information to be required of pipelines. Without further discussion, the House agreed to drop this requirement. The Senate accepted the amended version May 14, 1874, by a vote of 24 to 0.[20] The governor signed the bill into law the next day.

The new statute called for the posting of a sworn statement by the fifteenth of each month on the amount and location of oil in the possession of the person or line making the statement and the amount of oil due producers in outstanding acceptances, certificates, and vouchers of the pipelines at the end of the previous month. A report on the amount of oil stored and shipped was to be filed with the state's Bureau of Statistics. Various provisions aimed against fraud in the handling of oil certificates were also included. Infractions were punishable by a fine of up to $1,000 and imprisonment for a period of up to one year.[21] It was significant, however, that the law made no provision for gauging tanks by state appointees. The accuracy of the reports depended upon the honesty of the management of the pipeline companies and the vigilance of their patrons. Nevertheless, the law constituted a new and important assertion that pipeline operations were a legitimate sphere of public policy and subject to the regulatory action of the state.

The provisions of the new law regarding the fraudulent handling of pipeline certificates were important, for the certificates had become the negotiable instruments of the petroleum industry. Representing 1,000 barrels of oil credited by a pipeline to the account of a producer, an endorsed certificate was as negotiable as a certified check and became the basis of oil exchange operations. The producer's interest in the oil represented by the certificate ended with its sale; the final purchaser paid the costs of piping the oil and also storage costs, if any. Since many of the pipeline companies had their own buying departments, they opened themselves to charges of speculation such as that aired by John Zane. The legislation of May, 1874, was aimed at abuse of the certificate system whether by producers, pipelines, oil brokers, or refiners.

To many producers it looked as though a minor skirmish had been won and a major battle lost in the 1874 legislature, for the enactment of the Wallace Corporation Act in the same session appeared to threaten the validity of the limited free pipe law of 1872. The Wallace Act was one of a series of measures designed to carry the new Pennsylvania constitution into effect. A Senate committee, headed by William A. Wallace, in February, 1874, had reported this general incorporation bill to give effect to the constitutional prohibitions on granting special charters to corporations. Although the measure, which became law April 29, 1874, made provision for companies chartered under the 1863 act, of which the free pipe law was an extension, it failed to mention pipelines specifically.[22] It was an open question, therefore, whether the 1872 law still applied to the eight counties it had named. Certainly, the effort of a pipeline company to utilize the Wallace Act in obtaining access to Pittsburgh during the summer of 1874, ended in failure.

Although the legislative session of 1874 had brought mixed comforts to harassed producers, the hope of breaching the Pennsylvania Railroad's hold on the Pittsburgh oil traffic by means of a trunk pipeline cheered Butler County oil operators and Pittsburgh refiners. The vehicle for this enterprise was the Columbia Conduit Company, incorporated in 1872 by a special act of the legislature. Allegheny County was outside the scope of the free pipe law of that year, but the Conduit was authorized to lay pipes from any point in Butler County to, at, or near Sharpsburg in Allegheny County by any route deemed best suited for the purpose.[23] By January 1, 1874, seven thousand dollars had been spent on surveying routes for the line and preparing for operations. Construction along a route between Millerstown in Butler County and Pittsburgh was commenced the following June.

The leading figure in this project was "Doctor" David Hostetter, who had a colorful and varied business career. His title was a token of the fact that he was the originator of Hostetter's Bitters, a medicinal brew of wormwood and whiskey. He had been a member of a ring which attempted, unsuccessfully, to corner the oil market in 1869, and he had served as head of the Pittsburgh Gas Company, where his efforts to suppress competition had not been forgotten.[24] As an owner of wells in Butler County, seeking to escape the toils of the Pennsylvania Railroad, he turned to pipelines.

The importance attached by producers to the right of eminent domain for pipelines was increased as a result of the Columbia Conduit's experience in attempting to cross a branch line of the Pennsylvania Railroad in Butler County. The road refused to accept a bond for damages on the grounds that the pipeline was a private corporation not entitled to the right of eminent domain and that there was no provision in its charter for the assessment of damages. Although the Court of Common Pleas for Butler County ordered acceptance of the bond, the railroad tore up the pipes laid by the Conduit. New legal action before the same court resulted in a verdict favorable to the pipeline.[25] Meanwhile, construction of the line toward Pittsburgh continued, and Hostetter sought to bolster his position by obtaining a new charter, carrying the right of eminent domain under the terms of the Pennsylvania Constitution and the Wallace Corporation Act. The governor granted this petition, and letters patent were issued in July, 1874.[26]

A month later a new controversy arose when the West Penn Railroad sought to prevent the Hertz refinery from connecting with the Columbia Conduit under the tracks at Fairview Station on the outskirts of Allegheny County. The railroad asserted that the refinery was owned by the Conduit and that Hertz had unlawfully laid and relaid pipes under its tracks. Since the West Penn was built on the route of the old Pennsylvania canal, which had been sold to the Pennsylvania Railroad and was then held in fee simple by the West Penn, the railroad requested that an injunction be issued against laying pipes across its property. Although the Columbia Conduit denied any interest in Hertz's action, the court granted an injunction against both Hertz and the pipeline.[27]

In a separate action Hostetter failed to force the West Penn to accept a bond for possible damages resulting from construction at Fairview Station. In this instance the railroad challenged the application of the Wallace Corporation Act to pipelines by arguing that the act specified the class of corporations entitled to the right of eminent domain and that conduit companies were not included. The pipeline's attorneys maintained, on the other hand, that the act gave the right of eminent domain to companies furnishing light and heat. Since the Conduit transported oil for this purpose, they reasoned that the pipeline was covered by this provision.[28] Nor did they back down on the assertion that the company's charter both originally and as approved by the governor in July, 1874, conferred the right of eminent domain. The District Court of Pittsburgh, which was later sustained by the State Supreme Court, held otherwise, and the railroad's defenses stood firm.

Railroads, Refiners, and Pipelines Try to Suppress Competition

The Pennsylvania Railroad's opposition to the Columbia Conduit was heightened by the latter's threat to the most recent effort to stabilize railroad rates by means of a joint railroad-pipeline pool. A favorable contract between Standard Oil and the Erie in April, 1874, had given the Pennsylvania and New York Central cause for concern. The generally low level of freight and passenger rates for all three roads led to their making rate agreements in the summer of 1874, including one on oil. To maintain it, however, past experience had shown that the co-operation of the principal oil refiners was essential to success. Also, by mid-1874 pipelines had become such an integral part of oil transportation that they had to be taken into account when estimating the chances for the pool's success.

The provisions of the railroad pool, organized by Joseph D. Potts of the Empire Transportation Company, eliminated the matter of distance from the oil fields as a factor in the competition of refiners. In the effort to end their own unprofitable competition, the roads agreed that half the oil traffic should be allotted to the Pennsylvania and one-quarter each to the Erie and the New York Central. Rates were to be increased, and the whole Oil Regions was to be treated as one station from which there should be uniform rates to the seaboard via refining points. The new railroad compact thus promised to shift refining even farther away from western Pennsylvania.

Railroad pools, however, had proved notoriously unstable, and Potts was well aware of this weakness. It was not at all inconceivable that the New York Central, aided by United Pipe Lines, might break the compact and challenge the Pennsylvania Railroad–Empire

Transportation Company–Union Pipe Line combination. Consequently, there was a good reason for bringing the major pipelines into the railroad pool, and conditions in the pipeline business favored such a development.

Despite the heavy production of 1873–1874, the rapid expansion of pipelines had created a capacity nearly double what was required. An uneconomical network of competing pipes had given rise to many of the devices employed by railroads to attract business away from rivals. Rate-cutting by pipelines was a familiar tactic.[29] As a result, there was as much need to stabilize the pipeline industry to make it profitable as there was for the railroads to take such a step.

While Potts was organizing the railroad pool, Henry Harley was busy with its pipeline counterpart. He boldly proposed to the representatives of the trunk railroads, assembled at the West End Hotel, Long Branch, New Jersey, in the summer of 1874, that the pipelines make through rates from the wells and constitute themselves the exclusive feeders of the oil traffic to the roads.[30] George Blanchard of the Erie, which still had an interest in Harley's Pennsylvania Transportation Company, was outraged. He later declared that he regarded the pipelines' proposal "as the most spasmodic and violent attempt on the part of the tail to wag the dog that I had ever seen." [31] Nor were the other railroad executives overly enthusiastic about Harley's proposition.

Harley was persuasive, however, in his argument that "the rail arrangement could only be maintained by including the transportation rates by pipes as well as by rail." It made sense to the railroad men that the inclusion of pipelines in a pool connected with that of the roads themselves would be a guarantee against rate-cutting. On the other hand, they were wary of creating a pipeline monopoly, which might dictate to them. Accordingly, they rejected the part of Harley's plan which they deemed to tend in this direction and accepted the rest.

The plan accepted by the railroads still appeared well calculated to eliminate pipeline competition either by crushing opponents or forcing them to join the pool. The standard charge for transporting oil to the railroad depots was to be 30 cents a barrel with some temporary exceptions to take care of existing commitments. The line performing the transportation was to retain eight cents and turn the remaining 22 cents over to a committee consisting of one representative from each of the member companies. The committee in turn was to distribute its receipts among the member lines in accordance with specified percentages.[32] The railroads agreed to add 22 cents to the through rates on all oil carried by them, refunding this amount only to shippers who used pipelines maintaining the 30-cent pipage rate. Theoretically no competing pipeline could survive charging only eight cents a barrel, which was the rate necessary to make the cost to the shipper the same as though he had used the pool's pipes.

The role of Standard Oil in these arrangements is not clear. According to George Blanchard, "the railroads proceeded without any reference to the Standard Oil Company."[33] Still, the provisions of the railroad pool clearly eliminated Standard Oil's disadvantage of being farther from the oil fields than some of its competitors and farther from the seaboard than others. It scarcely seems likely that Harley failed to consult Standard Oil men before proposing his pipeline pool, which allocated 36.5 per cent of its business to United Pipe Lines and the American Transfer Company. Certainly Standard Oil stood to profit from both railroad and pipeline efforts to suppress competition.

The existence of the pools was revealed in a circular issued September 9, 1874, by James H. Rutter of the New York Central. It embodied the agreements reached during the summer, specifying a uniform rate to the seaboard on refined oil from Cleveland, Titusville, and refineries in or adjacent to the Oil Regions. On crude oil rates of $1.75 to Boston and $1.50 to New York, Philadelphia, and Baltimore from the Regions, 22 cents a barrel was to be refunded "only on oil coming from pipes which maintain the agreed rates of pipage."[34]

The initial reaction of the Oil Regions to the Rutter circular was reminiscent of the days of the South Improvement Company. A mass meeting at Titusville on September 28 condemned the railroads and their pipeline allies. The *Oil City Derrick* called for organization against the new threat. Members of the pipeline pool attempted in vain to turn the anger of a mass meeting at Parker's Landing on October 2. Resolutions were again passed condemning the railroad and pipeline rates, urging that action for conspiracy be instituted and inviting extension of the Columbia Conduit's line. The producers, however, were either unable or unwilling to make another fight like that of 1872, and, despite the efforts of the editor of the *Titusville Courier* to rekindle that spark, a mass meeting on October 23 showed a noticeable lack of zeal.[35]

Pittsburgh refiners were alarmed and angered at the news of the pools. The city had from four to five million dollars invested in the oil business and a refining capacity of 10,000 barrels per day, which was far from being fully utilized. The new rates, effective October 1, 1874, reportedly would enable Cleveland to send refined oil to Philadelphia even more cheaply than the alleged 42 cents a barrel advantage that it already had over Pittsburgh.[36] Even before the appearance of the Rutter circular the Pittsburgh refiners' organization had voted its support of the Columbia Conduit's effort to enter the city.[37] The Rutter circular spurred them to new action.

At a meeting on September 18 the Pittsburgh refiners agreed that it was essential to break the Pennsylvania Railroad's hold on the city's rail shipments of oil. The group resolved to ask the city government for the right to lay a pipeline for refined oil from a point near Negley's Run to the Connellsville branch of the Baltimore and Ohio Railroad, which was not a member of the pool. To aid refiners outside the city in reaching this road, the Pittsburgh refiners voted to seek petitions from the public requesting the legislature to extend the free pipe law to Allegheny County.[38]

Elements of the Pittsburgh press lent enthusiastic support to the refiners' pipeline project. In an editorial on October 5, the *Daily Dispatch* declared: "Only one avenue leads to relief. That is the pipe line. . . ." The *Gazette* accused the Pennsylvania Railroad of working against Pittsburgh's interests and blamed the officials of the Empire Line for catering to the Cleveland trade for their own benefit while overcharging Pittsburgh refiners in an attempt to pacify stockholders. The paper laid the exclusion of Allegheny County from the free pipe law at the Pennsylvania's doorstep and came out strongly for the proposed refined oil pipeline.[39] Both papers stressed the decay of Pittsburgh's oil trade, and both urged the benefits of supporting the efforts to save this home industry, which used a million barrels annually, consumed a ton of hoop iron daily, and provided employment in these and other industries related to refining.

The Pittsburgh Common Council passed the pipeline ordinance October 5, 1874, and the Select Council followed suit a week later.

Although the *Gazette* hailed the step as a "new policy" based on "invoking the competition of rival railroad lines," actual construction of the refined oil pipeline was not pushed. Apparently the refiners were awaiting the outcome of the Columbia Conduit's struggle with the West Penn Railroad.[40]

While the Pittsburgh Councils were considering the refined oil pipeline ordinance, Hostetter was laying the groundwork for a new attack on the West Penn. He purchased land on both sides of the railroad's tracks at Powers Run, a stream over which he believed the railroad had only a right of way. The West Penn, suspecting that the Conduit intended to use the culvert under the tracks, required each train using the route to stop and investigate.[41]

Unsuccessful in court actions to force the West Penn to accept a bond for damages and to refrain from interference with the laying of pipes at Powers Run, the Conduit officials finally decided to attempt a tour de force. On the night of November 27, 1874, 250 men were scattered through the area in the vicinity of Montrose Station awaiting an opportunity to rush the pipeline to completion. Their chance came early in the morning of the twenty-eighth, and they completed laying the vital 100 feet of pipe through the culvert in an hour's time. By 8:00 A.M. oil was flowing through the line. On discovering the *fait accompli*, the railroad commenced to gather its forces for a test of strength, but violence was averted when it was agreed to take the matter to court. Again the legal decision went against the pipeline.[42]

In early December a new case developed when a railroad crew moved in and tore up the Conduit's pipe, allowing oil to flow in profusion before it could be shut off. The Conduit charged that this action was a breach of the agreement to stop operations in an orderly manner and once again went to court, this time demanding damages. Meanwhile, the railroad erected six small "forts" from railroad ties and established a guard force at the scene of the pipeline crossing. Pickets even patrolled the neighboring woods, demanding countersigns from all who approached.[43] Seemingly the Pennsylvania's defenses were impregnable both physically and legally—at least for the time being. So far the Butler County oil operators had gained less from the pipeline efforts of Dr. Hostetter than they had from the 1874 legislative session, small as was the triumph there.

Up to the end of 1874 the railroad-refiners' combination, its position buttressed by the pipeline pool, had been more successful than any of its predecessors. Pipeline access to Pittsburgh and competing refineries, as well as to the Baltimore and Ohio, had been blocked. Despite strident blasts from the Pittsburgh press, refiners there were avoiding precipitate action. The producers seemed unable to organize themselves for a fight. In short, Potts's plan for stabilizing a ruinously competitive situation in favor of the railroads, a select group of refiners, and the major pipelines was bearing fruit. The key to success, however, was control of pipelines, and this control was vulnerable both to public policy and to competition made possible by pipeline enterprise.

Public Policy and Pipelines as Weapons against Combination

With prices for crude hitting new lows and with the railroads and major pipelines blocking access to new markets, the producers desperately sought counterweapons in the fall of 1874. For a time, before ice closed navigation, barges were employed to carry crude to Pittsburgh, and this expedient provided a measure of relief. Since there was insufficient tankage to store the flood of crude in the producing area, the sale of oil at a reduced price became the condition of transporting it—the so-called practice of "immediate shipment." [44] By December, 1874, the price of crude was at its lowest point in more than a decade.[45] Eager to escape the consequences of the glut of oil as well as the tentacles of the railroad and pipeline pools, producers sought allies among Pittsburgh refiners and turned to the state for aid.

On January 28, 1875, a bill was introduced in the Pennsylvania State Senate to extend the eminent domain provisions of the Wallace Corporation Act to crude and refined oil pipelines, to declare such lines common carriers, and to fix maximum pipeline rates on a scale graduated according to distance. The *Pittsburgh Gazette* reported that the bill had the support of twenty thousand people "representing the very best business element in Allegheny County and the oil region." The paper argued for the bill in these words:

It will benefit oil producers, as the oil will reach refiners at less cost, and therefore will enable them to pay better rates to producers. The cost of transportation, and expense of marketing every production invariably comes out of the producer, and oil is no exception to the general rule. It will benefit our refiners, in that it will enable them to compete against the world.[46]

The *Dispatch* declared: "Its main features are just what are needed to make the Columbia Conduit Company of practical use to Pittsburg." [47]

The pipeline measure was of sufficient significance to justify front-page coverage by the *New York Tribune*. That paper reported that the outstanding opponent of the bill was the Pennsylvania Central Railroad, whose strength would be augmented by that of other members of the railroad pool if need be.[48] This prediction was well founded, but in addition to engendering railroad opposition the measure also became the center of a controversy between the rival refining interests of Pittsburgh, Philadelphia, and Baltimore.

Support for the bill, which reportedly originated in the Pittsburgh Chamber of Commerce, was the subject of divided opinion among Pittsburgh refiners when they came to realize that the encouragement of pipeline construction might mean that crude oil would be transported elsewhere for refining. At least William Frew explained an alleged switch in his position on the measure in these terms. The *Gazette* hinted that his connection with Cleveland interests might better explain his motives. Although Frew's firm with seven refineries in Pittsburgh and extensive works in Philadelphia had elected to cast its lot with Standard Oil the preceding October, Frew ignored this point in his rebuttal. He declared that far from being the "sole" opponent of the pipeline bill among Pittsburgh refiners, twelve out of thirty-four of them had voted against a resolution in favor of it.[49]

The progress of the pipeline bill in the Pennsylvania Senate was carefully watched by business circles in Philadelphia and Baltimore and by oil shipping interests in New York and Cleveland, as well as in Pittsburgh. Philadelphia and Baltimore oil exporters had an especially good reason for their interest since the trend of oil shipments during the past year had favored the Maryland city. In January, 1874, Baltimore had exported only 3,315 barrels, but in the corresponding month of 1875 the amount had risen to 37,331 barrels.[50] This remarkable increase in Baltimore's favor was a result of the fact that, even including the pipeline pool's rates, oil could be shipped more cheaply to tidewater via the Baltimore and Ohio than by the Pennsylvania.[51] A pipeline law enabling shippers to use the Baltimore and Ohio even more or giving encouragement for the construction of a pipeline to the seaboard might tip the scales farther in this direction.

The competition of the Baltimore and Ohio was already worrying Tom Scott, and he was already preparing steps to counter it. An angry blast against the other road in mid-February, 1875, was soon followed by reduced rates on the Pennsylvania, which thus violated the terms of the railroad pool.

Meantime, opposition to the pipeline bill was strengthened by the rivalry of Pittsburgh and Philadelphia refiners. By seeking escape from the grasp of the railroad-pipeline pools through this legislation, Pittsburgh refiners ran the risk that refining at the seaboard might be encouraged at their expense. This danger was minimized by advocates of the pipeline measure who charged that freight rate discriminations and pipeline control were already being exercised to the disadvantage of both Pittsburgh and Philadelphia. Passage of the pipeline bill, they maintained, would destroy the unnatural stimulus given to Cleveland and New York refining by the railroad pool.[52]

This argument was not convincing to Philadelphia refiners and exporters, who were losing business to Baltimore. Their objection that completion of Columbia Conduit's pipeline would accentuate the current trend was difficult to counter. Again the rebuttal took the form that a bad situation might be improved by passage of the bill. As long as the Pennsylvania remained in the pool, it was pointed out, Philadelphia was bound to suffer. Completion of the Conduit's pipe would make little difference, since the Pennsylvania owned the tracks between Baltimore and Philadelphia and could therefore levy tribute on Philadelphia oil whether shipped directly or via the Baltimore and Ohio.[53] The passage of the pipeline bill, however, might force the Pennsylvania to change its ways.

Nevertheless, Philadelphians were of divided opinions about possible benefits of the pipeline legislation. Although the Philadelphia Board of Trade endorsed the measure, it did so with the proviso that rates on refined oil should be at least 10 per cent higher than on crude.[54] The Philadelphia City Councils protested the passage of the bill in any form.

The arguments in favor of the pipeline bill always returned to the central issue of the Pennsylvania Railroad's membership in the railroad-pipeline pools. In both the Senate and the House it was suggested that the passage of the bill would permit the railroad to break the Saratoga compact and begin to make money on the oil traffic. The declining position of Pennsylvania refining was attributed to the limited effectiveness of the 1872 free pipe law, together with railroad-pipeline alliances that favored shipment of crude out of the state. The Pennsylvania Railroad's participation in these arrangements was attributed to its connection with the Empire Line.[55] Maintaining that the existing situation was proving costly to the railroad as well as to Pennsylvania oil interests, representatives of the producers demanded that the state help save the railroad from itself.

Tom Scott, however, had good reasons for opposing the pipeline measure. In the first place, it might create pipeline rivals to his railroad and his pipeline system, and from his point of view it was sound policy to guard against such a possibility. The *New York Tribune* recognized this motive when it reported: "The establishment of pipe lines modified somewhat the transportation system, but the influence of the roads and the restrictive legislation adopted in their interest made the pipes feeders to them instead of rivals. . . ."[56] Since the railroad pool provided that 37.54 per cent of the oil traffic to Philadelphia and Baltimore should go via the Pennsylvania, the management of that road did not propose to lose this share through legislation which would aid the Baltimore and Ohio. Secondly, Scott felt capable of meeting his rival's competition without strengthening pipeline competition for the oil traffic, and by March 1, 1875, he was ready to engage the Baltimore and Ohio in a rate contest even though his action violated the pool agreement. Finally, the Pennsylvania may have been contemplating support of a pipeline to the seaboard, without utilizing the provisions of the proposed law, if such a step should become necessary.[57]

Without revealing these motives, railroad spokesmen in the Senate had plausible grounds for opposing the general right of eminent domain for pipelines as a public policy. Basing his argument on the history of pipelines up to that time, Senator David Maclay maintained that pipelines were not permanent assets to the areas which they served. As soon as oil production moved on, the pipes would follow. Railroads, on the other hand, remained to serve the needs of the community after an oil rush had subsided.[58] The *Butler Democratic Herald* indicated that arguments like this one had a telling effect. "What we want in this section," the paper said, "is to have a means of transportation for articles into the county as well as out of it. These railroads accomplish, but pipes do not." [59]

The proponents of the pipeline bill sought in vain for a formula that would reconcile the interests of Pittsburgh, Philadelphia, and the Pennsylvania Railroad. Representative Joseph S. Lusk of Butler County probably came the closest to summing up the producers' solution for this problem. He appealed to each party of the opposition in these terms:

I say to the gentlemen from Philadelphia, that the only possible way in which they can restore this [oil] trade to the city of Philadelphia, is by passing this free pipe bill. They will thus make Pittsburg that which naturally is the oil refining centre; and every barrel of that refined oil will be taken over the Pennsylvania railroad to Philadelphia, and shipped abroad from that point.[60]

The producers, however, were fighting a losing battle. Despite the inequities arising from the existing situation, Pennsylvania refiners saw more to be lost than gained by passage of the pending bill. The Pennsylvania Railroad, for reasons satisfactory to itself, took a similar position. Legislators were sensitive to the argument that passage of the measure would cost the state a loss of revenue from the railroad. Consequently, the Senate bill was defeated on March 4, 1875, by a vote of 27 to 15.[61] Although debate on the companion House measure continued, the Senate's decision had sealed its fate as well.

It seems surprising that in the debate on this legislation the proposal to fix maximum pipeline rates was not challenged; yet there was no discussion of the implications of governmental intervention in this field. The purpose of this section was to break the 30-cents-a-barrel rate of the pipeline pool, and the only questions that arose were whether the rates specified were sufficiently generous. The subcommittee of the House Committee on Corporations was virtually unanimous in approving a maximum charge of 15 cents a barrel for the first ten miles of pipeline transportation.[62] Despite efforts to raise this figure by three cents, the House apparently felt that there was no need for an increase in view of the fact that the pool estimated average costs at eight cents a mile per barrel regardless of distance. Consequently, no change was made in the rates reported out of committee.

There was no debate on the proposal that pipelines organized under the act should be limited to transportation activities. Producers had suffered from the speculative activities of pipelines,[63] and perhaps they may be credited with a legitimate desire to make pipelines perform solely as common carriers, rendering their services on equal terms to all comers in return for a reasonable compensation. Still, considering the sponsorship of the bill, the legislators' silence on this section is puzzling.

A bill authorizing the appointment of gaugers by the courts and inspection of crude and refined oil storage facilities also came before the 1875 legislative session. Unable to cope with the flood of oil, pipelines had required producers to pay pipage and storage charges on oil which was not quickly moved out of their tanks. This practice forced producers to sell pipeline certificates for whatever they would bring as an alternative to the unpleasant prospect of assuming charges that they might not recover.[64] Apparently the gauger and inspection bill was designed to force pipelines to reveal whether or not their tankage was actually as fully employed as this practice seemed to indicate. In essence the producers were challenging the accuracy of the reports submitted under the terms of the law of May, 1874. As originally drawn, the new measure applied only to Butler County, but at the suggestion of the Attorney General it was changed to apply to the whole state.[65] Although the bill passed first reading, refiners objected to its application to them, and nothing more was heard from it.[66] The Pennsylvania legislative session of 1875 thus ended in complete defeat for the producers.

The railroad-pipeline pools emerged unscathed from this attack, but they were suffering from internal dissension and worried about the prospects of increasing competition from the Baltimore and Ohio allied with the Columbia Conduit. Although a new effort in February, 1875, to complete the pipeline at Powers Run had failed, the Baltimore and Ohio was delivering 3,000 barrels of oil a day to Baltimore in March.[67] This was a challenge that the Pennsylvania could not ignore, and it meant the end of the railroad pool. This development in turn meant that members of the pipeline pool would have to cement new alliances with the railroads. The early spring of 1875, then, was a time of change in an industry which combination had only temporarily stabilized.

On the threshold of a new era in pipeline-railroad-refiner relationships, only Standard Oil was a stronger unit than it ever had been. Soon after the formation of the railroad-pipeline pools in the summer of 1874, executives of leading refining firms in Cleveland, New York, Philadelphia, and Pittsburgh decided to establish a close community of interest under Standard Oil's leadership. The agreement, concluded in mid-October, included Charles Pratt and Company of New York, Warden, Frew and Company of Philadelphia, Lockhart, Frew and Company of Pittsburgh, and The Standard Oil Company (Ohio). The community of interest between these firms was to be implemented in the spring of 1875 by the participation of stockholders and partners of each firm in all firms in the group. Once that took place the interests of their Cleveland and New York operations would not dominate the thinking of Standard Oil's leaders. Representatives of all four major refining centers, as well as others to be added later, would speak with a single voice to railroads and producers.

The events of 1872–1875 set the stage for this Standard Oil development, and pipelines played a leading role in those events. Gathering pipelines had become indispensable to crude oil transportation. Railroads found them essential to protect their oil traffic against rivals, and Standard Oil found them useful to cement ties with the northern trunk railroads as well as to assure its crude oil supply. In a little over a year Standard Oil had acquired pipeline interests which were larger than those of any railroad, and it handled a third of the crude moving from wells to railroad depots.

On every hand the effects of depression and overproduction made combination in oil refining and transportation attractive and attempts to undermine it inevitable. The pools of 1874 gave concrete recognition to the importance of pipelines in any arrangement affecting crude oil transportation. Feeling themselves victimized by the results, producers turned to the construction of a trunk pipeline and legislation for a remedy. Although in 1874 they had succeeded in obtaining legislation which recognized pipeline operations and oil storage as proper subjects for public policy, the law itself provided no effective relief. The producers' legislative program in 1875—eminent domain and common carrier status for pipelines throughout the state, maximum rate regulation, and official inspection and gauging of oil tankage—failed completely. On the other hand, pipelines, aided by other factors, were instrumental in breaking up the railroad-pipeline combination. Thenceforth pipelines played an even more important role in the petroleum industry than they had so far.

III

Pipelines as Competitive
Weapons, 1875-1878

THE producers' failure to obtain pipeline legislation in 1875 shifted
the struggle over pipeline power back into the arena of bare-
knuckled competitive strife. The next two years were crucial in this
contest, which arrayed the producers against the growing Standard
Oil alliance and provided them with unexpected aid from the Pennsylvania Railroad. Allied with producers and independent refiners,
the Pennsylvania challenged the Standard Oil group, which was
backed by the northern roads. In the ensuing conflict pipelines were
important weapons, and Standard Oil's dominance in crude oil
transportation between the wells and railroad shipping points was
strengthened by the outcome of the struggle.

The Changing Scene, 1875

The spring of 1875 was a time of rapid change in the unstable
alliances which characterized the petroleum industry. The breakup
of the railroad pool, initiated by the Pennsylvania's rate cuts on
March 1, was the signal for each road to reconsider its competitive
position. The Erie had already expressed its displeasure with the
Pennsylvania Railroad's relationship to the Empire Transportation
Company, which George Blanchard of the Erie believed to be the
recipient of secret rebates. As he put it in 1879, "It was clear that,

as the Empire Line added to its already large resources not only this commission upon the oil business excepting Pittsburgh, but the added profits upon its pipe lines, that its combined operation and profit united to control an increasing share of the entire trade. . . ." [1] The Erie, therefore, in March, 1875, exchanged membership in the pool for a new contract with Standard Oil, whereby the railroad was to carry 50 per cent of Standard Oil's refined oil shipments and in return was to give a 10 per cent rebate on the open rates of the other trunk lines.[2]

Meanwhile the Pennsylvania was attempting to counter the Baltimore and Ohio's growing threat.[3] Completion of the Columbia Conduit's pipe, which was barred from Pittsburgh by only the width of the West Penn's tracks, would increase the seriousness of this challenge. To forestall this development, the Empire Line entered into negotiations for the purchase of Hostetter's company, reportedly offering $400,000 for it. The sale was scheduled to be completed April 27, 1875, but at the last moment the Empire asked for more time.[4] The offer of sale was then suddenly withdrawn. Instead of selling the pipeline to the interests that had thwarted him at every turn, Hostetter leased it to three young men who were to play an important part in pipeline development: Byron D. Benson, Robert E. Hopkins, and David McKelvy.

Undoubtedly, as contemporary reports stated, the Baltimore and Ohio was behind the moves which denied control of the Columbia Conduit to the Empire Line.[5] The problem of connecting the pipes at Powers Run, which remained securely in the hands of the West Penn Railroad, was temporarily solved by pressing tank wagons into use to cross the railroad tracks. Meanwhile, the rival railroads reached a settlement of their differences, and the *Titusville Courier* on June 21, 1875, reported that the Pennsylvania had agreed to permit completion of the pipeline. Within a month the Conduit was delivering oil to Pittsburgh refineries at the rate of 500 barrels an hour.[6]

Pipeline construction had threatened the Pennsylvania Railroad's position not only in Pittsburgh but also in Clarion County. Producers had organized the Atlantic Pipe Line, which tapped two-thirds of the Clarion field, and the Pennsylvania's Allegheny Valley Railroad had refused to connect with it at Sligo. While the producers' lawyers in-

stituted a damage suit against the railroad,[7] the producers turned to
ways of reaching the Baltimore and Ohio. By May 15, 1875, $170,000
of a $300,000 goal for extending the Atlantic Pipe Line to Freeport on
the Baltimore and Ohio's line had been subscribed.[8] Although some
attention was given to the possibility of extending the pipe to the
seaboard if the connection at Freeport were frustrated,[9] such a step
proved unnecessary. The conclusion of the Baltimore and Ohio-
Pennsylvania struggle in June apparently ended the Allegheny
Valley's reluctance to connect with the Atlantic Pipe Line. By the
end of July this link was completed, and the pipeline was reported
to be planning an extension to Karns City, where it could connect
with the Conduit.[10]

The completion of the Atlantic Pipe Line helped to undermine
the effectiveness of the remnants of the pipeline pool. In July the
Pittsburgh *Dispatch* reported that these lines were feeling the effects of the producers' control of the Atlantic Line.[11] A few weeks
later the same paper reported that the associated lines were receiving only five cents pipage. The situation was comparable to the one
that had inspired the pool a year before.

In the interim, however, the Standard Oil alliance had grown in
size and power. This fact was the governing one in the jockeying for
position that accompanied the collapse of the railroad and pipeline
pools. In March, 1875, Standard Oil increased its capital stock ten
thousand shares to take care of the purchases and exchange of shares
projected the preceding fall. In addition to Warden, Frew and Company of Philadelphia, Lockhart, Frew and Company of Pittsburgh,
and Charles Pratt and Company of New York, all of whom had acted
in concert with Standard Oil since the inauguration of the pools,
other firms were brought into the alliance during the spring and
summer of 1875.[12]

Despite its growing power, the Standard Oil group was threatened
on its southern flank by the possibilities inherent in the alliance between the Columbia Conduit and the Baltimore and Ohio Railroad.
This threat could be offset and the security of the refining combination safeguarded by a campaign to acquire refineries south and east
of Pittsburgh. The first step in this direction was taken in the spring
of 1875 with the addition to the combination of the refinery of
Johnson N. Camden of Parkersburg, West Virginia. Camden was

then assigned the task of eliminating any challenge to the alliance from refineries along the Baltimore and Ohio's route to the seaboard. Unaware of the change in the ownership of the Camden firm, the railroad concluded a very favorable contract with that concern in the fall of 1875. In the next two years Camden completed his assignment efficiently.[13]

With the new firms added to the Standard alliance came outstanding managerial talent. From Porter, Moreland and Company of Titusville, for example, came John D. Archbold. Alert, aggressive and ruthless, Archbold was destined to succeed Rockefeller as head of Standard Oil. With Charles Pratt and Company came Henry H. Rogers. A gambler by instinct, iron-nerved, Rogers later managed Standard Oil's pipeline holdings in the National Transit Company. With men like these, Standard Oil could count brains and business talent as well as physical facilities among its new assets.

The moves of early 1875, which included acquisition of an interest in a leading independent pipeline system, were one facet of the Standard Oil plan to dominate American refining. News of the "grand design" began to filter to the public in March, 1875. It was rumored that a combination of refiners was in the making to reduce the cost of crude and raise the price of refined oil. John D. Rockefeller publicly scoffed at the idea of an "Oil Ring," but he told a *New York Tribune* reporter that he favored an organization to "protect the oil capital against speculation, and regulate prices." [14]

With refined oil selling in New York at 15 cents a gallon, refiners had a motive for favoring organized action that might improve their revenues. Standard's Henry H. Rogers told a *Tribune* reporter that oil should sell for at least 25 cents a gallon to yield a fair profit. He also hinted at the broad outlines of Standard Oil's plan to achieve that goal. Rogers declared that an organization of the five principal refining centers was indicated: Pittsburgh, with its advantage of cheap coal; Philadelphia, well situated for export operations; the Oil Regions, close to crude; Cleveland, with its cheap barrels and canal and railroad connections; and New York, situated in the best market area.[15]

Actually plans for such an organization, under Standard Oil's auspices, were already well matured. The *New York Tribune* made them public on April 29, 1875, when it printed the articles of agreement of The Central Association. Refiners were to lease their facilities to the association, whose executive committee was to apportion refining among the five centers named by Rogers, control the purchase of crude and sales of refined, and negotiate all rail and pipeline rates. Rockefeller was president of the association, whose roster soon represented the refining power of the country.

The increasing significance of pipelines at this time did not escape notice. A correspondent of the *Pittsburgh Daily Dispatch* who toured the Butler oil fields in June, 1875, was distinctly impressed by the pipeline operations that he witnessed. He reported: "The whole producing region is brought in contribution to the pipe line companies, whose lines extend in every direction to the extreme limits of the territory." He placed the combined capacity of the lines at 60,000 barrels a day, their storage capacity at 4,800,000 barrels, and their capital at $4,750,000. "It will be easily seen," he wrote, "that these corporations have in themselves the controlling power of the oil regions." [16] Allied with a powerful combination of refiners and the railroads, pipelines under unified control could indeed be regarded as "the controlling power of the oil regions." But that time actually had not yet arrived.

The Erie's contract of March, 1875, with Standard Oil not only had taxed the road's facilities but also had brought a demand from the other trunk lines for a greater share in the oil traffic. Conversations among the roads in the summer of 1875 were followed by a new allocation of seaboard oil shipments. For the first time the Pennsylvania Railroad itself had a contract with Standard Oil. According to Vice-President Cassatt, the Pennsylvania received about 51 per cent of the oil destined for the seaboard, the New York Central and the Erie each received 20 per cent, and, later, the Baltimore and Ohio about 9 per cent.[17] For its services as an "evener" Standard Oil received a commission which amounted to a rebate of 10 per cent from all the trunk lines.[18]

The new railroad pool called for new pipeline alliances. Although Joseph Potts of the Empire disapproved of the Pennsylvania Railroad's new relationship to Standard Oil, which he believed would progress "toward a control of all cars, all pipes, all production, and finally of the roads themselves," he concluded an important contract with the Pennsylvania, November 4, 1875. The Empire Line agreed to build a pipeline from Limestone to Olean, New York, and to increase storage facilities to take care of this expansion. In return the fast-freight line was to receive 20 per cent of the through rate to New York on oil shipped eastward and 40 per cent of the through rate on oil shipped to Buffalo.[19] While the Pennsylvania and the Empire Transportation Company were thus strengthening their bonds, United Pipe Lines concluded an alliance with the New York Central and the Erie. Each road was to receive half of United's crude oil deliveries, and the Erie was guaranteed 27 per cent of all oil freights from the Regions. In return the pipeline company was to receive a 10 per cent rebate on the crude oil shipments of the two roads.[20]

By the end of 1875 the dissolution of the railroad and pipeline pools had resulted in the creation of two powerful railroad-pipeline groups. On the one hand, the Pennsylvania-Empire Line combination watched the growth of the Standard Oil alliance with misgiving; on the other hand, the close working relationship between Standard Oil and the New York Central and the Erie made a challenge to any one of them a challenge to all. It was a situation that called for caution, and for the time being both groups were content to await further developments.

The First Project for a Pipeline to the Seaboard

The events of 1874–1875, culminating in the railroad pool agreements of the latter year, had played into the hands of Standard Oil. When the Baltimore and Ohio joined the compact, producers and independent refiners had to turn elsewhere to escape the pool's levy on their shipments. For some refiners it was easier to capitulate. In mid-April, 1876, for example, it was reported that the Aladdin, Cosmos, and Vesta refineries in Pittsburgh and the Octave refinery at Titusville had been sold to Standard Oil.[21] If the process were not to continue, some means had to be found to transport oil to the seaboard free from the exactions of the railroads.

The usefulness of the Columbia Conduit for this purpose had been greatly lessened by the Baltimore and Ohio's participation in the pool. Pittsburgh refiners found a workable, though far from satisfactory, solution to their problem. Oil transported to Pittsburgh by the Conduit was refined there and then loaded aboard barges for the trip down the Ohio River to Huntington, West Virginia. At that point it was transferred to the Chesapeake and Ohio Railroad, which carried it to Richmond, Virginia, for export.[22] But this expedient could render only partially effective relief. As a New York *Daily Graphic* reporter put it, the success of pipelines "and the growing trammels of the Standard combination suggested a larger pipe and a line across the country to the sea, dispensing with cars, accidents, monopolies, freights, and all the brood of mischiefs which impede the free distribution of nature's distilled gifts." [23]

The occasion for this comment was an interview with Henry Harley, the pipeline pioneer, who had now undertaken the project of connecting the Regions with the seaboard by pipe. A charter for this purpose had been obtained by the Pennsylvania Transportation Company in 1875, and news of the enterprise began to appear in the Regions press in April, 1876. Harley had presented his plan to General Herman Haupt, an expert in railroad construction, for whom he had worked as an engineer on the Hoosac Tunnel, and had consulted Benjamin Butler as to its legal aspects. Both men had been enthusiastic. Haupt estimated the cost of a three-hundred-mile line and associated equipment at $1,250,000. Of this amount, $1,000,000 represented the cost of cutting out wagon roads to reach the route, and laying, ditching, and crossing streams with the line. Thirteen pumping stations along the way would cost $150,000, and $100,000 was earmarked for securing a right of way, constructing a telegraph line, and defraying the usual legal expenses.

The lack of a general free pipe law reportedly did not bother Harley. The Columbia Conduit was stopped because the route of the West Penn Railroad had been owned in fee simple by the Pennsylvania Railroad. This was not true, however, of the Pennsylvania's main line nor of those of its leased lines. Consequently, Harley was confident, at least for purposes of publication, that the problem of obtaining a right of way for his pipe was a minor one.[24]

The Pennsylvania Railroad and the Empire Line, now associated with Standard Oil and with an extensive pipeline network of their own, apparently opposed Harley's project. There had been a barrage of articles pointing to the risks invited by those permitting the pipeline to cross their property, and Harley attributed them to the efforts of Standard Oil and the Pennsylvania Railroad.[25] But there were other more basic factors threatening the success of the enterprise.

On August 1, 1876, the Oil City correspondent of the *Pittsburgh Daily Dispatch* reported that Harley's project had not created great excitement—first, because it was regarded as too large an undertaking for the parties involved, and, second, because another line proposed by New York parties, none of whom was identified, was regarded as more likely to succeed. Two weeks later the paper added to these views the rumor that, when the line was in operation, it would be sold to the Pennsylvania Railroad, and the producers would be in "as bad shape as ever."

The producers were actually not in "as bad shape" as this report suggested. Although in early July Standard Oil was accused of raising refined oil prices out of all relation to the price of crude,[26] by the middle of the month the price of raw petroleum was rising, and it was reported that the producers would not even oppose a resuscitation of the South Improvement Company if the margin between crude and refined prices was not made too great.[27] By September the *Oil City Derrick* was exulting over good prices, declaring: "We do not feel the full effects yet, but we perceive the brilliant dawnings of better days—days when the Oil Region and its product shall take its old rank of importance in the greatest industries of the world."[28]

Under these conditions it is obvious why Harley's projected pipeline did not call forth the same enthusiasm that accompanied construction of the Columbia Conduit and Atlantic pipelines. Moreover, there was growing suspicion, perhaps fostered by Standard Oil and the Pennsylvania Railroad, that Harley's Pennsylvania Transportation Company was being mismanaged.

During the spring and summer of 1876 there had been a rising demand for gauging of pipeline companies' tanks in the belief that the reports submitted under the law of 1874 were not correct.[29] Although the Pennsylvania Transportation Company's gaugers had reported that all was in order, by October 23, 1876, prominent oil dealers were refusing to accept the company's certificates.[30] Within a few days the company's directors acknowledged an overissue of certificates in the district below Oil City. By November 1 it was reported that the company had failed and that it had little, if any, oil on

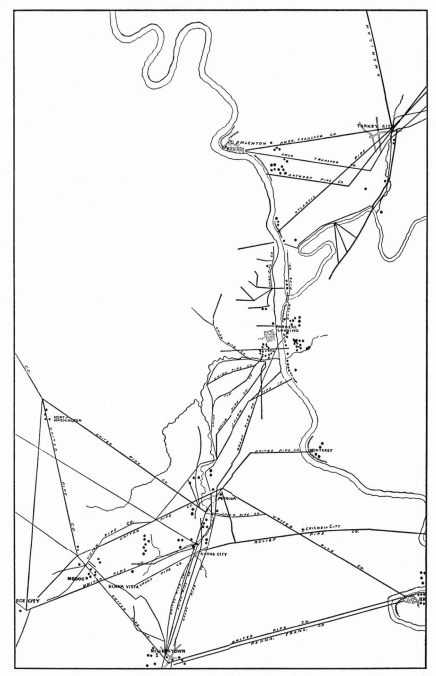

Location of pipelines and tankage in the lower district of the Pennseylvania Oil
Regions, 1876

hand.[31] Two days later General Haupt, the chief engineer for the seaboard line, resigned, and by the end of the month Harley had been indicted by a Venango County Grand Jury for obtaining money under false pretenses.[32] Harley's misfortunes ended the seaboard pipeline project for the time being.

Although Harley had been harassed at every turn and quo warranto proceedings had been instituted to test his right to lay a pipeline to the seaboard, there seems to be little ground for believing, as was later charged, that Standard Oil had to go out of its way to ruin him. Even Ida Tarbell declared that the Pennsylvania Transportation Company had been "grossly mismanaged." [33] The very characteristics that made Harley a promoter and innovator robbed his business ventures of success.

The Protagonists Seek Positions of Advantage

The failure of Harley's seaboard pipeline project seemed to confirm the helplessness of producers and independent refiners in the face of the railorad-refiners' combination. Moreover, the chief benefits were accruing to Standard Oil, as Joseph Potts had foreseen in 1875 when he had opposed the Pennsylvania Railroad's alliance with the combination. In the meantime, the Standard Oil group had grown steadily, purchasing or leasing refineries in the Oil Regions, Pittsburgh, New York, Baltimore, and at intermediate points.[34] Unquestionably Standard Oil intended to dominate refining, and unquestionably it was succeeding.

Potts feared for the future of the Empire Line as an oil carrier. He later told a federal investigating committee:

We reached the conclusion that there were three great divisions in the petroleum business—the production, the carriage of it, and the preparation of it for market. If any one party controlled absolutely any one of those three divisions, they practically would have a very fair show of controlling the others.[35]

Potts, therefore, proposed to challenge Standard Oil's rapidly increasing hold on refining. With the support of the Pennsylvania Railroad, he put the Empire Transportation Company into the refining business as a means of keeping its oil traffic profitable.

This move must have been influenced to some extent by the spectacular development of the Bradford field in McKean County, whose rich yield had not been foreseen when the railroad pool was formed in 1875. Production in that district shot up from 384,000 barrels in 1876 to nearly a million more barrels in the following year.[36] The Empire had thrown a network of gathering pipes into the area, and they carried for the New York Central as well as the Pennsylvania.

In the fall of 1876 a representative of the Empire approached George Blanchard with the suggestion that the Erie also utilize the Empire's pipes as feeders. Blanchard, however, was unwilling to be dependent on a rival's pipeline. Instead, he concluded a contract with Standard Oil's American Transfer Company, which he understood was opposed to the Empire.[37]

Under the terms of the contract, effective in early 1877, the already close relationship between the Erie and Standard Oil was strengthened. The pipeline company was to construct a three-inch pipe from Carrollton, on the Erie's main line, to Bradford as well as to provide necessary branch lines and tankage. All oil transported by these pipes was to be shipped over the Erie, which was to make through rates from the wells or tanks no higher than rates via other railroads. The American Transfer Company was to receive 20 cents a barrel for collecting, transporting, and loading oil aboard Erie cars.[38] According to President Jewett of the Erie, the through rate was to protect the railroad against the pipeline making improper exactions from producers. In return the Erie agreed not to charge less for transporting oil delivered at its stations than it charged for oil which came from the wells via the pipeline. Jewett said that the pipeline charge was paid by the railroad, which received compensation by making its own arrangements with shippers.[39]

Meantime, the Empire was preparing a position from which it might be able to challenge Standard Oil and the northern roads. Potts had acquired the Sone and Fleming refinery at Newtown Creek, Long Island, and he had a new refinery under construction near Philadelphia. At Communipaw, New Jersey, the Empire had a large, well-equipped oil terminal, where additional refining operations were contemplated.[40] With these facilities and also alliances with refiners outside the Standard Oil combination, the Empire would have a market for the oil transported by its pipes and tank cars. Potts, however, had to make sure of the Pennsylvania Railroad's support.

While the Erie was cementing its ties with the American Transfer Company, the Empire Line was strengthening its attachment to the Pennsylvania. By the terms of a contract concluded in January, 1877, the railroad agreed to provide transportation for all oil destined for refineries controlled or allied with the Empire. The fast-freight line was to receive all rebates and deductions made by the Pennsylvania to other oil shippers, and in return the Empire from its refinery profits was to make up any losses incurred by the railroad if it were forced to reduce its net rates on petroleum and its products below those existing in December, 1876.[41]

This situation was intolerable to the northern roads. As President Hugh J. Jewett saw it, the Erie could not permit the Pennsylvania through the Empire Line to build up facilities which, when completed, would permit it to go into the Oil Regions with an advantage over the Erie.[42] The New York Central took a similar position. William H. Vanderbilt later recalled "that the Erie Road and the New York Central protested against any competitor of theirs in the way of railroads being engaged in pipe lines—being engaged in transportation, refineries, etc.; that was the fight; the Standard Oil Company had nothing to do with it." [43]

It is inconceivable, however, that Standard Oil should have remained aloof in the face of a growing threat to its hold on refining. Nor was this the case. Officials of the combination complained to the Pennsylvania, before the other railroads brought pressure to bear, that the Empire Line was not according fair treatment to Standard Oil in cars or rates.[44] Henry M. Flagler testified in 1888 that the Empire had favored its own refineries in the matter of rates, allegedly enabling Standard Oil's competitors to undersell the oil alliance. "That, of course," he said, "was the main point which brought about the issue in 1877." [45]

The Pennsylvania, attempting to extricate itself from a difficult position, urged the Empire to lease its refineries to Standard Oil or place them in other hands. Potts, however, would do neither. When he offered to sell out to the railroad, which was an option in the terms of their contract, the Pennsylvania declined to exercise its option.[46]

In the face of protests by Blanchard of the Erie and Rutter of the New York Central, Potts maintained his stand. In mid-March Standard Oil, counting on the support of the northern roads, cut off its oil shipments via the Pennsylvania. Jewett of the Erie recalled the situation in these words: "I have no doubt—because it would be but natural and therefore I say I have no doubt—that we demanded of the Standard Oil Company, during that contest, to withdraw its shipments from the Pennsylvania Railroad." [47] Alexander J. Cassatt, third vice-president of the Pennsylvania, declared: "They [representatives of Standard Oil] simply insisted that they could not make any arrangements with us for the transportation of their oil so long as that transportation was carried on by an organization which was their rival in the refining business." [48]

Neither side could have entered the fray without pipelines. By March 22, 1877, the United, Sandy, Antwerp, Oil City, Atlantic, and some of American Transfer's pipelines had completed arrangements to consolidate their interests in a single corporation to be known as the United Pipe Lines, organized under the Wallace Corporation Act of 1874. Its charter, enrolled March 27, 1877, authorized it to engage in exploring for, producing, purchasing, refining, transporting, and dealing in petroleum in accordance with the supplement to the mining and manufacturing law of July 18, 1863, approved April 9, 1873. It was specifically stated that the company was authorized to lay pipes and erect telegraph lines, tanks, and other facilities in accordance with the pipeline law of March 12 and 19, 1872. Capital stock in the amount of $3,000,000, divided among 30,000 shares, was authorized. Jacob Jay Vandergrift was named president, and John D. Rockefeller, Henry Flagler, Jabez Bostwick, and Daniel O'Day were among the directors.[49] A bonus of $12,500 was paid to the state upon the company's incorporation.[50]

The Empire did not formally reorganize its pipeline holdings until the contest with Standard Oil was well under way. In early April, however, its Union Pipe Line Company extended a line into the booming Bullion pool in Butler County, and in May it absorbed the Karns Pipe Line.[51] On June 30, 1876, the company gave notice that its lines would be reorganized as of July 1 in the following manner. The Union Pipe Line Company would be known as the Union Division of the Empire Pipe Company; the Titusville Pipe

Company would be designated the Titusville Division; the Warren Pipe Line would become the Warren Division; and the Olean Pipe Company would be renamed the Olean Division.[52] The battle of Standard Oil and its railroad allies against the Pennsylvania was equally one of United Pipe Lines against the Empire Pipe Company.

The War on the Empire Line

Termination of Standard Oil's shipments over the Pennsylvania meant that Potts had to make strenuous efforts to take up the slack. Arrangements had to be made to obtain oil from the producers and to effect alliances with refiners. An agreement was reached with a body of producers and embodied in a contract negotiated by Charles P. Hatch, the Empire's chief oil agent, with Benjamin B. Campbell and Elisha G. Patterson. Under its terms the producers were to run their oil through the Empire Pipe Line, and the Empire Transportation Company was to transport that oil at rates as low as any offered by its competitors. The Empire also agreed to continue purchasing oil for the next six months as it had in the past in order that the producers might establish relations with independent refiners. The contract, concluded in early July, 1877, was guaranteed by the Pennsylvania Railroad and its affiliated lines.[53]

Standard Oil reportedly cut the price of refined oil in every market served by the Empire.[54] To attract business from independent refiners and other shippers the Pennsylvania was forced to offer larger and larger rebates. Vice-President Cassatt of the Pennsylvania recalled:

We paid very large rebates; in fact, we took anything we could get for transporting their oil; in some cases we paid out rebates more than the whole freight. I recollect one instance when we carried oil to New York for Mr. Ohlen, or some one he represented, at 8 cents less than nothing.[55]

Standard Oil's railroad allies suffered nothing like this loss. The Erie, for example, never received less than 35 cents a barrel, net, during the height of the contest.[56]

Added to the Pennsylvania's losses on the oil traffic were those resulting from the railroad strike and riots of July, 1877. The results were catastrophic. The net earnings of all the Pennsylvania's lines east of Pittsburgh and Erie showed a decline of $423,440 in August,

1877, as compared with the same period the year before.[57] By September it was reported that the road was in "sore straits for money," had borrowed $300,000 on stock of the Pittsburgh and Fort Wayne, and was willing to borrow smaller amounts from anyone who would lend it.[58]

Furthermore, there was growing discontent among stockholders of the railroad with its relationship to Potts's company. In 1874–1875 the course of the Pennsylvania in supporting Standard Oil had been attributed by the press and in the legislature to its connections with the Empire. Now a cry arose against the road for sacrificing its profits for the sake of the fast-freight affiliate. Reporting that the Baltimore and Ohio had severed its connections with the Adams Express company, the *Philadelphia Record* of August 6, 1877, for example, observed editorially: "Millions of dollars have been made by the transportation, express and other corporations having the privilege of running their cars on our railroads, which ought to have gone into the coffers of the railroad companies." The application of this stricture on railroad management to Tom Scott's situation is unmistakable. On virtually all counts it seemed advisable for the Pennsylvania to end a struggle which was only adding to the deficits created by the Pittsburgh riot and by declining revenues elsewhere in its operations.

In August, 1877, Rockefeller and Flagler extended the olive branch, inviting Scott to send a representative to Cleveland to discuss termination of the conflict. Satisfactory conversations between Scott's emissary, Alexander Cassatt, and the Standard officials in Cleveland were followed by further negotiations in Philadelphia during September. According to Cassatt, Standard Oil's basic condition for resuming oil shipments over the Pennsylvania was that the Empire cease refining.[59] Potts was unwilling to concede this point, insisting that, if the Pennsylvania was to capitulate, the railroad must buy out the Empire under the terms of the contract between the two transportation agencies. Potts had foreseen the consequences of bowing to Standard Oil as far back as 1875, and he did not intend to be a party to it without adequate remuneration. Scott, on the other hand, hard pressed financially, had the offer of an attractive contract with Standard Oil dangling before his eyes and was ready to surrender.

The existing railroad situation also favored a settlement on the Empire issue. Since April, 1876, the trunk lines had been engaged in a ruinous struggle for traffic between New York and western points. By the summer of 1877 the roads were seeking relief by means of a pool, which would include the oil traffic. Standard Oil's pipeline power as well as its large refined oil shipments insured its inclusion in the pool as "evener" of the oil traffic.

The Pennsylvania, however, had suggested that the roads agree to divide the oil freights in fixed proportions with equal rates charged to all shippers. As one method of accomplishing this, it proposed that a joint agent be assigned to the Oil Regions and empowered to issue bills of lading for shipments over any one of the roads and to be responsible for a division of the business. According to Cassatt this proposal was rejected because the other railroads felt that Standard Oil, if left out of the agreement, would seek other outlets than the trunk rail lines, and the result would be a decrease rather than increase in freight rates.[60]

The northern railroad presidents may have feared the expansion of Standard Oil's pipeline network, which was both technologically and financially feasible. They were certainly unwilling to risk such an obviously unprofitable course of action as the Pennsylvania had been following. Therefore, having agreed upon a division of the oil traffic, each road made its own arrangements with Standard Oil.[61]

The usefulness of the Empire's pipelines to the Pennsylvania was now at an end. With the prospect of receiving a minimum shipment of 2,000,000 barrels of oil per year guaranteed by Standard Oil, Tom Scott was ready to liquidate the Empire's entire holdings.

It was a foregone conclusion that Standard Oil would buy the refineries, but this left the matter of the pipelines and tank cars. Cassatt declared that representatives of the oil combination offered to let the Pennsylvania buy the pipelines.[62] Flagler backed this interpretation in later testimony, declaring: "We were not interested in transportation at all."[63] On the other hand, the *Philadelphia Record* of September 19, 1877, reported: "In order to get these [Empire] pipe lines in hand it has been necessary to cook up the purchase of the Transportation Company, and that is all the milk contained in that cocoanut." There was probably more truth in this statement than in Flagler's assertion that Standard Oil was not interested in transportation. In any event he testified that since Scott did not want the pipelines, "we finally yielded that point." [64] If it was indeed a concession, it was a magnificent one. The Empire's pipelines cost Standard Oil $1,094,805.56, by far the largest amount involved in the whole transaction.

The formalities were concluded in Potts's office, Girard Street, Philadelphia, on October 17, 1877. In addition to agreeing to the purchase of the pipelines, Standard Oil was to pay $501,652.78 for the Empire's New York and Philadelphia refineries, $900,000 for its share in the Oil Tank Car Trust, and $900,000 for other items.[65] In return William Rockefeller and Tom Scott exchanged letters confirming the Pennsylvania's share in the oil trade in return for a 10 per cent commission to Standard Oil for its services as "evener." [66]

The pipeline transaction apparently was concluded without reference to the other railroads; in fact, these roads, which claimed credit for starting the war on the Empire, declared a complete lack of concern with its outcome. William H. Vanderbilt of the New York Central testified in 1879: "We never insisted that he [Cassatt of the Pennsylvania Railroad] should sell to the Standard; we did not care whom he sold to; never made that point; never did, and I don't think Mr. Jewett did." [67] George Blanchard of the Erie corroborated this testimony by saying: "It was no part of our stipulation that the Empire Line should go out of the transportation business or sell either its pipes, refineries or cars to the Standard Oil Company or anyone else, and we were not to my knowledge, consulted by the Standard Company, the Empire Line or the Pennsylvania Railroad upon any of those points." [68] Thus the railroad managers who had expressed fear of a pipeline monopoly in 1874 now appeared indifferent to Standard Oil's rapid progress in this direction. Content with the existing situation, they placed the origination of their oil traffic irrevocably in the hands of Standard Oil.

During the remainder of the year Standard Oil consolidated and expanded its pipeline holdings. The success of Camden's campaign to secure the oil combination's southern flank against the sniping of independent refiners had removed the threat of the first trunk pipeline, the Columbia Conduit. In the late summer of 1877 David Hostetter was seeking a purchaser for the line. He had approached the Empire Line,[69] but its capitulation to Standard Oil left only the latter's United Pipe Lines in a position to purchase. On October 2, 1877, the Regions press reported that Standard Oil had absorbed the Conduit. The Baltimore and Ohio thus joined the list of roads almost completely dependent on the oil alliance for their petroleum shipments. In November the American Transfer Company completed a line from Butler County into Pittsburgh,[70] thereby suggesting that Standard Oil intended to take the crude oil traffic to the Smoky City entirely away from the railroads.

In late October a reporter for the *New York Tribune* interviewed Henry C. Ohlen, an independent oil broker, on his reactions to Standard Oil's recent conquest. His reply summed up the situation in these words:

I can ship no oil from the Oil Region now without paying a royalty to the Standard Oil Company. . . . The Standard Company now controls all the pipe lines, but it is not likely that at present it will discourage the producers by making an extravagant charge for transporting oil through the pipes.[71]

This was an accurate statement in regard to Standard Oil's policy on pipeline charges. Effective November 20, 1877, United Pipe Lines confirmed a standard rate of 20 cents per barrel from the wells to all delivery points on railroads in Butler, Armstrong, Clarion, and Venango counties.[72] Standard Oil did not attempt to exploit its pipeline power in these counties directly at the expense of the producers who might have attempted to exercise countervailing power. Instead the alliance chose a more vulnerable target—the railroads.

Standard Oil's Pipeline Power and the Railroads, 1877–1878

In a statement submitted to the United States Industrial Commission in 1899, John D. Rockefeller declared, "To the best of my recollection the greatest rebates [to Standard Oil] were paid from 1877 to 1879." [73] Beginning on October 17, 1877, the day of the Empire's sale to Standard Oil, the New York Central and the Erie commenced paying a commission on the oil they carried, regardless of its origin, to the American Transfer Company.[74] This organization's pipes had been transferred to United Pipe Lines except for those connecting with the railroads at Oil City, Olean, Salamanca, Kane, and Pittsburgh.[75]

American Transfer was in a key position to exact the "royalty" of which Ohlen spoke. The general manager of the company, Daniel O'Day, called this fact to the attention of Alexander J. Cassatt of the Pennsylvania Railroad in a letter dated February 15, 1878. He declared:

I here repeat what I once stated to you and which I asked you to receive and treat as strictly confidential, that we have been for many months receiving from the New York Central and Erie Railroads certain sums of money, in no instance less than twenty cents per barrel on every barrel of crude oil carried by each of those roads.

Cooperating, as we are doing, with the Standard Oil Company and the trunk lines in every effort to secure for the railroads paying rates of freight on the oil they carry, I am constrained to say to you that, in justice to the interest I represent, we should receive from your company at least twenty cents on each barrel of crude oil you transport.[76]

The significance of Standard Oil's victory over the Empire Line and its control of pipelines was now clear. As Cassatt later testified, the alternative to accepting the demands made on him would have been to see the American Transfer open its pipelines for transportation to the Ohio River. This would not only have cost the Pennsylvania the patronage of Standard Oil but would have forced the railroad's rates down on all its other oil shipments.[77] O'Day carefully pointed out in his letter that the purchase of the Columbia Conduit had cut off the shipments that it had been making via the Ohio River and the Chesapeake and Ohio Railroad, and he concluded, "I may add that the Baltimore and Ohio road are wholly dependent upon us for any oil they may carry." The implication was that the new pipeline into Pittsburgh could ruin the Allegheny Valley Railroad's oil traffic but was being restrained by Standard Oil's role as "evener."[78] Cassatt, therefore, consented to a payment of 20 cents a barrel on all crude oil carried to New York, Philadelphia, and Baltimore by the Pennsylvania.[79] Under Standard Oil's auspices, the potentialities inherent in the pipeline-railroad pool of 1874 were now being fully realized.

The New York Central and the Erie both attempted to justify their payments to the American Transfer Company when the matter was aired before a committee of the New York legislature in 1879. President Jewett of the Erie declared that his road had never paid the

American Transfer for any services that it had not rendered.[80] George Blanchard explained the situation in some detail. He pointed out that all the crude coming over the Erie system from Oil City passed through the American Transfer Company's lines at that shipping point and that the payments on that oil represented compensation for the pipeline's paying the charges of the Allegheny Valley Railroad, storing the oil, transferring it across the river by pipe, and loading it aboard cars of the Atlantic and Great Western.[81] In regard to payments made by the Erie on shipments through the pipeline from Carrollton to Bradford, Blanchard declared that they were "always regarded by us as a portion of our actual expense of doing the business, and worth as much or more to our increased miscellaneous traffic than the amount paid for bringing the oil to Carrollton." [82] Accordingly, it was his view that such payments did not represent a form of rebate, concession, or drawback but rather an "item of requisite working expense." [83]

Similar explanations were forthcoming from representatives of the New York Central, which was served by the American Transfer Company at Salamanca, where deliveries were made to its Rochester and State Line Railroad. In his testimony James H. Rutter, the Central's freight agent, at first denied that his road had paid 20 cents a barrel to the American Transfer. He qualified this, however, by admitting that the Rochester and State Line might have made such payments.[84]

William H. Vanderbilt, on the other hand, denied ever hearing of the American Transfer Company as "connected with oil." [85] He maintained that he had no knowledge of its being paid 20 cents a barrel on oil transported over the New York Central and testily declared: "I don't know Mr. O'Day from a side of sole leather." [86]

Against these denials and explanations we have Cassatt's testimony that he had personally examined receipted bills showing that both the New York Central and the Erie had paid commissions to the American Transfer.[87] In view of O'Day's letter to Cassatt stating that this was the case and demanding similar payments from the Pennsylvania, there can be little doubt that the American Transfer Company was the medium through which Standard Oil collected a levy on all crude oil shipments over the trunk line railroads. In some instances it was perhaps a legitimate payment for services rendered. In others it was simply an exaction made possible as a result of Standard Oil's pipeline power. Certainly from Cassatt's own testimony it is obvious that Standard Oil's control of pipelines influenced the Pennsylvania in yielding to O'Day's demands.

The events of 1875–1877, resulting in Standard Oil's acquisition of the Columbia Conduit and Empire pipelines, removed the railroad threat to Standard Oil's goal of predominance in refining. Playing on the roads' chronic inability to end ruinous competition, the oil alliance was able to expand its power over refining and to add dominance in pipeline transportation to railroad delivery points. The collapse of the seaboard pipeline project, the defeat of the Empire, and the resulting arrangements whereby the trunk railroads paid rebates to Standard Oil on not only its own but its competitors' oil shipments placed the alliance close to its goal. But the producers and the remaining independent refiners still had public policy and pipeline innovation as weapons against the increasingly powerful and unified refining combination.

IV

Pipelines and the Producers'
Attack on Standard Oil, 1878-1880

BY THE end of 1877 Standard Oil seemed to have a clear field in consolidating its predominant position in refining. The trunk line railroads were its allies, and Standard-controlled pipelines served the railroads. The only major antagonists still in a position to upset this picture were the producers, and they needed transportation and refining facilities to offer a serious challenge. The Empire Line had offered these resources, but now its facilities were added to those of Standard Oil. A dwindling number of independent refiners and exporters, chiefly in New York, still provided the producers with a market for crude outside the Standard Oil alliance, but their survival and the producers' deliverance from a dependence on the alliance similar to that of the railroads did not seem likely.

During the next two years the producers probed desperately for weak spots in Standard Oil's armor. They sought access to the seaboard by pipeline, public policies which would offset the advantages of the oil alliance in transportation, and the creation of a public opinion hostile to that group.

A Pipeline Answer to Standard Oil's Victory over the Empire

The Bradford field in McKean County, close to the New York State line, had developed rapidly since 1875. The hilly, wooded tract of oil land between the Allegheny and its tributaries yielded an ever-increasing flow of oil. By November, 1877, pipeline runs were averaging 8,200 barrels daily,[1] and the Standard Oil lines were feeling the strain. Although United Pipe Lines attempted to fulfill its usual functions, connecting with new wells, providing storage, and acting as banker for all oil delivered, it could not keep up with the demand for its services. On December 27, 1877, the company announced that it could not provide tankage for production at the current rate and shortly thereafter invoked its "immediate shipment" requirement, whereby producers had to sell their oil at a discount to have it moved from the wells.[2]

This situation was anathema to producers. They were faced with the alternatives of selling at depressed prices, having the oil run out on the ground, or stopping the drill only to have competitors benefit by the "law of capture." Again they organized and turned to pipeline construction and public policy for an escape from their predicament.

The vehicle for action was the Petroleum Producers' Union, which was vitalized after the collapse of the Empire Line. Its proposed course of action was veiled in secrecy until late in December, 1877. The press then revealed that the Grand Council of the Union had a seaboard pipeline project under consideration.[3] On January 10, 1878, the Council voted full support to an enterprise already under way.[4]

Even before the formal surrender of the Empire Line, the producers had been considering a new proposal for reaching the seaboard by pipeline. They had been promised assistance by Andrew Banks, president of the only company holding a pipeline charter in Maryland.[5] Byron D. Benson, Robert E. Hopkins, and David McKelvy, who had operated the Columbia Conduit prior to its acquisition by Standard Oil, were the key figures in the new undertaking. They had sufficient experience with trunk pipeline operation to appreciate the possibilities of constructing a line to the seaboard, and they engaged Herman Haupt, chief engineer of Harley's abortive project, to handle the construction. On January 3, 1878, the *Baltimore American* reported that Haupt had secured a right of way from Butler County, Pennsylvania, to Anne Arundel County, Maryland, a distance of 230 miles. He had also filed deeds on 300 acres of land where reportedly a refinery was to be built to offer a challenge to Standard Oil.

The undertaking called for a considerable amount of capital, but it promised good returns. The *Bradford Era* declared that the Producers' Union was considering the purchase of the pipeline's right of way and the organization of a company in which any of its members could hold stock. The purpose of this arrangement would be to furnish trunk pipeline transportation to the members of the Union at a maximum charge of one dollar a barrel.[6] If, as the *New York Tribune* reported, oil could be pumped from the Regions to Baltimore for six cents a barrel as compared with the railroad charges of $1.20 to $1.45, the enterprise looked like a profitable one. Although Standard Oil prepared to counter this threat,[7] the producers' project remained dormant for the next six months.

Meantime, another avenue of escape from the tightening web of Standard Oil's influence was being investigated. In this case the objective was to reach Buffalo by pipe and then to use the Erie Canal for the remainder of the trip to New York. The possibilities offered by this route had been discussed by producers in the Bradford area since early 1877, and Lewis Emery, Jr., now assumed the lead in such an enterprise.

Born at Chautauqua, New York, in 1839, Emery had come to the Oil Regions in 1865. His first producing venture had been at Pioneer in Venango County; later he established a refinery at Titusville. In 1875 he entered the Bradford field, which was just opening up, and had been very successful. A resident of Bradford, he was elected to the Pennsylvania House in 1878, to the Pennsylvania Senate in 1880, and was re-elected to that body in 1884. A tenacious, hard-hitting businessman and politician, he proved himself a worthy opponent of Rockefeller and his associates.[8]

In early 1878, Emery was the leading figure in the organization of the Equitable Petroleum Company (Limited), which proposed to link the Bradford field with Buffalo by pipeline.[9] This was a private venture outside the Producers' Union, and Emery reportedly was considering the erection of a refinery at Buffalo.[10] The two approaches to evading Standard Oil's advantages in transportation— one a collective effort by the producers, the other a private venture involving refining—divided the forces which opposed Standard Oil's single-minded drive to power.[11] The diversity of opinions about the proper strategy to employ in dealing with Standard Oil manifested itself in the major conflict which broke out between the producers and the refining combination in the spring of 1878.

By that time the producers in the Bradford field were suffering acutely from the consequences of overproduction and the lack of a route to the seaboard free from the combination's influence.[12] Although New York refiners also found themselves being squeezed in Standard Oil's vise, they were at first reluctant to support Emery's project.[13]

Josiah Lombard, Rufus T. Bush, and George F. Gregory were among the group of refiners that approached Alexander J. Cassatt of the Pennsylvania that spring and asked for the same rates as those given Standard Oil. Since it was obviously impossible for the group to generate the same amount of traffic as the Standard Oil alliance, Cassatt curtly dismissed the proposal. When the refiners queried him on his reaction to their building a pipeline, Cassatt snorted: "Well, you may lay all the pipe lines you like and we will buy them up for old iron." [14]

Emery's Equitable Petroleum Company was even then completing arrangements to reach New York by a pipeline-barge route. By May, 1878, the project was under way,[15] but construction of a pipeline to Buffalo was an expensive and slow operation. In August the *New York Tribune* reported that the new route, including alterations to oil boats, railroad extensions, and pipeline construction, already had cost $500,000 and that twice that amount was to be expended in the next year.[16] Standard Oil was reported earlier to be doing its best to increase the company's financial difficulties by threatening to boycott pipe manufacturers who extended credit to it.[17]

By midsummer a makeshift route was in operation. Oil was brought by pipe to Fisbie's Station on the Buffalo and McKean Railroad. From there it was transported by rail to Buffalo, where it was transferred to barges for the remainder of the trip. The first shipment via this route, 1,919,000 gallons of crude, arrived in New York on August 7, 1878.[18]

The New York refiners, with an eye to the problems that winter would bring to barge transportation, actually would have preferred to use the New York Central from Buffalo to tidewater. They sounded out William H. Vanderbilt on this possibility in July, 1878.

Like Cassatt, Vanderbilt demanded that the refiners provide an amount of freight equal to Standard Oil's if they were to enjoy the same rates accorded that group.[19] A promoter of the new route summed up the situation for a *New York Tribune* reporter on the occasion of the arrival of the first shipment by barge:

At present, they [the railroads] are moving oil under an apportionment agreement, and when dealers and producers desired to engage tank cars to be filled through the United Company, the railroad agents threw every obstacle in the way. We simply demanded equal rates with other operators in proportion to the gross amount of oil shipped, which were refused.[20]

To protect Standard Oil against the threat posed by the competition of the canal route and to retain their share of the oil traffic, the trunk line railroads granted additional rebates to the alliance. According to George Blanchard's later testimony, this amounted to 20 cents a barrel on refined oil.[21] The roads made the net rate on crude shipped to New York 88.5 cents a barrel as compared with the open rate of $1.40.[22] When the canal route was closed by ice in December, the rates were restored to their prior levels.[23] Only a pipeline to the seaboard, immune to weather and the exactions of Standard Oil's railroad allies, seemed to offer a satisfactory answer to the producers' transportation problems.

The project for a pipeline route to the seaboard from Butler County had languished during these months. Its promoters, Benson, McKelvy, and Hopkins, had been reassessing their undertaking. Since the tide of oil production was now definitely centered in McKean County, and the Philadelphia and Reading Railroad offered financial support as well as connections to Philadelphia and New York at Williamsport, the whole project was reoriented.[24]

The Tide-Water Pipe Company, Limited, with Benson as president, was organized in November, 1878, to undertake the new venture.[25] It was a partnership under the Pennsylvania law, and the Reading Railroad provided about $250,000 of the company's $625,-000 capitalization.[26] Under the terms of the pipeline's agreement with the railroad, the pipeline was not to approach closer to tidewater than Williamsport for its first eight years on the penalty of forfeiting $100,000.[27] On April 1, 1879, the Equitable Petroleum Company was consolidated with the Tide-Water,[28] which thus acquired the Equitable's line connecting Rixford, Pennsylvania, with Coryville.

In the absence of a free pipe law, the acquisition of the remainder of the route to Williamsport was a difficult matter. The task was entrusted to Herman Haupt, who had demonstrated his ability in securing the right of way for the proposed Baltimore pipeline. Haupt lived up to the expectations of him. To throw Standard Oil off the track as to the planned location of the pipeline, he communicated with sellers through third parties and wrote to his agents in cipher. By a minute search of boundaries and titles in Lycoming County he found a gap in Standard Oil's right of way across the state and obtained a patent for the creek bed where it was located.[29] But he still had to reckon with that old adversary of eminent domain for pipelines, the Pennsylvania Railroad. One of its branch lines tore up the Tide-Water's pipe where it crossed the road's rail bed, and time was consumed while the case went to court, where the pipeline won its case.[30] The delay was increased by challenges to the line's title to land in Potter County, strikes by teamsters hauling pipe, and procrastination by the railroad in unloading it.[31]

Finally, the line was completed and proved itself a complete success. The first oil commenced to flow from the pipeline at Williamsport at 7:10 P.M., June 4, 1879, 147 hours and 10 minutes from the time that it had left Coryville.[32] Two 80-horsepower pumps lifted the oil more than 1,200 feet to a point 31 miles east of Coryville, whence it flowed by gravity the remainder of the distance.[33] From Williamsport the oil was transported in tank cars via the Philadelphia and Reading and the New Jersey Central to the seaboard.

The 115-mile pipe from Rixford to Williamsport, capable of transporting 6,000 barrels of crude oil per day, had involved a considerable investment, estimated at $700,000 to $800,000.[34] Only the expectation of commensurate profits justified the expenditure. Despite the disappearance of independent refiners in increasing numbers, the Tide-Water found a market at Williamsport in the Solar Oil Company. At the seaboard there was still a nucleus of hardy independents, and as their number dwindled in the next few years, the Tide-Water in self-defense engaged in refining the product transported by its pipe.[35]

The *Pittsburgh Daily Dispatch* reported on January 6, 1879: "The leading producers who are in the enterprise say that the movement is not intended as a means of obtaining cheaper rates to the seaboard, but with a view of establishing equal rates and fair trade." A letter published in the *Oil City Derrick*, May 12, 1879, declared that the Tide-Water was not built in the interest of the Oil Regions but "originated wholly for the benefit of those who have invested their capital in it." Another producer told a reporter later that same month that the Tide-Water would not accord producers the treatment that they had a right to expect.[36]

These comments reflected the fact that in the face of overproduction producers were far from united on what course of action would improve their position the most. Some, like the vocal ones who communicated with the newspapers about the Tide-Water, were suspicious of privately sponsored pipeline ventures. On the other hand, there had been a marked lack of interest in the proposal by the Grand Council of the Producers' Union in midsummer, 1878, that local associations be formed into limited partnerships to handle oil from the crude state to the manufactured product.[37] A group, led by John P. Zane, who had ardently attacked the "oil monopoly" in 1874, favored co-operation with Standard Oil. In fact, so divided were the oilmen that Zane later charged Lewis Emery, Jr., with organizing a group to terrorize producers against accepting a plan for selling oil to Standard Oil at $2.50 a barrel.[38]

Despite charges that the Tide-Water would be of little value to producers as a whole, its completion presented a clear challenge to the railroads' and Standard Oil's hold on the crude oil traffic. In the meantime, the Producers' Union had confronted the combination with a menacing array of legal actions and legislative proposals.

Proposals for Pipeline Legislation, 1878

In support of the pipeline projects to reach the seaboard, the Petroleum Producers' Union had requested the Pennsylvania legislature for a law granting the general right of eminent domain to pipelines. A bill embodying the necessary provisions was introduced in early January, 1878. This move was the signal for a propaganda campaign on both sides which put the efforts of 1875 to shame. Within ten days the *Oil City Derrick* reported that Standard Oil was soliciting signatures to petitions requesting the Pennsylvania legislature to defeat the bill.[39] Nor were the producers idle. By the end of the month they had reportedly obtained the signatures of eight thousand people to a petition requesting passage of the bill.[40] The battle of words had a familiar ring.

The *Railway World*, owned by S. S. Moon, who was closely associated with the Pennsylvania Railroad, launched an attack on the bill, pointing up the dangers involved in pipeline construction. An article in this journal declared that pipes were liable to burst, that the oil would destroy the fertility of the soil, that leakage from them would kill cattle, that insurance costs on buildings would be increased, and that pipeline employees would be a constant and costly nuisance while inspecting the lines. The article concluded that "in short, a pipe line, whether upon the road or farm, is evil, nothing but evil, and every wise man will keep it off his property at all hazards." The *Railway World* denied the producers' assertion that monopoly was the cause of "cheap oil" and attributed the low price of crude to the producers' own overproduction.[41]

Other typical arguments appeared in this publication. For example, it maintained that passage of the pipeline bill would divert the oil business to Baltimore at the expense of Philadelphia.[42] It also charged that the adverse effect on the railroad oil traffic might result in increased rates on other commodities to make up the deficit.[43] In the event that the bill passed despite such objections, the *Railway World* urged that a heavy tax be placed on pipelines to compensate the state for loss of railroad taxes.[44] This argument, a *Philadelphia Times* correspondent thought, would mean defeat of the bill.[45]

The producers worked hard to counteract such effective propaganda and especially to win the support of Pittsburgh and Philadelphia. A committee headed by David Kirk presented the case for the bill to the Board of Directors of the Pittsburgh Chamber of Commerce on January 14, 1878. Kirk charged that the Pennsylvania Railroad had been engaged for the past year in securing an exclusive right of way to Rochester. "They [the railroaders] have got it so that no corporation can get from the farmers the right to lay a pipe across their land," Kirk said.[46] The producers' arguments were apparently convincing, for the Chamber adopted a memorial to Allegheny County representatives in the legislature which read in part: "We deem it apparent that with a free pipe law, and open competition in carrying rates, our city and county has the natural advantages, which will enable us to regain at least a large portion of the refining business, which has so unjustly been diverted from us to other States." [47]

On the other hand, there was general uneasiness in Pittsburgh about the results of supporting the bill. Standard Oil, as well as the producers, was reported to be toying with the idea of a pipeline to Baltimore,[48] and, if the free pipe bill and the railroad anti-discrimination bill linked with it passed, it was feared that the net result would be a decline in Pittsburgh refining. Thus, in mid-January the *Pittsburgh Daily Dispatch* found: "Most citizens interviewed on the subject express themselves strongly as ever against the Standard Company as a monopoly, but they are not ready to *Assume a Quixotic Role* and fight their neighbors' battles at their own expense." [49] The Chamber of Commerce shortly reversed itself and came out in opposition to the bill.[50]

Both opponents and supporters of the pipeline bill turned to Philadelphia for support. A. J. Ringwalt of the *Railway World* presented the railroaders' position to the Legislative Board of the Philadelphia Commercial Exchange. He denied the producers' claims that the Pennsylvania's rates were ruining Philadelphia's refining business, and he denounced the producers' efforts to build a pipeline to Baltimore as detrimental to Philadelphia's interests. John A. Warden of Pittsburgh declared that the producers themselves had opposed a seaboard pipeline when appearing before the Pittsburgh Commercial Exchange, because support of it would spell ruin for Pittsburgh's refining business.[51] Although the representative of the Producers' Union did not specifically deny this assertion, its validity is questionable. At least when the Pittsburgh Chamber of Commerce took its stand against the bill, the local lodges of the Union retaliated with a boycott of Pittsburgh commercial houses.[52] This pressure was such that in early February the Chamber again reversed itself and came out for the bill,[53] but it was an inexpensive gesture, since for all practical purposes the State Senate had already killed the measure.

Meantime, the producers continued their effort to win Philadelphia's support. They offered the following proposed amendments to the pending bill for the approval of a committee appointed by the Commercial Exchange to investigate the matter. According to the *New York Tribune,* these proposals were:

First—That the proposed pipe line to Baltimore shall never be organized or receive any right from the passage of said bill.

Second—That the first free pipe line laid to the seaboard shall have its terminus in Philadelphia.

Third—That the above amendments shall be put in form by attorneys selected by the Commercial Exchange and Board of Trade of Philadelphia.[54]

This offer did not, however, convert the opposition. On the day of the Senate's debate on the bill, January 30, 1878, a large Philadelphia delegation appeared to oppose the measure.

The producers were also present in force. They presented a memorial charging that Standard Oil was using its control of pipelines to supply independent refiners with low-grade oil and was forcing producers to sell their oil at a discount. They demanded rigid inspection of pipelines, publicity as to their activities, and passage of the free pipe law.[55]

The Senate debate raged for four hours. A senator from Warren County attempted to convince the legislators that the bill would not harm Philadelphia's interest. He declared that a "foreign corporation" was reported to own "every rod of pipe almost without exception" and that it had the power to cut off Philadelphia. He pointed out that the protectionists who believed a seaboard pipeline would result in the export of crude oil instead of refined had little to fear since the percentage of crude exports had dropped from 10 per cent in 1876 to 7 per cent in 1877. Furthermore, as things stood, Philadelphia was being discriminated against. In the past year only one-twentieth of the trade had gone to Philadelphia, as contrasted with one-third to New York and one-fourth to Cleveland.[56]

Opponents of the measure attacked its constitutionality and the general policy that it represented. They were successful, and the Senate voted 27 to 19 to postpone indefinitely further consideration of the bill.[57]

Although this decision made it clear that no bill could be passed in that session, the House continued consideration of a free pipe bill, and a new measure was introduced in the Senate. Various efforts were made to embarrass supporters of the pipeline legislation. Representative Henry M. Long of Allegheny County, brother-in-law of

William Frew of Standard Oil's Warden, Frew and Company, proposed an amendment imposing a tax of three mills per mile on every barrel of oil transported by pipe. He introduced a letter from Daniel O'Day of the American Transfer Company saying that rates were uniform and service was available to all who cared to use it. He also asserted that he had seen a letter from "D. V. Campbell" [Benjamin B. Campbell, president of the Producers' Union] favoring the antidiscrimination bill but declaring the pipeline bill a dead issue.[58] The Long amendment was soon dead itself, and the Senate refused to consider the pipeline bill after it had passed the House.

It seems probable that the producers were no more united in support of this pipeline measure than they were on other strategy against Standard Oil. Benjamin B. Campbell of the Producers' Union admitted in 1879 that he had "foolishly" underestimated the importance of pipelines.[59] Many producers put more faith in a bill aimed at requiring equal railroad freight rates and facilities for all shippers than in pipeline legislation which might have enabled them to escape, at least in some measure, from dependence on the railroads. If a choice had to be made between the two, it seems likely that advocacy of the former was better calculated to appeal to the refining and exporting interests of Pittsburgh and Philadelphia as well as to the general public. Nevertheless, the antidiscrimination bill failed in the Pennsylvania House on May 10, 1878. A gauging law providing for court-appointed examiners of pipeline storage facilities at the request of a holder of certificates for 10,000 barrels did manage to pass, but it was merely a police measure supplementing the law of 1874.

In Pennsylvania, then, the efforts to achieve a legislative remedy for the producers' problems failed almost completely in 1878. The committee of the Producers' Union which guided these efforts reported to its parent body:

How well we have succeeded at Harrisburg you all know. It would be in vain for your committee to describe the efforts of the Council in this direction. It has been simply a history of failure and disgrace. If it has taught us anything, it is that our present law-makers, as a body, are ignorant, corrupt and unprincipled; under the control of the very monopolies against whose acts we have been seeking relief.[60]

There was undoubtedly some justification for this outburst, but the legislature could not rightfully be made to take the entire blame when the producers themselves were divided in sentiment toward a legislative program.

Although in New Jersey the alleged unconstitutionality of a free pipe bill caused the legislature in March, 1878, to postpone consideration of such legislation indefinitely,[61] the picture was not completely bleak. Proposals to build pipelines from the Bradford field to Buffalo had led to a demand for a free pipe law in New York State. The legislature had obliged in 1877, but the bill had been vetoed.[62] In 1878, however, Governor Lucius Robinson, although he felt that the measure was unconstitutional, refrained from vetoing a new pipeline bill on the ground that it was a matter for judicial interpretation.[63]

The producers also obtained at least one consolation from their defeat at Harrisburg. They had awakened sufficient interest in their transportation difficulties to lead Governor John F. Hartranft to suggest that a commission be appointed by the legislature to investigate the oil traffic and to recommend "a plan to prevent unjust discrimination in charges and facilities for the transportation of oils." [64] This action gave the producers a new opportunity to continue their attack on Standard Oil and the railroads with the aid of the executive branch of the state government.

The Oil Trade and Proposals for an Interstate Commerce Law

Meantime, the demand for legislative action against transportation discriminations had been carried from western Pennsylvania to Washington. The independent oil interests' attack on railroad discriminations fitted in well with a growing national concern about this problem. Congressmen from western Pennsylvania made the most of the situation, urging adoption of an interstate commerce law directed against the more flagrant railroad abuses. Although Standard Oil's pipeline power had contributed directly to the discriminations in question, this fact received no notice in congressional debate.

In the spring of 1876, Representative James H. Hopkins of Pittsburgh introduced a bill forbidding railroad discriminations, requiring that shippers be provided with information on established rates, banning sudden changes in these rates, and providing penalties for failure to comply with these provisions. In a speech prepared for the House on May 29, 1876, he declared that in the two years between 1873 and 1875 Pittsburgh's crude oil receipts by rail had declined two-thirds. He attributed this decrease to the railroad agreements which made it possible to ship oil to the seaboard more cheaply from Cleveland than from Pittsburgh. He quoted a report to the Pittsburgh Chamber of Commerce indicating that twenty-one Pittsburgh refineries were idle and more than three thousand men were directly affected.[65]

Earlier, Hopkins had asked that a select committee be appointed to investigate the whole problem of railroad discriminations and the possibilities of remedying them by control of interstate commerce. According to Hopkins' later recollection, Representative Henry B. Payne, father of Ohio Standard's treasurer, had opposed the formation of a select committee on the grounds of its cost. Instead, he had suggested that the matter be referred to the Committee on Commerce, and Hopkins had agreed.[66] The resolution was passed in that form.[67] Johnson N. Camden of the Standard-affiliated Camden Consolidated Oil Company appeared as adviser to the Committee's chairman. Cassatt, Rutter, and Devereux were summoned to appear before the group as were Oliver H. Payne of Standard Oil, Elisha G. Patterson, and Frank Rockefeller. Of the railroad men only Cassatt appeared, and he refused to answer questions concerning the Pennsylvania's contracts with Standard Oil.[68] Patterson and Frank Rockefeller gave the independent oilmen's version of developments in the industry since the South Improvement Company. Payne refused to discuss Standard Oil, and the investigation soon came to a halt.[69] Hopkins declared much later that when he tried to find the testimony taken during the investigation he discovered that it had disappeared.[70]

Hopkins' interstate commerce bill of 1876 never got beyond committee, but in 1878 the Petroleum Producers' Union revived interest in a similar measure. Elisha G. Patterson was appointed head of a committee to draft a bill.[71] With the assistance of George B. Hibbard, a Buffalo attorney, a measure calling for federal regulation of interstate commerce was drawn up and introduced in the House of Representatives in January, 1878, by Lewis F. Watson, of Warren

County, Pennsylvania.[72] While this bill was in the Committee on Commerce, the so-called "Reagan Bill," named after John H. Reagan of Texas, chairman of the committee, was substituted for it.

Reagan frankly admitted that his proposal was substantially the same as that offered by Hopkins in the Forty-fourth Congress. It called for equal rates to all shippers, prohibited rebates and drawbacks, forbade long haul–short haul discriminations, banned combinations for the purpose of discriminating against persons or places, and forbade higher charges for interstate shipments than for intrastate ones. In defense of his proposal, Reagan said

One of its objects is to defeat that very abuse which was called to our attention by the oil interest during the Forty-fourth Congress, one of the largest interests in the country, which was smothered out, choked to death—which died in the hands of its legitimate owners through the efforts of a monopoly [referring to the "evener" functions of Standard Oil] of that very kind combining with the railroads.[73]

Representative John M. Thompson of Butler, Pennsylvania, came to Reagan's support. He declared that drawbacks to shippers on transportation from the Regions to the seaboard amounted to as much as $1.10 on the open rate of $1.50 a barrel.[74] Discrimination against localities and in the matter of rates on the oil traffic, he said, had given rise to the bill. This was a matter of the utmost importance, the congressman maintained, because oil ranked second in the list of exports for the year 1877, and he introduced some very interesting statistics in support of his position. As of May 1, 1878, Thompson reported, there were 9,000 wells representing an investment of $49,500,000; 2,500 miles of pipelines worth $7,000,000; refineries with a capacity of 60,000 barrels a day worth $6,000,000; and 6,000,000 barrels of tankage worth the same amount. For the year ending March 1, 1878, pipeline receipts for the carriage of oil between the wells and the railroads totaled $3,121,364.75 at 25 cents a barrel. The railroads, charging $1.50 a barrel, had collected $18,728,-294.50.[75]

Despite the obvious importance that might be attached to the role of pipelines in contributing to railroad discriminations, they were not injected into the discussion of the bill. Reagan's measure was doomed to failure in that session, but it was significant that it came to the fore as an acknowledged child of a segment of the producing interest in Pennsylvania. The Pennsylvania legislature, although it rejected an antidiscrimination bill for its own state, went so far as to pass a resolution favoring the Reagan bill.[76]

The Producers Turn to Legal Action, 1878–1879

Defeated in the legislature, the producers sought redress through the executive arm of the state government. Governor John F. Hartranft's message to the legislature in May, 1878, suggesting the appointment of a commission to investigate transportation conditions, gave the producers an opening for which they had been looking. A committee of eight representatives of the Petroleum Producers' Union, headed by Benjamin B. Campbell, met with the governor and his Attorney General one afternoon in July, 1878, to present their grievances. Campbell pointed out that the Pennsylvania constitution contained clear provisions against rebates; yet time and again the legislature had failed to enact laws which would enforce them. This failure was attributed by the committee to bribery of the legislators, either by the railroads or by Standard Oil.[77] The oilmen suggested that if public interest were aroused by the calling of a special session of the legislature, the legislators could not fail to do their duty.

The Governor appeared impressed with the producers' charges. He seemed convinced, however, that the existing laws of the commonwealth, if properly enforced, were adequate to safeguard the producers' rights. As Campbell recalled it, the Governor "pledged himself that the whole power of the executive and his legal adviser should be used for the redressing of those wrongs in the manner most likely to insure success." [78] The producers were asked to prepare a memorial covering the points they had made, and this was furnished to the Governor in mid-August, 1878.

The so-called "Producers' Appeal of 1878," prepared by Roger Sherman, counsel of the Petroleum Producers' Union, was a detailed recounting of the wrongs they believed themselves to have suffered at the hands of the Pennsylvania Railroad and the Standard Oil group.[79] Significantly, a major portion of the memorial was devoted to the role of pipelines in building up Standard Oil's power and to the Pennsylvania Railroad's opposition to a free pipe law. The producers saw in the railroad-pipeline pool of 1874 a major turning point in the history of the petroleum industry. In their words, "The scheme was a success, pipe-lines one after another succumbed, and refiner after refiner was bankrupted and his works absorbed." The producers declared that the surrender of the Empire Line in 1877 meant that "The South Improvement scheme (less its chartered organization as in 1872) was at last an accomplished fact, and in the successful designing, prosecution, consummation and operation of which it is impossible not to believe that railroad officials were personally interested."

The "Producers' Appeal" maintained that the railroad and pipe-line companies were not fulfilling their obligations as common carriers. The producers charged:

By their use of the petroleum of others stored in their tanks and lines; by the overissue of Pipe Line Certificates; by refusal to perform their public duties; by open defiance of the law and impudent evasions of its provisions, the pipe-line and railroad companies leave to the people, whose creatures they are, but two remedies—an appeal for protection, first to the law of the land, next to the higher law of nature!

The memorial concluded with the request

that immediate steps be taken to enforce by legislative enactment the wise provisions of our State Constitution, and by such legal processes as are necessary, compel obedience to law and the performance by chartered companies of their public duties.

Governor Hartranft, however, had already indicated that he did not deem it necessary to call a special session of the legislature. Although a petition was circulated in Pittsburgh during September in an attempt to arouse support for such a move,[80] no action was forthcoming on the legislative front. On the other hand, the producers had been promised legal action which they now began to receive. A two-pronged attack was launched—quo warranto proceedings against United Pipe Lines and suits against the Pennsylvania, Lake Shore, and Atlantic and Great Western railroads to enjoin them from making discriminations.

The first move was made barely ten days after the producers had sent their appeal to the Governor. The state's Assistant Attorney General applied to the Venango County Court for a writ of quo warranto against United Pipe Lines, charging that it had repeatedly violated the law and was doing business in McKean County without any proper authority.[81] The case, however, was delayed again and again in the courts on technical grounds.

At the outset of the legal action the *Parker's Landing Daily* shrewdly observed: "While a writ of quo warranto against the United Pipe Line may do some good, a writ of quo shut down drilling against every sea-cook in the drilling business would be an act to be commended even beyond the measure against the line."[82] Indeed, for lack of transportation or storage space, oil had been going to waste in the Bradford field. There was a reported surplus of 5,000,-000 barrels of oil in the Regions in mid-July, 1878,[83] and United Pipe Lines, which had revoked its immediate shipment order early in the spring, was again requiring sale of oil as a condition of moving it.[84] Charles Pratt of Standard Oil declared: "We relieve the market as fast as possible, but oil is produced faster than it can be consumed. If the producers can work out a remedy for the evil we shall be satisfied."[85] While vainly attempting to solve this problem of overproduction, the producers pressed the executive branch of the state government for action.

In response to the producers' charges, William McCandless, Secretary of Internal Affairs for the Commonwealth, ordered an investigation of discriminations in the oil traffic. Judge James Atwell was appointed to hear testimony on the matter, and hearings were held in Titusville, Harrisburg, and Pittsburgh. After studying the findings, McCandless reported in mid-October, 1878, that the charges of the oil producers had not been substantiated in any way that called for action.[86] This pronouncement threw the Oil Regions into an uproar. McCandless was burned in effigy at the Oil Exchange in Parker on October 19, and effigies were also found hanging at Bradford and Tarport. The anti-Standard producers believed that the Secretary's report was the result of a $20,000 bribe, and one of the effigies had attached to it a check made out to "Buck" McCandless, signed by John D. Rockefeller, and endorsed by the Pennsylvania Railroad.[87]

The producers charged that McCandless' report was designed to influence the State Supreme Court, which then had under consideration the question of assuming jurisdiction in the producers' requests for injunctions against the railroads.[88] If so, the move failed. On October 17, Chief Justice Daniel Agnew handed down a decision

allowing the bills to be filed and announcing that motions for preliminary injunctions would be heard in early November. Meantime,
the producers' counsel, who were handling the commonwealth's case,
decided that it would be advisable to withdraw motions for preliminary injunctions in favor of relief on final hearings. The defendants agreed to answer immediately and have the cases referred to a
master and examiner. Late in November, 1878, J. Bowman Sweitzer
was appointed master to hear the five cases placed at issue.

In subsequent hearings John H. Hampton, counsel for the Pennsylvania Railroad, charged that the legal proceedings undertaken
by Hartranft were politically inspired "for the purpose of carrying
the State for the Republicans in the approaching election." Hinting
that the objective of the actions was not redress of grievances but
defeat of the Democrats, he cited the fact that the Attorney General
had not examined a witness in this case and had only appeared on one
or two occasions during the trial.[89]

Benjamin Campbell, however, denied that politics was a factor in
the producers' case. Moreover, he had letters from the Republican,
Democratic, and National party nominees for governor promising
their support for enforcement of the constitution in the event that
they were elected. Both the Republican and the Democratic nominees promised specifically to work for the alleviation of the
producers' grievances as set forth in their appeal to Governor
Hartranft.[90] In any event, the Republicans carried the state in the
election of November 7.

The cases against both United Pipe Lines and the railroads
dragged along at a snail's pace. Attorney General George Lear de-
creed that the producers would have to make their case before representatives of the Pennsylvania Railroad would be called. John D.
Archbold of Standard's Acme Oil Company, and Jacob Jay Vandergrift of United Pipe Lines, though subpoenaed, refused to testify,
claiming that Lear had indicated that other witnesses would first
have to appear to substantiate the producers' charges.[91] Benjamin
B. Campbell and other producers made the most of their side of
the story, describing the arrangements made by Standard Oil after
the purchase of the Empire Line.

The climax came on March 4, 1879, when Alexander J. Cassatt,
third vice-president of the Pennsylvania, revealed the details of the

railroad's arrangements with the American Transfer Company, whereby it received rebates on all oil carried by the Pennsylvania. The day after this sensational testimony Governor Henry M. Hoyt ordered the case adjourned, but in response to a violent protest from the producers he reversed himself. On May 3, 1879, the commonwealth closed its case against the Pennsylvania Railroad, though retaining the right to recall Cassatt and another witness.

The defense did not immediately undertake its case but was granted until September and then until December, 1879, to take testimony. Finally, on December 10, the Pennsylvania's counsel appeared before the master and stated that the Governor had instructed the Attorney General not to require the defendants to close the taking of testimony until the commonwealth had concluded presenting its evidence in all the related cases then pending.[92] This was virtually a complete reprieve, since these cases included bills in equity against United Pipe Lines and three railroads.

Furthermore, key witnesses were keeping themselves well beyond the arm of Pennsylvania law. Daniel O'Day, for example, established himself at Olean, New York, confining his visits to Pennsylvania to Sundays. It was equally hard to reach the officers of the Lake Shore Railroad, which had its offices outside of Pennsylvania, and James H. Devereux, receiver of the Atlantic and Great Western, maintained that he was responsible only to the court which appointed him to the position.

While the quo warranto proceedings against United Pipe Lines made little progress and the case against the Pennsylvania seemed endless, it was proposed that new equity proceedings be instituted against the American Transfer Company, the Erie Railway Company, and the Baltimore and Ohio Company. In the view of the producers, if these cases were decided favorably and enforced, they "would have had all the effect as to the petroleum traffic of a law regulating commerce between the States." Although the producers provided the Attorney General with proposed bills for this purpose, he failed to take action.[93]

Meanwhile, on the basis of Cassatt's testimony and that of other railroad employees, a majority of the Grand Council of the Petroleum Producers' Union and its legal committee concluded that criminal conspiracy proceedings could be instituted against individual Standard Oil officials. Since there seemed to be an inclination on the part of the railroads to disassociate themselves from Standard Oil, railroad managers such as Scott and Cassatt were not included in the indictment. The conspiracy action was commenced in Clarion County, and on April 29, 1879, the Grand Jury found an indictment against John D. Rockefeller, William Rockefeller, Daniel O'Day, Jabez A. Bostwick, William G. Warden, Charles Lockhart, Henry M. Flagler, Jacob J. Vandergrift, and George W. Girty. In summary, they were charged with conspiring to secure a monopoly of the buying and selling of crude petroleum, eliminating others from this business, diverting traffic from Pennsylvania carriers to those of other states, extorting unreasonable rebates and commissions, and fraudulently controlling the market prices of crude and refined petroleum to acquire unlawful gains.[94] Since trial of the case would preclude any other business at the regular session, further action was postponed until fall. Meantime, Standard Oil officials under indictment for conspiracy used this fact to avoid giving testimony in the equity cases.

Public Opinion and Public Policy Proposals, 1878–1879

Although the direct results of the producers' legal attack on Standard Oil had so far proved barren, public interest in the company's relations with the railroads had been aroused. The producers' complaints to Governor Hartranft and their sequel in McCandless' investigation were considered of sufficient interest by the New York *Sun,* for example, to warrant assignment of a reporter to the story for four weeks. In a series of front page stories during November, 1878, the *Sun* recounted the producers' grievances and provided an interpretation of Standard Oil's rise in terms of railroad discriminations. The article in the issue of November 23, 1878, however, dubbed the capture of pipelines as "a most important" step of the Standard Oil people.

The hearings in the suit against the Pennsylvania Railroad provided interesting documentation of the charges of discrimination by the railroads in favor of Standard Oil. Cassatt's testimony on the payments made to the American Transfer Company on crude oil carried by the railroads, as well as on the great difference between open rates and Standard Oil's rates on refined oil, naturally received wide press coverage, and all of the testimony taken in the case was later made available as a state document.

A conjunction of circumstances aided the producers in publicizing their case against Standard Oil and the railroads. Railroad discriminations had affected New York City, and the Chamber of Commerce and the Board of Trade and Transportation of that city had called on the Assembly for an investigation. The Assembly responded in February, 1879, with the creation of a special committee on railroads to investigate alleged abuses in railroad management. Alonzo B. Hepburn was chairman, and Simon Sterne, representing the New York Chamber of Commerce and the Board of Trade and Transportation, guided the investigation. The *Railway World* naturally was bitter about this development and declared: "The New York Chamber of Commerce has probably been betrayed into an endorsement of the allegations presented in its name by insidious efforts of the communistic zealots of the Board of Trade and Transportation." [95] George R. Blanchard of the Erie also resented the aggressiveness of these organizations and wrote: "The investigating committee in New York was appointed mainly because of the gravity of charges preferred against the railways by the Chamber of Commerce and Board of Trade and Transportation, the latter without a transportation man in it, and both being trade organizations local to New York City." [96]

The key figures in the railway world, representatives of the producers and of Standard Oil were brought before the committee which heard testimony from June to December, 1879. The various versions of the major events in Standard Oil's development were put into the record, much of which has been utilized in the preceding chapters of this study. Archbold's biographer, on reviewing the testimony of Standard Oil's officials at the hearings, concludes: "It was as though a conspiracy was on foot to hoodwink the investigators at every possible turn, although the letter of the law was usually observed." [97] Nevertheless, a study of the testimony given in these hearings is basic to any account of petroleum transportation prior to 1879.

When Ida M. Tarbell commenced work on *The History of the Standard Oil Company,* she experienced great difficulty in locating copies of the Hepburn Committee's report. She declared later that the noted bibliographer of state economic materials, Adelaide Hasse, told her that only one hundred copies were printed and that the railroad presidents who had testified had bought up and destroyed as many of these as they could obtain.[98] Such precautions perhaps seemed warranted by the fact that the Hepburn investigation had contributed to the mounting public demand for regulation of the nation's railroads.

Unquestionably there was more united support among oilmen for antidiscrimination legislation aimed at the railroads on the state and national levels than there was for legislation on pipelines. Commenting on the introduction in Congress of the Watson antidiscrimination bill, the *Pittsburgh Daily Dispatch* declared on January 22, 1878: "It appears to have been primarily introduced in the interests of the oil men, and surely it will be of infinitely more advantage to them than the adoption of a free pipe law could be, and, besides, it will have a baleful effect upon no class of tradesmen nor upon citizens of any locality." The producers continued to push for federal antidiscrimination legislation. In December, 1878, the Grand Council of the Union was reported as "jubilant" over the progress of the Watson bill,[99] now sponsored by Chairman Reagan of the House Commerce Committee.

On January 15, 1879, the *Pittsburgh Daily Dispatch* predicted that the oilmen would not ask the current legislature for a free pipe bill —first, because it might jeopardize the success of a proposed antidiscrimination bill, and second, because experience in New York State indicated that no pipeline would be built under a free pipe law. The prediction was wrong, as was the second reason summoned in support of it. Only a few weeks before, the New York law of 1878 had been tested and upheld in connection with a Buffalo-to-New York pipeline.[100] The *Dispatch's* view that pipeline legislation was subordinate to measures against the railroads, however, proved correct.

In his message to the legislature at the opening of its 1879 session, Governor Hartranft had taken note of the growing feeling against transportation companies. Referring to the producers' appeal of the preceding August, he said: "It is to the interests of the stockholders of the railroads, and of deeper interest to the people of Pennsylvania, that the bitter and growing prejudice against transporting corporations should be proved to be unfounded and unjust, or the causes thereof be speedily and effectually removed." [101] Hartranft declared that he had long been convinced that the question of general government supervision of interstate and overland commerce was pressing and that he had used the first opportunity to seek a judicial declaration on the matter.

It was natural that in the Pennsylvania House, Lewis Emery, Jr. should take the lead in attempting to turn these generalities into concrete statutory provisions. As a producer and promoter of the Equitable Petroleum Company he had experienced the effects of railroad discriminations, and he was as aggressive a legislator as a businessman. Three years before he had been virtually penniless, but now by his own estimate he had an income of $125 a day. It was rumored that he employed as a private secretary a correspondent for Oil Regions, Washington, and New York papers, who saw to it that Emery's name was mentioned in his dispatches whenever possible.[102] It was far from being beneath Emery's conception of a legislator's dignity to involve in fisticuffs in the legislative chamber, and he used this method of persuasion more than once in his legislative career. In this very session, for example, he broke a reporter's desk in the course of a scuffle.[103]

Emery had followed closely the Reagan bill, and his antidiscrimination measure, introduced in the 1879 session of the Pennsylvania legislature, was modeled on it. He put his support behind a joint resolution to instruct Pennsylvania's senators to support the Reagan bill and presented a history of the measure to the Pennsylvania House on February 3, 1879. The resolution passed that body a week later by a vote of 117 to 50,[104] but Emery was not destined to be so successful in promoting his own antidiscrimination bill.

The oilman attempted to gain support for his bill by testifying before the committee investigating the Pittsburgh riots of 1877. He declared that Benjamin B. Campbell of the Producers' Union had told him that if the oilmen would go along with the Riot Bill compensating the Pennsylvania Railroad for its losses, it might be possible to secure passage of the antidiscrimination and free pipe bills.[105] There is no way of substantiating this claim, but the scandal resulting from efforts to secure passage of the Riot Bill lends credence to Emery's charge.[106] Nevertheless, the antidiscrimination bill failed in the House on May 13, 1879.[107]

Pleased with the bill's defeat, the *Railway World* declared: "In many respects the railway problem must be left to work out itself, especially in this widely-expanded free country, where that course is adopted in reference to nearly all other subjects." [108] In support of its laissez-faire argument the railroad journal contended that a Pennsylvania antidiscrimination law would place Pennsylvania at a disadvantage in relation to states that did not have such a law. In the view of the Pittsburgh *Dispatch*, however, Cassatt's testimony before the Hepburn Committee on the nature of the Pennsylvania Railroad's discriminations showed the need for both congressional and state action.[109]

Although the 1879 free pipe and antidiscrimination bills in Pennsylvania failed, a comprehensive pipeline law was enacted in that year by the West Virginia legislature. This law was placed on the statute books almost unnoticed in the public furor over the discriminatory practices of the Baltimore and Ohio Railroad. The new statute established maximum pipeline rates, prohibited discrimination between persons, and fixed wastage and evaporation allowances.[110] Since Camden, partly by the use of pipeline power, had largely succeeded in eliminating the independent refiners of West Virginia, and since producers in that state were in large measure dependent on Standard Oil, the law proved to be nothing more than an empty statement of public policy.[111]

Despite the growing public concern over railroad discriminations in the oil trade, there seemed to be little public recognition of the fact that Standard Oil kept the railroads in line by means of its dominance of gathering pipelines. Johnson N. Camden late in 1878 urged that Standard Oil ought to increase the potency of this threat by making some gesture toward the construction of trunk pipelines.[112] But as far as public policy was concerned, even the producers seemed hypnotized by the thesis that railroad discriminations were the primary source of their difficulties.

The Railroads, Standard Oil, and the Tide-Water Pipe Line

The completion of the Tide-Water Pipe Line in June, 1879, posed a far more serious threat to both the railroads and Standard Oil than

the host of inconclusive legal actions and public policy proposals
of the past two years. The oil alliance's best efforts to cajole and
then to hinder the pipeline proved disappointing. As in the case of
the Empire fight and the contest with the Buffalo barge route, however, the railroads cut their rates to meet the Tide-Water's challenge.
After hearing extensive testimony on the point, the Hepburn Committee of the New York State Assembly concluded: "Opposition, of
course, was not to be brooked, and again the Standard called upon
the railroads to protect them 'against injury by competition,' and
again the railroads responded." [113]

Testifying before a congressional committee nearly ten years later,
Henry M. Flagler of Standard Oil told a different story. He declared
that amicable discussions had taken place between representatives
of the Tide-Water and his company which "would have removed all
unnecessary competition." [114] He maintained that the New York Central, the Erie, and the Pennsylvania were adamant in their refusal
to recognize the pipeline and the Reading as oil carriers, despite
Standard Oil's promise to continue shipments over the lines even
if it reached agreement with the newcomers. In Flagler's version of
the story, the oil alliance was placed in the position of acquiescing
in a rate battle which it would have preferred to have avoided. As
he recalled it, his colleagues, "like fools," yielded to the railroads.[115]
Unquestionably Standard Oil was interested in shutting off or neutralizing competition, as were the railroads, but the approach here
may well have differed, as Flagler stated.

The railroads were anxious to protect their traffic against invasion
by the Tide-Water and the Reading and apparently preferred the
elimination of their rivals rather than a compromise. If this was indeed the case, it represented a serious miscalculation as to the degree
of effective rate competition that the pipeline could offer. The testimony of the Erie's George Blanchard before the Hepburn Committee
certainly reflected such a miscalculation. He prophesied that when
winter came on, the pipeline would run into difficulties. Furthermore, the Erie official made it clear that he regarded pipelines as
neither technically nor economically capable of competing with the
railroads. Blanchard declared that pipelines were more subject to
tampering along their routes than were railroads. He believed that
leakage from the pipes would prove objectionable, and he argued

that pipelines had limited utility, since they were incapable of taking "return business" as could the railroads. Blanchard maintained that pipeline transportation was uncertain as compared to railroad transportation and predicted that the cost of pumping oil through the pipe would make the line unprofitable.[116] The Tide-Water, however, proved him wrong on all these counts.

Blanchard testified that it was Standard Oil which had presented a conference of railroad trunk-line representatives at Saratoga, New York, June 5, 1879, with the rates that it thought necessary to meet the Tide-Water's threat.[117] The result was a drastic reduction in existing charges. The Pennsylvania's open rates, for example, were dropped from $1.10 a barrel to 55 cents on crude from the river district to New York, and the rate from Bradford was lowered to 30 cents.[118] The Erie and the New York Central similarly were hauling crude for Standard Oil at reduced rates.[119] In the oil fields United Pipe Lines cut its charge for collecting oil from 20 cents to 5 cents a barrel.[120] As John D. Archbold cogently expressed it, "The tide water line was a vastly disturbing element in the trade this year."[121]

Standard Oil's railroad allies certainly had reason to subscribe to this statement if we may believe the figures of Franklin B. Gowen, president of the Reading, as to his opponents' losses. In his annual report to stockholders for 1879 he stated that the oil rates of the opposing railroads had been reduced to such an extent that at times they yielded about one-sixth of a cent per ton-mile. This, he estimated, was about one-quarter of the actual cash cost of the transportation. The loss was further compounded by the size of the oil traffic which diverted motive power from more remunerative traffic.[122]

The Hepburn Committee was incensed at the size of the railroads' losses. It declared that oil shipments could have borne a charge of a dollar more per barrel and that the roads' connection with Standard Oil forced them "to forego all these millions they might have earned and look to other produce of the country for their revenues."[123]

As the months after the opening of the Tide-Water passed, it became obvious that the railroads had underestimated the "staying power" of the pipeline and the Reading. The last two mentioned were earning expenses while Standard Oil's railroad allies suffered losses. The significance of this development was not lost on William H. Vanderbilt. He told the Hepburn Committee: "The oil business is sealed; that is settled; there is no question about that; we won't any of us have the oil business long; they [Standard Oil] will build their own pipe lines to the sea board." [124] The *Railroad Gazette* drew a similar conclusion in these words:

THE RAILROAD OIL TRAFFIC seems finally doomed. Not that there will not always be a vast traffic in the distribution of refined oil, which will take care of itself very well, and probably command pretty good rates everywhere, but that the enormous traffic in carrying crude oil to the refining centres at Cleveland and Pittsburgh and to the sea-ports where oil is exported will henceforth go mostly by pipe-lines.

The *Gazette* pointed out that the railroads were fighting a losing battle with the Tide-Water. The railroad journal declared:

The force of gravitation has worked in favor of the pipe-line, its working expenses are insignificant, and while the extremely low rates might not yield any profit on the investment in it, they were likely, at least, to cover expenses.[125]

These were sound observations. Although railroad men like Blanchard seemingly failed to realize it, the successful completion and operation of the Tide-Water Pipe Line marked a turning point in the history of oil transportation. Just as pipelines had supplanted teams as a means of collecting oil in the fields, so now they were commencing to prove their potentialities as competitors of the railroads in long-distance crude oil transportation.

The Producers and Standard Oil Compromise, 1880

While the Tide-Water's pipeline was proving itself an able competitor of the railroads in the carriage of crude oil, the legal actions of the Producers' Union against the railroads and Standard Oil had been stalemated in the courts. By December, 1879, the time appeared ripe for a settlement out of court, and this the defendants' counsel offered to do on the basis of Standard Oil's abandoning the practices of which the producers complained.

A meeting was arranged between representatives of the two groups at the Fifth Avenue Hotel, New York City, January 7, 1880. There Standard Oil offered to renounce the entire system of rebates and drawbacks, except those that the railway companies were at liberty to give to other shippers. Furthermore, it agreed to provide pipage and storage on reasonable, uniform terms without discrimination between patrons. It also agreed to pay $40,000 to cover the expenses of the producers in their legal actions.[126]

The terms of Standard Oil's proposal relating to pipelines provided a concise answer to the producers' complaints in that field. Standard Oil offered to make no differentiation in the price of crude except on a quality basis as determined by tests; to make every reasonable effort to receive, transport, store, and deliver all oil tendered, provided it did not exceed 65,000 barrels per day during fifteen consecutive days; to change rates only after thirty days' notice; and to pay the same price for "immediate shipment" oil as for certificate oil, provided it was not sold to other parties at a lower price. Until production reached a daily maximum of 65,000 barrels, certificates or vouchers would be given for all oil taken into custody of the pipelines. Transfer of the certificate or voucher was to represent delivery of the oil between the pipeline and the seller, subject to the provisions of the certificate or other vouchers.[127]

On February 5, 1880, a contract embodying these provisions was accepted by Rockefeller, Flagler, Warden, Lockhart, Vandergrift, Archbold, and others, and the producers withdrew their suits in equity, the quo warranto proceedings against United Pipe Lines, and the conspiracy prosecution against the Standard officials.

The Grand Council of the Petroleum Producers' Union accepted the result somewhat reluctantly. In a resolution adopted with only five dissenting votes, it condemned William McCandless' part in the 1878 proceedings, the hesitation of Governor Hoyt in the extradition of out-of-state defendants in the conspiracy trial, and the role of some of the judges in the trial. The resolution declared:

While we accept the inevitable result forced upon us by these influences, we aver that the contest is not over and our objects not attained, . . . that the system of freight discrimination by common carriers is absolutely wrong in principle and tends to the fostering of dangerous monopolies, and that it is the duty of the Government, by legislative and executive action, to protect the people from their growing and dangerous power.[128]

The bitterness of this resolution came from the council's dissatis-
faction with the "escape clause" which Standard Oil insisted upon,
namely, that it would not receive rebates that "the railway companies were not at liberty to give other shippers." This left an opening for Standard Oil "big enough to drive a train of cars through,"
and the producers recognized the fact.

On the other hand, shortly after the contract was signed, Benjamin B. Campbell, on behalf of the producers, came to an agreement
with Tom Scott whereby the Pennsylvania Railroad agreed not to
allow a shipper a rebate or drawback larger than that granted any
other shipper offering to ship a like quantity.[129] This agreement was
in effect a concrete acknowledgment of the inadequacy of the February contract with Standard Oil and placed the rate problem where
it had been in 1878. The railroads had offered then to carry for
others at the same rates that they gave Standard Oil—provided that
the same quantity of oil was furnished. In 1880, as two years before,
the possibility of meeting these conditions was negligible. The producers' attack had ended in a compromise which gave them paper
promises. Only time would tell if they would be made good. Meanwhile, Standard Oil's power was being increased by a major program
of trunk pipeline construction.

The events of 1878–1880 demonstrated beyond question that the
Empire's defeat had been a defeat for all segments of the petroleum
industry except Standard Oil. The railroad managers, by casting
their lot with Standard Oil and abandoning the Empire's pipelines
to the refining alliance, made an irrevocable decision. Opponents of
the combination thenceforth had to operate pipelines in conjunction
with refining operations if they were to avoid paying gathering and
storage charges to United Pipes Lines. To avoid the Standard Oil–
railroad grip on the transportation of crude oil, producers and refiners opposing the dominant group had to build a trunk pipeline.
The trunk railroads then discovered that they could not compete
on equal terms with the trunk pipeline in alliance with the Reading.
This situation further increased their dependence on Standard Oil
as the deliverer of oil to loading points.

Producers discovered that public policy was a weak reed on which
to lean in opposing Standard Oil at that time. Much of their diffi-

culty, however, came from disagreement among themselves as to whether it was the proper weapon to employ and, if so, which facet of it would be most effective. The result was a shotgun approach with increasing emphasis on state and national legislation against railroad discriminations rather than against the abuse of pipeline power or in support of pipeline enterprise. Only the legal actions against Standard Oil, its pipelines, and railroad allies bore immediate fruit, but even the limitations of that gain left a bitter taste.

In the course of these developments one important advance was made by the producers. They had succeeded in awakening public interest in Standard Oil's competitive practices and thus laid the groundwork for future ventures against the combination through public policy.

V

Standard Oil's Pipeline Empire and Pipeline Legislation, 1880-1883

THE success of the Tide-Water Pipe Line, as William H. Vanderbilt foresaw, "sealed" the doom of the railroads as primary crude oil carriers, for Standard Oil was compelled to meet this new challenge on its own ground. As long as the combination had favorable rates from the railroads and its competitors had no alternative method for the long-distance carriage of crude, it had no incentive to build trunk pipelines. Now the situation was changed. Continued predominance in refining required possession of such lines. Standard Oil's managers, with typical efficiency, turned the resources of their organization to the development of a great trunk pipeline system, and they fought the Tide-Water to a standstill. In the political area, however, they were less successful in blocking state legislation favorable to their opponents, who profited from mounting public criticism of Standard Oil—now organized as the Standard Oil Trust. Still, the Trust's predominant power in crude oil transportation was no more threatened by public policy than by competition.

Standard Oil Creates a Trunk Pipeline System

As the first step in the creation of a trunk pipeline system Standard Oil officials proposed to connect their Cleveland refineries with the

Oil Regions by pipe. By the end of October, 1879, contracts had been let for the construction of a five-and-one-half-inch line, estimated to cost $500,000.[1] The right of way was provided by the Chicago and Great Western Railroad. In the contract covering this arrangement it was specified that should Standard Oil extend its pipe to Chicago along the railroad's route, the road was to receive in return a guarantee of one-third of the oil shipped to the west and southwest. When the Lima, Ohio, field came in later in the eighties, this contract was put to use.[2]

The Cleveland pipe commenced delivering oil in the spring of 1880, charging the chief independent refiners in that city, Scofield, Schurmer, and Teagle, 20 cents a barrel for transporting crude from the Regions as contrasted with the railroads' rates of 35 to 50 cents.[3] Standard Oil, however, later utilized its control over this method of crude transportation to cut off the firm's supply when it exceeded the quota assigned to it under a restrictive refining agreement. Whereas previously pressure had been applied to competitors through United Pipe Lines' refusal to load tank cars,[4] Standard Oil was now also in a position to cut off its Cleveland competitors from the cheapest means of receiving oil from the Regions.

The federal census of 1880 reported that there were ten important pipelines in the Pennsylvania Oil Regions, representing a capital investment of $6,347,930 and controlling 2,286.85 miles of pipe. Analyzing these statistics and the developments of the next two years, Samuel F. Peckham declared:

At the present time the pipe-lines not only form a complete network throughout the oil regions, but there are trunk lines which extend from the oil regions to Pittsburgh, Cleveland, Buffalo, New York, and Williamsport. These trunk lines transport the oil of large areas to those cities under a high pressure, delivering thousands of barrels daily.[5]

The trunk pipelines, with the exception of the Tide-Water's to Williamsport, were the property of the National Transit Company, a part of the newly formed Standard Oil Trust. In the years 1879–1883, Rockefeller and his associates had applied with skill the Tide-Water's lesson that the long-distance transportation of crude oil by pipeline was both feasible and more economical than by tank car. Ida M. Tarbell observed: "Never, indeed, has the ability of the

men Mr. Rockefeller gathered into his machine shone to better advantage than in the building up and management of the pipe-line
business." [6]

Standard Oil pipeliners did a thorough job. When they purchased
a right of way across private property, they sought to obtain good
will with it by liberal payment for the privilege. They built for
permanence, laying the pipe at least eighteen inches deep except
where solid rock was encountered. Tankage of the latest and best
type was provided along the trunk line routes. In each department of
construction and operation the Standard Oil men strove for efficiency.

Administration of Standard Oil's gathering and trunk pipeline
systems was centralized, prices were stabilized, and practices were
uniform. United's gathering lines connected with wells upon request
and collected oil at a charge of 20 cents a barrel for transportation
between the well and storage tanks regardless of the distance.
Storage was free for thirty days, and thereafter at the rate of 1.25
cents per barrel per month. Detailed statistics on these operations
were maintained at district pipeline headquarters. Trunk pipeline
operations proceeded with similar smoothness. [7]

The problem confronting the public and independent oil interests
was not the technical efficiency with which Standard Oil executed
its pipeline operations. It was the cost at which this efficiency was
obtained. These achievements involved the elimination or neutrali-
zation of competing pipelines and the refineries that they served;
they also involved agreements with the railroads resulting in pipeline
charges which kept the less efficient railway crude oil carriers in
the trade. The public, however, was understandably indifferent to a
situation which opponents of Standard Oil did not analyze in pipeline terms.

Unsuccessful in its initial efforts to deal with the Tide-Water,
Standard Oil had commenced to buy up other pipeline properties
while simultaneously inaugurating a vast construction program and
continuing to harry its newest opponent. Since March, 1879, the
River Division of the Pennsylvania Transportation Company had
been under lease to United Pipe Lines. A year later the franchises, real
and personal property of the Pennsylvania Transportation Company,
including ninety-one miles of pipe with pumping stations, telegraph
lines, and accessories, plus a franchise for a seaboard pipeline whose

right of way was already secured, were sold to Kemble and Wright for $79,995.[8] Whether this firm was acting for Standard Oil or not, by the fall of 1880 the franchises and properties of the old Abbott and Harley firm were in Standard Oil's hands.[9] By the end of the year several other small lines had also been acquired.

In the face of this trend, New York, Buffalo, and Oil Regions parties undertook the construction of a pipeline from Rock City, near Bradford, to Buffalo, where it was planned to serve three independent refineries.[10] Although the line used the New York free pipe law, it met opposition from the Erie Railroad, whose right of way it crossed between Olean and Carrollton, New York.[11] Litigation over the pipeline's right to cross the railroad delayed its going into operation. When the pipe was finally opened, it carried oil at the rate of 10 cents a barrel.[12] The cause of the railroad's opposition soon became apparent, for the pipeline's competition forced railroad oil freight rates down.

Standard Oil, however, restored these rates and eliminated competition by means of pipeline power. Securing a right of way along the Buffalo, Southwestern and Erie Railroad, Standard Oil built its own pipeline into Buffalo. It then purchased the Atlas Oil Company and the Rock City pipeline, later pulling up its own line.[13] Trunk pipeline rates to the remaining independent refineries rose to 25 cents a barrel, and railroad oil freight rates advanced to the same figure.[14] Trunk pipelines clearly could now call the tune on the price of transporting raw petroleum, and it was more than ever to the advantage of oil-carrying roads to co-operate with rather than to antagonize Standard Oil.

At one crucial point Standard Oil was dependent on a hostile railroad, and in 1879 the oil alliance began a campaign to eliminate this weak link in its projected seaboard pipeline chain. The Pennsylvania Railroad had arrangements with the Central of New Jersey, the Tide-Water's ally, for making deliveries to Standard Oil's refineries at Constable Hook and tanks at Communipaw, New Jersey. Furthermore, pipes connecting the tanks and the refineries passed through the Central's property. At the outset of the struggle with the Tide-Water, the Pennsylvania made plans to lay its own tracks into Communipaw, while Standard Oil, faced with the Central's threat to remove the pipes running across its property, petitioned the Common Council of Bayonne to authorize the laying of pipelines under the city streets. The measure was passed by the council only to be vetoed by the mayor. A second petition was submitted and then, for reasons which are not clear, was withdrawn in June, 1880.[15]

The following September the desired authorization was granted. In a single night, before the Central of New Jersey was able to discover the stratagem, Standard workmen had completed laying a pipe through Thirtieth Street.[16]

Meantime, the laying of the seaboard pipelines was under way. By July, 1880, construction of a six-inch pipe from Olean, New York, near the Bradford field, to Saddle River, New Jersey, was well started.[17] It was completed by December, 1881, and a second six-inch line was being laid down beside it, giving Standard Oil by January, 1883, the capability of delivering 32,000 barrels of oil a day to New York harbor.[18] This freed Standard Oil almost completely from reliance on the railroads for delivery of crude oil to this important center. At the same time it gave the combination a tremendous advantage over the Tide-Water Pipe. Still another trunk line was constructed from Colegrove, McKean County, Pennsylvania, to Philadelphia, where it served refineries at Gibson's Point. From the main line a branch was completed to Baltimore in 1883.[19]

In May, 1881, when Standard Oil's first seaboard pipeline did not extend beyond Hamilton, New York, the oil combination reached a significant agreement with the Pennsylvania Railroad. The Pennsylvania's good will was important in carrying through the trunk pipeline program, especially since the road had a right of way through New Jersey where there was no free pipe law. Furthermore, with the through pipelines still unfinished, Standard Oil relied on the rail carrier for conveying oil between the ends of the pipes and for transporting construction materials. After construction was completed, there would be a continuing need for the railroad's services in carrying coal for the boilers of pipeline pumping stations as well as in the carriage of refined products.

The contract provided for a through rate on pipeline-rail crude oil shipments, with the Pennsylvania fixing the amount. If this rate dropped below 40 cents, the railroad was to receive part of the gathering pipeline charge as compensation.[20] Thus Standard Oil, which had profited from railroad rebates in the past, now stood ready to pay rebates, or their equivalent, to a railroad. The full significance of this arrangement, which was later duplicated with the Erie, did not become apparent to other oil shippers until several years later.

As Standard Oil entered on its program of pipeline expansion, a reorganization of its pipeline interests became necessary. Up to that time these interests had been managed by United Pipe Lines and the American Transfer Company. The latter, under Daniel O'Day, built the new trunk lines. Laying a six-inch line, costing $5,000 to $6,500 a mile, was a major undertaking, and the resources of the existing companies were not deemed adequate for the pipeline program already outlined.[21] United, for example, already had its hands full collecting and storing oil in the Bradford field.

There was another consideration which Standard Oil officials kept in mind when weighing a reorganization plan. The National Storage Company, in which Joseph Potts, the former president of the Empire Line, was deeply involved, had built up a sizable oil storage business and in early 1881 was expanding its own refineries and pipelines. In the Empire contest Potts had shown himself to be a wily antagonist, and the possibilities of bringing him into the Standard Oil group were not to be overlooked. Moreover, Potts was receptive to the idea.[22]

The instrument chosen for the projected reorganization was the charter of the Southern Railway Security Company. This charter, created by special act of the Pennsylvania legislature, April 7, 1870, was a mate to that of the notorious South Improvement Company. It was seized by the state in 1873 and was brought forth in March, 1881, when it was sold at public auction for $16,250.[23] The rights and franchises granted by this charter were transferred to the National Transit Company, which was organized by Standard Oil in April, 1881, with an authorized capital stock of $100,000. This amount was increased to $30,000,000 in January, 1882, to meet the needs of the ambitious pipeline program.[24]

National Transit thus became the parent company of Standard Oil's burgeoning pipeline empire. Potts's National Storage Company was brought into it. A steamship, the *Vaterland*, for the European trade, and Standard Oil's pipeline properties completed National Transit's holdings. United Pipe Lines, however, retained its corporate individuality until 1884.[25] Potts became a director but declined the opportunity to become president of the new company. That position went to Clement A. Griscom, who had a large interest in the National Storage Company and in shipping enterprises. The vice-presidency went to Benjamin Brewster, whom Rockefeller once described as "a rugged man, one of the old type of successful merchants." Daniel O'Day, the builder of Standard Oil's first pipeline, became general manager.[26]

The organization of the National Transit Company was but one of the steps being taken to organize the far-flung enterprises of Standard Oil into a centrally controlled structure. As the concern had acquired enterprises outside Ohio, it had developed a complex system of relationships which was by no means ideally suited to efficient management. Credit for knitting the Standard Oil empire together in a new form belongs—next to Rockefeller, who dealt chiefly with the over-all problems—to Flagler and Samuel Calvin Tate Dodd.

Dodd was born in Franklin, Pennsylvania, in 1836, was graduated from Jefferson College in 1857, and was admitted to the Venango County bar in 1859. A delegate to the Pennsylvania constitutional convention in 1872–1873, he had vigorously attacked the South Improvement Company and had sponsored an antirebate provision in the constitution. He had joined Standard Oil in 1879 with the understanding that he would be free to fight rebating. In 1881 he was appointed general solicitor, and he, more than any other member of the combination, provided the public defense of the Standard Oil Trust in the years that followed its formation in 1882.[27]

When Dodd joined Standard Oil it already had in operation a form of trust arrangement. Various officers and lawyers of The Standard Oil Company (Ohio) acted in their individual capacities as trustees of the stock of allied companies, whose owners were also stockholders in Ohio Standard. This system had been employed, for example, in the acquisition of the Vandergrift and Forman pipelines.[28]

At no time had the trustees under this system held the stock of The Standard Oil Company (Ohio), and this was crucial to the trust plan which emerged in January, 1882. A board of nine trustees was then established to hold the stocks and bonds of Ohio Standard and other companies in the combination. Forty-one investors in forty companies surrendered their stock to the trustees and received trust certificates in return.[29] The trustees received dividends from the companies thus combined and distributed dividends to the certificate-holders.

Equally important, they were given power to exercise general supervision over the constituent companies of the combination.

An analyst of the trust agreement, which became public property in 1888, commented: "Whatever the theory, whatever its status in law, the trust is, in actual fact, a solid, organic, efficiently centralized structure." [30] He also noted that "the business over which this trust presides is primarily oil refining; but its pipe-line transportation has become an enormous ancillary industry." [31] Dodd himself gave as one of the justifications for the combination the claim that "they [Standard Oil managers] have cheapened transportation, both local and to the seaboard, by perfecting and extending the pipe-line system." [32] In an affidavit submitted to the United States Industrial Commission in 1899, Rockefeller declared: "To perfect the pipe-line system of transportation required in the neighborhood of fifty millions of capital. This could not be obtained or maintained without industrial combination." [33] Clearly the expansion of Standard Oil's pipelines had contributed to the need for the centralized organization which took the form of the Standard Oil Trust.

Standard Oil and the Tide-Water Pipe Line

While Standard Oil expanded its pipeline network, the Tide-Water Pipe Line continued to prosper. Having reached an understanding with the railroads, which had been forced to abandon their costly rate war with the pipeline in early 1880, the Tide-Water set about consolidating its position. Backers of the pipeline had a refinery at Williamsport, but it was sold to Standard Oil in 1880. [34] The Tide-Water offset this loss by construction of a new refinery, the Chester Oil Company's, near Philadelphia in the same year. In 1881 the pipe was extended seaward, reaching Tamanend in Schuylkill County, Pennsylvania, where it made a direct connection with the Central of New Jersey. [35] Although Standard Oil's purchases of independent refineries were stepped up, another outlet for the Tide-Water's oil was provided at Communipaw, New Jersey, with the organization of the Ocean Oil Company, and efforts were made to open the European market. [36]

These developments were watched closely by Standard Oil, which even contributed to the Tide-Water's expansion through a loan made in the fall of 1881. In return for its assistance Standard Oil received a share of the Tide-Water line's profits and "a certain representation in the Board of Managers." [37] Whatever the nature of this representation, Standard Oil was kept in touch with a growing rift in the Tide-Water's management through Joseph Potts, in whom the company's malcontents, led by Hascal L. Taylor and John Satterfield, confided.

Apparently Taylor, Satterfield, and John Pitcairn had hoped to obtain control of the Tide-Water and then come to a profitable agreement with Standard Oil.[38] In this design they were frustrated by the Tide-Water's able president, Byron D. Benson. Their differences came to a head in January, 1882, over the question of borrowing $2,000,000 from the First National Bank of New York to finance further expansion. The Taylor-Satterfield group attempted to prevent the loan by charging that the company was virtually insolvent. Benson and Franklin B. Gowen of the Reading replied with charges that their opponents were tools of Standard Oil. The Benson group was finally successful in convincing the bank of the soundness of the company, and arrangements for the loan were completed in October, 1882.[39]

Meanwhile, the attack on the Tide-Water's management had been carried into court. In September, 1882, Elisha G. Patterson, who had been a leader in the producers' attack on Standard Oil in 1878–1880, requested the Court of Common Pleas, Crawford County, Pennsylvania, to appoint a receiver for the Tide-Water.

Patterson's new role had an interesting explanation. He had been thoroughly disgusted by the producers' decision to compromise with Standard Oil in February, 1880, and he saw in the state's effort to collect back taxes from the combination during the following year an opportunity to avenge himself.[40] When the state refused to pay Patterson for collecting evidence in the case, he had turned to Archbold. The latter, apparently to avoid harassment, in April, 1882, agreed to give Patterson fifteen thousand dollars and a job carrying a salary of five thousand dollars a year.[41] Although Lewis Emery, Jr., who had also given Patterson money, admitted later that Patterson had received fifty-five hundred dollars from Archbold, he denied that Standard Oil's old foe had sold himself to the "octopus." [42] Nevertheless, Patterson paid for fifty shares of Tide-Water stock, to which he had subscribed at the organization of the company, with money received from Archbold.[43] With these shares in hand he had instituted the charges against the Tide-Water in September, 1882.

In court Patterson failed to make good his case against the Tide-Water's management. One of the charges, for example, was that the pipeline should be taken out of the hands of its owners because its capacity fell below the demands made upon it. The defendants, on the other hand, claimed that a plug had been placed in the line, cutting its capacity by one-third, and they left no doubt that they regarded it as deliberate sabotage.[44] On January 16, 1883, Judge Pierson Church denied Patterson's request for dissolution of the Tide-Water with the intimation that the case involved a form of blackmail to which his court would not be a party.[45]

Just before Judge Church's decision on this case, rumors began to circulate in the Oil Regions that United Pipe Lines did not have in its possession the amount of oil indicated by its outstanding certificates. The *Pittsburgh Daily Dispatch* took up these charges and editorially suggested that the pipeline company did not have more than 20,000,000 barrels of the 32,000,000 it claimed.[46] The paper demanded an investigation and on January 6 declared:

There is so broad a field for research, and specific proof of the allegations is so difficult to secure, that the investigators hardly known [sic] where to begin, but it will be strange, indeed, if those who are interested in holding the gigantic monopoly within legal limits do not find the means to expose its practices.

The Oil City Oil Exchange was so angered at these charges that at its meeting on the same day resolutions supporting the United company were adopted, and copies were supplied to the Associated Press in the hope of wide dissemination. The Exchange expressed faith in Standard Oil's pipelines and pointed out that court-appointed examiners could determine the amount of petroleum in storage upon petition of a holder of a voucher for over 10,000 barrels.[47] Three days later an Oil Exchange was opened at Franklin by persons who believed the Oil City Exchange to be dominated by Standard Oil.[48]

A battle of the press ensued. The *Pittsburgh Daily Dispatch* made numerous demands that United Pipe Lines' reports be checked, and the *Leader* took Standard Oil's side. The *Dispatch* retaliated with the publication of charges by the Oil City *Evening Blizzard* that the Oil Regions' press was controlled by Standard Oil. According to this account the *Oil City Derrick* had been purchased by Standard Oil interests on January 1, 1879. The *Sunday Call* was similarly alleged to be under the combination's control, as was the *Bradford Breeze* and the *Bradford Era.* John D. Archbold was alleged to control the *Titusville Herald.* The *Dispatch,* which consistently opposed Standard Oil, affirmed its belief in the accuracy of these charges.[49]

Although United Pipe Lines was fully vindicated by a subsequent investigation, the Pittsburgh paper's assertion that the pipeline company did not have in storage the amount of oil represented by its outstanding certificates had an unexpected result. According to the Oil City correspondent of the *Dispatch,* the publication of these figures had caused producers to attempt a connection with the Tide-Water at the expense of the United. This move, he wrote, had led directly to the latest effort to wrest control of the Tide-Water from the anti-Standard group.[50]

This time a bold attempt was made to seize power in the line's board of directors. Following the court decision against Patterson in mid-January, 1883, the local managers of the Tide-Water had requested postponement of the scheduled annual meeting until they had an opportunity to consult with the nonresident managers. On January 17, however, while the Titusville group was in New York, the Taylor-Satterfield faction, with Patterson in their train, appeared at the Tide-Water's offices, which were occupied by Benson's associates, David McKelvy and Andrew N. Perrin. Ignoring the fact that the annual meeting had been postponed, the Taylor-Satterfield group proceeded to organize a stockholders' meeting. Permitting one of their group, who was acting as teller, to vote five hundred shares of which he was but one of five co-trustees, they went through the formality of ousting Benson, Perrin, and Hopkins from the management. Satterfield was then elected chairman; Thomas S. MacFarland, treasurer; David B. Stewart, secretary; and James R. Keene and Franklin B. Gowen, managers. Upon notification of their election, the latter two men refused to recognize the new board.[51]

Satterfield and MacFarland were officers of the Union Oil Company, which was reported to have a $250,000 interest in the Tide-Water and to be closely allied with Standard Oil.[52] It is not surprising, therefore, that the *Pittsburgh Dispatch* remarked editorially that this coup was not unexpected, for there "were influences which rendered the line almost as close in some phases of relationship to the Standard as the United Pipe Line Company itself." [53]

Members of the Benson group did not propose to allow the management of the Tide-Water to be stripped from them, and they took the matter to court. Again the scene was the Court of Common Pleas, Venango County, with Judge Pierson Church, who had ruled against Patterson's demand for dissolution of the Tide-Water, presiding. The request of Benson and his associates for a temporary injunction was granted, pending a hearing which commenced in late February, 1883. The case had excited such interest that representatives of some of the larger newspapers in the country were on hand at Meadville when the proceedings began. The trial itself hinged on the technicalities of the election procedure, which were unusual because the Tide-Water was organized under the Limited Partnership Law of 1874 and not under the general corporation act of that year.

The real interest, however, centered on the relationship of Standard Oil to the Tide-Water and its new board. "Jim" Keene, one of the promoters of the Tide-Water's National City Bank loan, testified that Standard Oil had systematically tried to hamper the Tide-Water and then had attempted to obtain control of it.[54] Gowen asserted that the oil combination had offered 200 per cent of the Tide-Water's worth to get control of it, and this within the last ten days.[55] On the other hand, an affidavit submitted by John D. Archbold denied that Standard Oil had sought to undermine the Tide-Water. Rather, he charged that Benson and McKelvy had approached him on various occasions in the past several years with proposals to combine the Tide-Water with the Standard Oil group and also had sought agreements with him on rates and charges for refined oil. He declared that he had not answered any of these proposals.[56] Benson replied with an affidavit that he had never made the alleged advances. The truth probably lay somewhere between these extremes.[57]

On March 16, 1883, Judge Church rendered his decision, which was in favor of the old board. He termed the election of January 17 "farcical, fraudulent and void" and ordered the continuance of the injunction against the board elected at that meeting. The Philadelphia *Press* hailed the decision with satisfaction, declaring:

Without any reference to the legal merits of the controversy, it is enough
that the decision will keep the Tidewater Pipe Line free from the control
of that overshadowing corporation of the State of Ohio which has swal-
lowed up or strangled every other competitor in the business of transporting, storing and refining oil but this.[58]

For the time being the Tide-Water remained a challenge to Standard
Oil's predominant position in crude oil transportation.

Standard Oil and the Literature of Exposure

The expansion of Standard Oil's power, the source of that power,
and the significance of the contest with the Tide-Water had not
gone unnoticed in the national periodical press. Although various
episodes in the combination's development had long received attention in the newspapers, in Congress, and in state investigations,
it was 1881 before a comprehensive survey of Standard Oil's development in terms of railroad discriminations appeared in a magazine
catering to a nation-wide reading public.

Ten months before the formation of the Trust, an author who was
to make that term one of reproach, launched his first attack on
Standard Oil. Henry Demarest Lloyd told the "Story of a Great
Monopoly" in the March, 1881, issue of the *Atlantic Monthly*. Lloyd,
the son of a Dutch Reformed Church minister, had been admitted
to the bar in 1869. From the law and politics he had turned to journal-
ism, accepting a position with the *Chicago Tribune*. He had become
interested in the subject of monopoly, and in this article he declared:
"Very few of the forty millions of people in the United States who
burn kerosene know that its production, manufacture, and export,
its price at home and abroad, have been controlled for years by a
single corporation,—the Standard Oil Company." [59]

Lloyd's theme was that Standard Oil had achieved monopoly by
conspiracy with the railroads and that pipelines aided it in exploiting
this position. He charged that Standard Oil had "done everything
with the Pennsylvania legislature, except refine it." He concluded:

The time has come to face the fact that the forces of capital and industry
have outgrown the forces of our government. . . . The nation is the
engine of the people. They must use it for their industrial life, as they
used it in 1861 for their political life. The States have failed. The United
States must succeed, or the people will perish.[60]

Abbott & Harley pipeline terminal, Shaffer Farm on the Oil Creek Railroad, ca. 1867

A pipeline challenging a railroad, 1875. Oil is being transported by wagon across the tracks of the West Penn Railroad, which temporarily balked completion of the Columbia Conduit, the first trunk pipeline

This was the opening gun of an attack on Standard Oil, which the "literature of exposure" was to make a symbol of corporate greed and evil in the eyes of the American public.

Two years passed, however, before the next virulent magazine attack on the combination came in February, 1883. This time it was in the form of a printed debate appearing in the *North American Review*. John C. Welch reviewed the Standard Oil's growth in terms of railroad discriminations, citing the use of the American Transfer Company to collect rebates from the railroads and the Tide-Water's beneficial effect in forcing the reduction of railroad rates.[61] In the same issue of the magazine Senator Johnson N. Camden offered a defense of Standard Oil.

Camden was president of the Camden Consolidated Oil Company of Parkersburg, West Virginia, and of the Baltimore United Company, members of the Standard combination.[62] With the decline of Baltimore as a refining center, these firms had taken a place in the rear ranks of Standard Oil's growing army, and Camden had turned to politics. Although elected to the United States Senate from West Virginia in January, 1881, Camden continued to keep an eye on his oil interests. For example, he claimed credit for killing bills in the 1882 session of the Maryland legislature which would have regulated pipeline and oil storage rates.[63]

Camden was the first spokesman to break Standard Oil's self-imposed silence in the face of increasing public criticism, and his observations are worth noting. He argued that Standard Oil had brought stability and progress to an industry which had been tottering on the verge of bankruptcy. Pointing out that there were more than 4,000 miles of pipeline, 20,000 wells, and 100,000 people involved in the oil business, Camden declared:

It may be admitted, then, that to our national characteristics is to be largely attributed the unprecedented development of the American petroleum industry. The specific agency through which this development has been mainly effected is the organization known as the Standard Oil Company, which may be defined to be an association of business houses united under one management in such a manner as to insure harmony of interests, and a consolidation of capital adequate to any possible business emergency, yet each retaining its individuality, and even competing sharply with the others.[64]

The Senator asserted that Standard Oil had made an important contribution by its consolidation of pipelines, which rendered certificates uniformly negotiable and permitted oil to be delivered at any railroad shipping point without extra charges.[65] Further, he maintained that every foot of the right of way for Standard Oil's pipes had been purchased.[66]

Camden attributed the attack on the oil combination to the "Anti-Monopoly" racket of politicians who had been aided by Standard Oil's silence, which was popularly interpreted to be an admission of guilt. The *Pittsburgh Daily Dispatch,* on the other hand, observed, "As for Senator CAMDEN, he has well earned his retirement from office by this one effort, in which he exhibits himself as a legislator capable of using his office in any way to usurp the rights of the mass and give them over to monopolies." [67]

The Senator's effort was not followed up by other Standard Oil officials. Five years passed before another such systematic defense of the Trust appeared from the pen of one of its key figures. Meanwhile, as the Trust gathered strength so did popular sentiment against it.

Pennsylvania Pipeline Legislation, 1883

The year 1883 had opened in the Oil Regions of Pennsylvania with a mounting attack on Standard Oil and its United Pipe Lines, to which was added the acrimony resulting from the struggle for control of the Tide-Water. This situation offered a fertile background for legislative efforts to bring the Standard Oil colossus to earth.

Before leaving office, Republican Governor Henry M. Hoyt had recommended that action against transportation discriminations be taken under Article XVII of the State Constitution, and the incoming Democratic governor, Robert E. Pattison, vigorously supported such proposals. Legislative efforts centered on antidiscrimination legislation, a proposal for semiannual gauging of pipeline tanks, and a free pipe bill. One antidiscrimination bill was introduced January 11, 1883, and was followed by others. The number of these bills led the Philadelphia *Press* to observe: "The fever for railroad regulation has seized upon the Legislature."

There was even greater excitement over proposed pipeline legislation. Influenced by the charges that the United Pipe Lines did not have the amount of oil in its possession indicated by its outstanding certificates, Lee Thompson of Armstrong County introduced a bill in the Pennsylvania House on January 11, 1883, to provide official gaugers and to require semiannual gauging of pipeline tanks. In the Senate on March 13 a new free pipe bill was introduced by Lewis Emery, Jr.

The rural press of the eastern counties generally opposed Emery's bill. The *Media American* argued that the right of eminent domain should not be given to pipelines because they were not common carriers and did not confer any benefits on the communities through which they passed. The *Lancaster Examiner* referred to the bill as that of the "oil kings in the Senate" and opposed it because it would give the right to lay pipe through private property anywhere in the Commonwealth. The *West Chester Village Record* also opposed the bill and urged farmers to close ranks against it.

Emery, who was leading the fight for the measure, charged that the farmers' opposition was systematically encouraged by handbills distributed by opponents of the bill. Before the Industrial Commission in 1899, he cited the contents of such a handbill as declaring: "These people are endeavoring to pass a law that will destroy the springs on your farms; it will blow up your houses; it will create havoc in your fields, when the pipe bursts, by killing the grass. The most dangerous of all laws." [68]

In the Senate, opposition was spearheaded by Thomas V. Cooper of Delaware County. He and Emery got into a spirited argument over the latter's charges that Standard Oil was deliberately stirring up the farmers against the measure. The following exchange is typical:

Senator Cooper—All the eastern counties are opposed to the bill. It proposes to confer no great public good. The only one who would profit by it would be those engaged in the oil business. Owners of land under which it would pass would be punished by it by having their property damaged, as I learn that land soaked with oil becomes non-productive for years.

Senator Emery—Why, oil is the greatest fertilizer in the world.

Senator Lee—The pseudo farmers here a few years since had their expenses paid.

Senator Cooper—Not the farmers of my county (Delaware). I know they paid theirs.

Senator Greer—They were badly bitten.

Senator Emery—Well, I know through Allan Pinkerton's Agency that the bills of farmers were paid at the hotels. . . .[69]

The focusing of debate on the farmers' opposition to pipelines is significant, for it suggests that the railroads had largely given up the fight against crude oil transportation by pipeline. In the dispute with Cooper, Emery pointed out that an officer of the Pennsylvania Railroad had told him there was no use opposing the bill because "the railroads could not compete with pipe lines in the transportation of oil." Even the *Railway World,* which continued to oppose the bill, acknowledged the transformation that had taken place in long-distance oil transportation. It declared: "It is noticeable that while disputes relating to methods of carrying petroleum have been fomenting bitter agitations in some communities, the entire movement from the producing regions has been rapidly transferred from railroad companies to the pipe lines." [70] The article cited figures which showed that nearly three-fourths of the oil leaving the Regions in January, 1883, went by pipe.[71]

Philadelphia, which had long opposed a free pipe bill, seemed now more sympathetic to the proposal. In the view of the Philadelphia *Press* the fact that the bulk of Pennsylvania crude oil reached the seaboard through New York State was evidence in favor of the pending measure. In an editorial on March 30, the paper noted that opposition to the bill came chiefly from farmers in counties east of the Alleghenies. It declared that the fears they expressed were scarcely justified, for the rights that would be conferred on pipelines were the same as those given railroads and under the same restrictions.

On April 5, the free pipe bill came up for its third reading in the Senate. Again the chief contenders were Cooper and Emery. Cooper stoutly maintained that his opposition to the bill was based on opposition to Standard Oil. "If I were that company," he declared, "and were given the right of eminent domain I'd buy up all competing lines. There ought to be an amendment to prevent that." [72] He maintained anew that it was the views of his farmer constituents which prompted his stand against the measure.[73] Emery countered with the charge that five hundred of these constituents had already granted an exclusive right of way to Standard Oil, which made their clamor about the effects of allowing pipelines to pass through their property ring hollow.[74]

Cooper then turned from blanket opposition to an attack based on amending the bill, proposing that all pipelines exercising the right of eminent domain be limited to serving refineries located within the state. This motion was lost.

When Emery resumed his personal attack on Cooper, his victim lost his composure. The irate senator shouted: "I hate the Standard Oil Company as a hydra-headed monster. Show me a way to get at it, and I'll throttle it to death. I'm tired of these sneers and innuendoes. I hope the senators will desist." [75]

Emery, however, followed up his advantage with a thrust which revealed his strategic appeals to sectional interests and his motivation —concern for his personal interests as well as the public's:

Had you given us this law ten years ago, you'd have fifty, seventy-five or one hundred vessels laden with oil in Philadelphia to-day. Twenty-six vessels are loading in New York and just one in Philadelphia. This is because certain senators and representatives could see too clearly the duty of serving corporate powers. The Senator from Delaware is serving in the same principle this afternoon.[76]

With anger in his voice, Emery shouted:

What right has that company to steal our business? It is an octopus that has driven me three times to bankruptcy. . . . The Standard has nearly got its clutches on the Tidewater, but this will permit others than the Standard to go over the Pennsylvania Railroad, which, so help me God, can't be done now. . . . Do we own ourselves? If we do let us give ourselves some rights.[77]

Despite the obviously personal basis of his argument, Emery was successful. The bill passed its third reading on April 6 by a vote of 31 to 12, through the efforts of a coalition of Senate Democrats and Independents.

The Philadelphia *Press* took the position that the public interest demanded passage of the free pipe bill. In an editorial on the day of the Senate vote it undertook to answer the argument that since pipelines were not common carriers, they were not entitled to the right of eminent domain. It pointed out that railroads which connected with mines and quarries were not common carriers; yet they enjoyed the right of eminent domain. Further, the editorial argued, it was desirable to increase the number of pipelines, and it was in the public interest to permit them to secure a right of way through reasonable payments.

On the other hand, the *Press* regarded the bill as a passive instrument of public policy. The paper's comment on the success of the bill's proponents in getting it through the Senate shows that the paper viewed Standard Oil as the real object of attack. "A Free Pipe law will bring the Standard to terms," the *Press* declared, "inasmuch as under the law the shippers of oil will always have a way of escape from the oppression of monopoly." [78]

The pipeline bill had a rough passage through the House. Before it passed a second reading there, the measure acquired an amendment which would force companies organized under its provisions to have their termini in the state. A Philadelphia representative proposed an amendment forbidding pipelines to connect with others beyond the limits of the state. This led "Uncle Jake" Ziegler, chairman of the Ways and Means Committee, to suggest sarcastically that the end of the pipe be left open "so that oil could squirt across the State line." [79] This amendment failed.

In May a bill proposing a tax on petroleum transported by pipeline was, in the words of its opponents, a "bombshell thrown into the House against the Free Pipe bill." [80] While clearly aimed at the "octopus," it threatened the potential beneficiaries of the pipeline bill. The new measure proposed a tax on pipeline companies, except those owned by individuals or ordinary partners, of one mill for every gallon of crude oil transported. To prevent the companies from passing on the charge, it was specified that the maximum rate for pipeline transportation was to be 20 cents per barrel, with no distance specified. The sponsors defended the proposition on the ground that it would force Standard Oil to pay taxes to the state in proportion to its business. At first the Philadelphia *Press* supported the idea as an avenue for tapping "a magnificent source of revenue." [81] Four days later, however, it adopted a more realistic attitude and pointed out that Standard Oil might evade the tax by piping oil out of the state through lines nominally owned by individuals. The legislature apparently adopted the same viewpoint. At any rate the measure died. [82]

The pipeline bill needed 101 votes to pass the House, but it failed on May 31, 1883, by a vote of 94 yeas to 88 nays. Emery's and James W. Lee's stand on congressional district apportionment, which was a major issue of the session, hurt the measure. Stalwart Republicans were reported to have voted against the bill simply because they knew the two Independents were interested in it.[83] All members of the Montgomery, Chester, and Delaware County delegations voted against it, as did the Lancaster representatives, with one exception.

W. J. Hulings, Republican sponsor of the antidiscrimination bill, was not ready to give up on the pipeline measure. He rallied his side of the House while Jake Ziegler and others whipped the Democrats into line. Representative Christopher Magee of Pittsburgh told the Allegheny County delegation that sentiment in the western part of the state would not tolerate any display of friendship for Standard Oil.[84]

On the other side the friends of the Pennsylvania Railroad, which, Emery to the contrary, was apparently determined to put up a fight, closed ranks with those who opposed the bill as a danger to farmers.[85] Their efforts were not sufficient, however, to stop passage of the bill in the House on June 1 by a vote of 107 to 73. The same day the antidiscrimination bill, with which even its proponents were not satisfied, passed the same body by a vote of 148 to 7. Furthermore, a resolution was adopted to investigate Standard Oil's payment of taxes and its relationship to the state.

The Senate concurred in these measures, which marked a legislative victory for the independent oil interest. The Philadelphia *Press* greeted passage of the free pipe bill with the comment: "In all probability very few pipe lines will be laid under the free law; the right to lay them is the important thing."[86] The *Pittsburgh Daily Dispatch* commented:

This ends a struggle against the monopoly of the oil trade by the Standard, which was established through the default of our legislators and railway men eight years ago. The Standard's growth was due to its control of the routes of transportation through the railways, in which it was upheld by the refusal of the Legislature, year after year, to put the pipe line business on a footing which give a fair chance to competition.

The paper concluded:

The passage of this measure affords independent refiners and producers a chance at competition after the Standard has had supreme control of the business for not less than six years.[87]

The latter observations were overly optimistic about the results of the free pipe bill, for Standard Oil's growth had been the product of other factors as well as transportation advantages. The lack of a free pipe bill, however, had certainly handicapped those who had undertaken to challenge Standard Oil. The new law would help the attackers, but it would take more than a statute to threaten seriously the lead that a combination of resources, including pipeline power, had given the Trust.

The pipeline law was followed on June 5, 1883, by enactment of a gauging law, which authorized holders of more than 2 per cent of the oil in a pipeline company's custody to request courts of common pleas for a gauging. Court-appointed examiners were empowered to measure pipeline tanks and the assistance of pipeline companies was enjoined. Actually, this law was only an extension of a similar measure enacted in 1878 and perhaps was even a little less favorable to producers.[88]

As it turned out, the session was not to end on June 6. Governor Pattison summoned the legislature into extra session the following day to deal with the troublesome problem of apportioning the state into electoral districts. Although nothing was accomplished in this direction, the session, which continued for six months, did produce a significant addition to the pipeline legislation passed earlier.

One of the provisions of Article XVII of the state constitution forbade the consolidation of competing transportation companies, and this prohibition was now specifically applied to pipeline companies. On June 13, 1883, "An act to prevent the consolidation of competing pipe lines for the transportation of oil, or to hold the controlling interest in the stocks or bonds of competing pipe lines, or the acquisition or control either directly or indirectly, by purchase or otherwise, and prescribing penalties for the violation thereof," became law. The law was a harsh one, for it provided that failure to observe its provisions was punishable by forfeiture of the stocks, bonds, franchises, and earnings of the illegally controlled company from the time of the violation. Conviction of violating this statute carried with it a mandatory requirement for the public sale of these assets.[89]

Recalling the circumstances attending passage of the bill, Pattison wrote ten years later that he regarded it as

a wise measure intended and necessary at the time to prevent a monopoly of the oil-carrying interests. The long agitation for legislation which would authorize the incorporation of oil pipe lines and invest them with the rights and powers necessary to their successful construction, eventuated in what was known as the "Free Pipe Line Bill." To protect and preserve the rights it secured, the Act of June 13, 1883, was an essential supplementary measure, else all the advantages of the Free Pipe Line Bill would have been lost, by permitting monopolies to consolidate and to acquire controlling interest in the competing pipe lines to be created under the salutary legislation of that session.[90]

For practical purposes the legislation was virtually a dead letter, although it did affect somewhat the Standard Oil–Tide-Water struggle. Standard Oil had long since absorbed all pipelines of any significance, except the Tide-Water. Having failed to conquer it and now by the new law denied the full fruits of a surrender, the oil combination reverted to its original strategy of coming to terms with its competitor. The Tide-Water was receptive. On October 9, 1883, the National Transit Company and the Tide-Water Pipe Company signed contracts effective the first of that month, dividing refining and pipage to the seaboard between them. Standard Oil was to have 88.5 per cent of the refining business done by the two groups and the Tide-Water 11.5 per cent. A similar division of the business of piping oil from Pennsylvania fields to the seaboard was also agreed upon. Both parties were to maintain the same rates for pipage. For collecting and delivering oil in the fields a charge of ten cents, half the normal rate to other patrons, was established.[91]

While the Tide-Water's independence was retained, it was effectively neutralized as a competitor of Standard Oil. For the producers there was no longer a choice among the railroads, the Standard Oil pipelines, or the Tide-Water. The legislative triumph which they had been seeking since 1868 and now had achieved proved empty. Standard Oil dominated refining and controlled, directly or indirectly, the pipelines which gathered the oil and transported it to the seaboard. Free pipe legislation at the state level could not now change this fact. The anticonsolidation law could only change the method by which control was exercised and maintained. Railroad antidiscrimination legislation was beside the point as far as crude shipments were concerned unless railroad-pipeline pooling were prohibited. Standard Oil's power had become a national issue, but the producers', and therefore the public's, attention was increasingly focused on railroad discriminations. The public interest continued to ride on the shoulders of oilmen, who so far had not suggested a national public policy toward pipelines.

VI

The Place of Pipelines in
Petroleum Transportation and
Public Policy, 1884-1887

IN THE years 1884–1887 Standard Oil's dominance in the transportation of crude petroleum continued undiminished despite the adoption of new public policies aimed against it. The Pennsylvania free pipe law and the prohibition against the consolidation of competing pipelines did not curb the Trust's pipeline power. Hurt by falling crude prices in the wake of overproduction, producers sought to subject the lines to regulation of rates and practices in Pennsylvania and Ohio in 1887. In the same year the passage of the Interstate Commerce Act crowned years of effort to outlaw railroad discriminations. While independent oilmen contributed significantly to this legislation, they made no effort to have it embrace pipelines. It soon appeared that economic self-interest weighed more heavily with the producers than the public interest which they claimed to champion.

Standard Oil's Pipelines in 1884

The extent of Standard Oil's pipeline empire was revealed to the oil industry in early 1884 when plans were under way to merge the United Pipe Lines with National Transit. A meeting of the Conference of Oil Exchanges, held at Oil City on March 10, 1884, resolved that a committee should investigate and report on the proposed transfer. A committee of three, including Joseph Seep, Standard's oil buyer, was appointed for this purpose. The committee proceeded to frame a series of questions, which were answered by Jacob J. Vandergrift and William T. Scheide for United Pipe Lines and by John D. Archbold, Samuel Dodd, and Daniel O'Day for National Transit.

The first question was carefully phrased to ascertain whether the National Transit Company was a common carrier "in the same sense as the United Pipe Lines." Both Vandergrift and Archbold agreed that this was the case. The second question and their replies indicated what they meant by this definition of common carrier. The two Standard Oil officials declared that the oil in the custody of their respective companies belonged to their patrons, that is, the owners of the oil. Archbold stressed this fact. When questioned as to whether the National Transit Company would deliver oil at the seaboard or intermediate points upon presentation of the certificate and payment of 20 cents local pipage, plus the trunk line transportation charges, Archbold declared that "the obligation of the company as a common carrier will govern that question." He indicated that this procedure was being followed and that he foresaw no reason for change.[1]

The question was then raised as to how trunk pipeline rates were to be determined. Archbold answered that railroad competition would form "a large factor" in determining the rates charged by National Transit. "The charge for transportation by our lines should be no higher than that charged by the railroads," he declared, "for, if higher, the railroads would perform the service. Competition in this, as in other matters, will largely govern." Archbold did not say what would be the result if pipeline rates were lower than the railroads' rates. Instead he chose to ignore the agreement of 1881 with the Pennsylvania Railroad to maintain rail and pipe rates on a noncompetitive basis. Within a few months, however, Standard Oil concluded a new contract with the road for the same purpose.

Although Archbold did not explicitly define "common carrier" in this instance, his testimony and that of other Standard Oil officials at one time or another clarifies their conception of the term. Archbold, Rockefeller, Dodd, and O'Day all said that Standard Oil pipelines were open to the public on the basis of uniform charges. This definition of a common carrier—one who carried for every person offering business and did so at the same rates under the same circumstances—was identical with the concept then being applied in the courts passing on railroad discriminations in the oil traffic. Producers generally agreed that the Standard Oil pipelines hewed to this practice. Their complaints, which were by no means universal among oilmen, were that premiums were paid to take oil away from other lines, that pipeline rates were too high, and that they were maintained by agreements with the railroads and the exercise of monopoly power in gathering oil. Some charged that on occasion pipelines of the oil combination delivered inferior oil to competitors and failed to make deliveries at points specified by the shipper.

These "violations" of the "obligations" of common carrier pipelines obviously relate to the specialized functions of the pipes as contrasted with the railroads. In some cases complaints against the pipelines could be explained away on the basis of the specialized service that they rendered; in others the lines were clearly used as competitive weapons. When trunk pipeline rates were held at the same level as railroad rates by agreement, there was reason to suspect that the latter explanation held true. Nevertheless, none of these practices was illegal as matters stood, and the complainants made little progress in having them declared so.

The transfer of United Pipe Lines' properties to National Transit more firmly integrated Standard Oil's pipeline holdings. The transaction, according to Scheide, would give National Transit an additional 2,200,000 barrels of tankage situated along its trunk lines and at New York and Philadelphia.[2] The oil held by the two companies was to be consolidated, but otherwise there appeared to be no significant changes contemplated in the mode of operation. The officers of the older firm continued as managers of the new United Pipe Line Division of the National Transit Company.

The size of United Pipe Lines' physical assets in 1884 gives some indication of its growth in the preceding decade. It had absorbed the following: Antwerp, Oil City, Clarion, Union, Conduit, Karns, Grant, Pennsylvania, and Relief pipelines; the Clarion and McKean divisions of American Transfer; the Prentice lines; the Olean Pipe; the Union Oil Company's line at Clarendon; and the McCalmont line at Cherry Grove. It reportedly possessed 3,000 miles of pipe, a storage capacity

of 40,000,000 barrels, and could move 10,000 barrels a day from producers' tanks. United Pipe Lines also had 51 pumping stations in the
Bradford and Allegheny fields; 32 in Warren and Forest County fields,
and 35 in the district below Oil City. Eighty-seven gaugers were employed in the first two fields mentioned and 32 in other areas. The results of their work were wired to the central office for the field
concerned, and books kept there showed each producer's balance at
the start and close of the day.[3]

The National Transit Company's holdings were equally impressive.
Its property was valued at $15,000,000 and included several thousand
miles of pipe and 15,000,000 barrels of iron tankage. Its New York
Division operated two six-inch lines from Olean, New York, to
Bayonne, New Jersey, and a connecting link to the refineries on Long
Island. The Pennsylvania Division, 280 miles long, operated a six-inch
pipe from Colegrove, McKean County, to Philadelphia, and a branch
pipe to Milton, Pennsylvania. In addition there was the trunk line to
Cleveland, 100 miles of five-inch pipe; the Pittsburgh Line, 60 miles
long; and the Buffalo and Baltimore Divisions, each about 70 miles
long.[4] In the next few years this impressive network was further expanded.

The National Transit Company and the Pennsylvania Railroad

The proliferation of Standard Oil's trunk pipeline system brought
new agreements with the railroads. The first contract between National Transit and the Pennsylvania Railroad had been made May 6,
1881. Although evidence submitted to the United States Industrial
Commission suggested that under this contract the Pennsylvania in
effect provided Standard Oil with a rebate,[5] if any rebate was involved, the railroad received it from the pipelines.[6] Starting in 1884, if
not earlier, this was also true for the Erie Railroad.[7]

New contracts between the National Transit and the Pennsylvania
were concluded in August, 1884. Under the first of these, pro rata payments on oil carried partly by pipe and partly by rail were to be continued, and the railroad was guaranteed the income on 26 per cent of
the traffic. The second contract demonstrated how superfluous railroad transportation of crude to the seaboard had become for Standard
Oil. It provided that should the railroad be unable to transport its full
quota of oil, the pipeline would do so, charging the Pennsylvania

only six to ten cents a barrel for delivering the oil to Philadelphia.[8] If this charge represented the pipeline's actual cost for the transportation, the open rate of 45 cents per barrel or more seemingly left a wide profit margin indeed.

Dodd later explained why the National Transit Company agreed to share this profitable traffic with the railroad. In the first place, since there was no free pipe law in New Jersey, the pipeline could not have easily reached the seaboard without use of the railroad's right of way. Secondly, there was need for a traffic contract with the railroad on oil shipped via Milton to Philadelphia.[9] Although Standard Oil's general counsel did not say so, other advantages accrued to the National Transit from the uniform railroad and pipeline rates on crude. This situation deprived other shippers of an opportunity to play one transportation agency against the other. At the same time Standard Oil stood to benefit in the road's treatment of its refined shipments.

The advantage of the contracts to the Pennsylvania is obvious. The railroad could share in the lucrative crude oil traffic without even the necessity of carrying the full amount of oil from which it would receive a revenue. According to Pennsylvania officials, the agreement became inoperative in 1892, but it was not formally canceled until 1905.[10]

The Rice Case

George Rice, a bitter critic of Standard Oil's relations with the railroads, was one of the most vocal of the independent refiners. A Vermonter, Rice had commenced his career in oil as a producer in the Pithole region in 1865. In 1876 he had established a small refinery at Marietta, Ohio, obtaining his oil from the Pennsylvania fields by pipe to the Ohio River and then by barge to Marietta. His experience with Standard Oil's pipeline power provides a documented record of how this weapon could be applied.

In late 1883 or early 1884, Daniel O'Day for undetermined reasons ordered the pipe serving the barges removed, and Rice was forced to ship his crude by rail into Pittsburgh. He soon began to take more oil from the Macksburg, Ohio, field, using the Cleveland and Marietta Railroad.[11] Standard Oil was also in this field, where pipeline construction multiplied.

National Transit moved smoothly and efficiently in eliminating pipeline competition in the Macksburg field. In the late summer of 1884 the West Virginia Transportation Company constructed a line from that field to the Muskingum River, which flowed into the Ohio at Marietta. This concern's difficulties shortly became overwhelming. National Transit, to maintain its foothold, offered a premium for oil considerably above that of the new line, whose pipe was torn up by the Cleveland and Marietta where it crossed the railroad's right of way. While awaiting court action on the latter problem, the West Virginia Transportation Company sold out to National Transit.[12] In January, 1885, Standard Oil had acquired another pipeline connecting the Macksburg field with tankage along the Cleveland and Marietta. The president of this concern, the Ohio Transit, later explained the sale in these terms: "We said we could not compete with the Standard Oil Company, and for that reason we sold out at a fair price." [13]

With these pipelines in hand, Standard Oil removed the premium on Macksburg oil, which in this light appears to have been a competitive device, and Daniel O'Day approached the receiver of the Cleveland and Marietta, Phineas Pease, with an interesting proposal. Pease was informed that O'Day was contemplating a trunk pipeline to connect the Macksburg field with Parkersburg, West Virginia. If the railroad would advance its rates to 35 cents a barrel, including a pipeline gathering charge, and remit 25 cents of this to the parties represented by O'Day, he said that the trunk pipeline would not be built and the railroad would have the traffic.[14] In effect this meant that shippers like George Rice, who had been paying 17.5 cents a barrel, would have to pay double the existing rate, whether they used Standard's gathering lines or not, and the bulk of the money would go to Standard Oil.

Assured by his attorney that the proposal was legal, Pease agreed to O'Day's terms. On March 20, 1885, a joint agent for Standard Oil's pipeline and the railroad commenced to collect the new charges.[15] Rice immediately turned to the construction of his own pipeline and by May, 1885, had it in operation. With this development it was neither necessary nor profitable for O'Day to continue shipments over the railroad. O'Day then completed a pipeline to Parkersburg despite alleged obstructive tactics by Rice. As a result, the Cleveland and Marietta soon lost all its oil shipments.

In October, 1885, Rice applied to the United States Circuit Court for an accounting by Pease, and the application was granted. Twelve days later a check for $340, representing Standard Oil's rebates on 1,360 barrels of oil shipped by Rice before he constructed his pipe-line, was returned to the railroad by the Macksburg Pipe Line Company.[16] The return of the rebates preceded the filing of Pease's report with the court. The judge found this report unsatisfactory, and further evidence convinced him that "the discrimination complained of in this case is so wanton and oppressive it could hardly have been accepted by an honest man, having due regard for the rights of others." [17]

The judge found that Standard Oil had desired to "crush" Rice and that the practices of the receiver were a "violation of sound public policy." [18] The decision was reported by *The New York Times*, December 11, 1885, in a front page article which said in part:

Gen. Pease was yesterday removed by Judge Baxter, of the United States court, for discriminating against a Marietta refiner in favor of the Standard Oil Company. Judge Baxter was very severe in his remarks on this kind of railroad management, and regretted that he could not punish Gen. Pease as he deserved, and at the same time characterized it as "robbing the poor and giving it to the rich, who did not need it."

Baxter referred the question of the amount of the rebates and their disposition to a special master, George K. Nash. Nash's investigation revealed the details of the surreptitious handling of the rebate arrangements and the fact that two firms besides Rice's had been similarly victimized. The rebates involved in these cases, however, were also returned.[19]

The Rice case became a *cause célèbre* in the annals of the growing public controversy over the Standard Oil Trust. The matter was aired in the House Trust Investigation of 1888,[20] and in March, 1890, John D. Rockefeller took special note of it in his famous interview with a New York *World* reporter. Rockefeller maintained that the agreement with the Cleveland and Marietta had been made by "our agent in that place" and that it had been disapproved in Standard Oil's New York office.[21] In any event, the significant role of pipeline power in extorting favors from Receiver Pease received little public notice; yet the power of the National Transit Company was becoming greater than any that the railroads had exerted over the crude oil traffic, except in its earliest days. In such a situation the company could have afforded to conduct itself with restraint, and O'Day's tactics in the Macksburg field were not typical of the finesse with which Standard Oil officials generally handled their problems.

The Billingsley Bill

The producers had certainly never been noted for finesse or even unity in dealing with their problems, and the manner in which they reacted to the glut of oil confronting them in 1887 was no exception to the rule. Oil had been brought to the surface at such a rate since 1882 that the amount in storage at the end of each year had never been less than the 33,395,885 barrels which were carried over from 1886 to 1887.[22] By July of the latter year the price of crude had dropped to 54 cents a barrel and the average for the year was the lowest since 1861.[23] Some producers naturally saw a causal connection between their plight and the obvious size and power of Standard Oil's pipeline system.

There was some justification for this view. A 20-cent charge for collecting a barrel of crude represented a high percentage of its cost to the purchaser at 1887 quotations. Storage charges of 40 cents per 1,000 barrels per day, with carry-overs of the magnitude already described, were scarcely calculated to win friends for Standard Oil. By reducing pipeline and storage charges, the producers believed that the demand for crude might be increased. Basically, overproduction was at the root of the producers' troubles. Nevertheless, some of them took advantage of the first opportunity that offered to renew the legislative attack on Standard Oil.

In his message to the Pennsylvania General Assembly on January 4, 1887, Governor Robert E. Pattison upbraided the legislators for failing to enforce Article XVII of the State Constitution forbidding discriminations in transportation. He declared that it had been a "dead letter" for twelve years, that the bills passed in 1883 had been impotent, and that no judicial action had been taken under them. In sum, "Discrimination in charges and facilities for transportation is as widespread and injurious as it ever was." [24] The producers scarcely needed such an invitation to loose their resentment against Standard Oil in legislative form.

This time the weapon of the producers was House Bill 104, introduced by James K. Billingsley of Washington County, January 27,

1887. Bill 104, popularly known as the Billingsley bill, became one of the most controversial and bitterly disputed measures of the session. Unfortunately for its future progress, the bill when introduced was a poorly drawn, partisan measure. Its title tells the story:

An act to punish corporations, companies, firms, associations and persons, and each of them engaged in the business of transporting by pipe-line or lines or storing petroleum in tank or tanks, under certain restrictions and penalties from charging in excess of certain fixed rates for receiving, transporting, storing, and delivering petroleum, and to regulate deductions for losses caused to petroleum in pipe-lines and storage tanks by lightning, fire, storm, or other unavoidable causes.[25]

Two concepts emerge clearly from this wording. The first, punishment of Standard Oil, was a reflection of the producers' desperation. The other, the regulation of pipeline and storage charges, was a logical reaction to Standard Oil's predominant power in crude oil transportation and was not inconsistent with the Trust's claim that its lines were common carriers.

The reasonable and the unreasonable, however, were closely intertwined in this measure. The provision calling for a maximum rate of ten cents per barrel for collecting and delivering oil within a given pipeline division and requiring delivery where the patrons wanted it does not seem unreasonable in view of the fact that Standard Oil carried for the Pennsylvania Railroad at this rate or less.[26] But the bill went on to impose almost impossible conditions on the pipelines. Each pipeline division was to establish and maintain one shipping point capable of accommodating the entire traffic within that division. All oil offered for transportation and storage had to be accepted and, if the owner desired, stored for at least a year at a specified rate, the first thirty days at no charge. Finally, the bill required that pipelines connect with any well upon application, regardless of its size or the revenue it could be expected to yield.

In effect the largest producer and the smallest, regardless of whether they brought oil to the surface out of all proportion to demand, were to be protected against the consequences of their action at the expense of the pipelines. Violations of the provisions of the bill were to be punishable by a fine of two thousand dollars for the first offense. A fine of two thousand to five thousand dollars, plus imprisonment for sixty days to one year, was provided for the second offense. The fines were to be divided equally between the prosecutor and the county in which the offense occurred. Furthermore, individuals injured by the violations were authorized to sue for double the amount of damages sustained.

The *Titusville Morning Herald* took the lead in attacking the bill. Although, as pointed out in the preceding chapter, Standard Oil's enemies maintained that the paper was controlled by Archbold, its comments had considerable merit. Late in January, the *Herald* declared: "The passage of the law, even were it not a monstrous travesty on the theory of legislation, would not advance the price of the producers' product a cent." A few weeks later the paper noted:

The use of the word *"punish"* shows the underlying notion of the bill, and in itself taints the whole act with a manifestly mischievous and vindictive purpose, entirely uncalled for and contrary to the whole spirit of commercial legislation, looking to the fixing of rates arbitrarily in a precarious and unexceptional business.[27]

Comments in the *Petroleum Age,* a periodical friendly to the producers, indicated some qualms about the bill as introduced. It was suggested that the requirement that pipelines connect with wells, no matter how far distant, combined with the low pipage rates specified in the bill, might discourage pipeline enterprise.[28] On the other hand, the *Age* declared: "While the present measure doubtless contains some objectionable and impracticable features, the motive of it is endorsed by the oil producer and the general oil trade." [29]

Actually, it is difficult to determine just how enthusiastic the majority of producers and speculative oilmen were. Apparently a sizable number of them were indifferent, maintaining that in the long run it was the consumer who paid the pipeline charges.[30] The speculators were not interested in pipeline regulation, and they felt that regulation of storage charges would "belittle the trade." [31]

With 30,000,000 barrels of oil in storage and the charges yet to be paid, Standard Oil had a powerful weapon with which to reinforce these views. National Transit let it be known that, regardless of whether the bill passed or not, it would charge the existing rate for storage of this oil.[32] Accordingly, many dealers in pipeline certificates expressed their opposition to the Billingsley bill.[33]

In addition to the weaknesses of the bill from a practical point of view, there were three other major objections to it. The first objection was that the measure would violate the obligation of contract involved in the National Transit Company's charter. The charter, originally granted in 1870, authorized its holder "to fix and regulate the tolls and charges to be charged or demanded for any freight, property or passengers traveling or passing over any improvement erected, managed or owned by the said company, or any merchandise or property transported over any road whatever by the said company." [34] The Billingsley bill, its opponents charged, would impair this right. The second objection was that the bill attempted to regulate commerce between the states, for the operations of the National Transit were certainly interstate in character. Finally, advocates of the laissez-faire philosophy objected that it was simply unwise to legislate on the subject of pipeline and storage practices and rates.

Various legal decisions were cited to refute these objections, [35] but the producers' basic answer lay in the argument that the bill was not designed to protect the existing system. Those who supported the measure demanded protection as citizens against the monopolistic power of Standard Oil's pipelines. Again they identified their welfare with that of the general public; yet, as will appear shortly, this identification was quickly forgotten when the opportunity offered to join Standard Oil in an effort to restrict production and raise crude oil prices. Meanwhile, the Billingsley bill had gone down to defeat.

Purged of its punitive title and the requirement that pipes connect with every well where their services were requested, the measure had little trouble in passing the House. Twenty-five of the thirty-nine opposing votes came from the Philadelphia area, repeating a pattern already familiar in past voting on the free pipe bill. [36] In the Senate the bill went through its first two readings without significant opposition, but feeling against it had risen by the time it came up for its final reading on April 20, 1887.

The center of the bill's support was naturally the oil-producing counties of northwestern Pennsylvania, whose independent political attitudes had won them the name "the independent Northwest." [37] In the campaign for passage of the measure, the Knights of Labor and other trade organizations lent their support, and this fact gave added political significance to debate on it.[38] In the Senate, Lewis Emery, Jr., used the independent political habits of the oil country to the utmost advantage, declaring as the bill entered its third reading:

I warn the Republican party that there are fifteen counties in the oil region, all of them now Republican but four. They ask relief. If you do not give it they will revolt. I am a good Republican, but I will myself lead this revolt. I acted independently in 1882 and I will act in the same way again.[39]

Emery, however, was under severe attack from both the *Oil City Derrick* and the *Titusville Morning Herald,* which he termed Standard Oil's "paid press." They charged him with using the Billingsley bill as a means of obtaining the sale to Standard Oil of a refinery in which he was interested. This refinery had been opened at Greenwich Point, Pennsylvania, near Philadelphia, following the dismissal of the suits against the oil combination in 1880 and the Pennsylvania Railroad's promise to treat all customers alike. The plant, which according to Emery represented a $250,000 investment, had received its oil via United Pipe Lines and the Green Line tank cars of the Pennsylvania Railroad.[40] Emery became dissatisfied with the quality of the oil which he received from United Pipe Lines' tanks, and he therefore laid a pipe twenty-five miles long connecting his own wells with a branch of the railroad. Thereafter, he testified, he encountered difficulty in obtaining cars from the Green Line, and his facilities were idle more than half the time.[41] The *Derrick* now charged that he was attempting to sell the refinery and his "friendship" to Standard Oil for $750,000.

As was usually the case when Emery was supporting an oil measure, debate on the Billingsley bill took on a personal note. The oilman defended himself at length, citing notarized statements by his partners, A. H. Logan and W. R. Weaver. Logan stated that Standard officials had approached Weaver and arranged a meeting at the Lafayette Hotel, Philadelphia, on September 24, 1886. John D. Archbold and Daniel O'Day were present on this occasion and made an offer to purchase the Logan, Emery, and Weaver business. As no conclusion was reached, another meeting was held September 30, 1886, at the Albemarle Hotel in New York City. There Emery, with the consent of his partners, had named a sum for which they would be willing to sell, but the Standard representatives had refused to purchase at that price. At a further meeting at the Astor House that November, they had offered the Emery firm $22,500 per year if it "would act in harmony with them." This offer was declined.[42] Weaver's notarized statement supported Logan's version of the story, and on the floor of the Senate Emery angrily denied that he was a "boodle taker." He climaxed his defense with the dramatic accusation that William T. Scheide, the general superintendent of National Transit, who was among the spectators, was responsible for the charges against him.

Senator Emery A. Walling of Erie reportedly gave the best speech in support of the bill. He pointed out that if there were a dozen competitors for crude oil transportation, rates might safely be left to the competitive result. When, as in the current case, there was only one transporter, the need for regulation of its rates was clear. Appealing to the popular belief that the Trust was becoming rich at the producers' expense, the Senator resorted to comparisons calculated to make Standard Oil's profits comprehensible to the dullest legislator. "The Standard Oil Company," he declared, "has made more money in five years than Cornelius Vanderbilt made in his life or than Jay Gould ever made or lost." He made explicit the producers' assumptions about the cause of their distress by asking why a company making these profits did not reduce charges when the oil country was suffering from low-priced oil, overproduction, and monopoly.[43]

Senator George W. Delamater countered Walling's appeal with the charge that the Regions' sponsors of the bill were far from the poor, oppressed men they claimed to be. Actually Emery was on his way to becoming a millionaire, but he and Delamater were naturally poles apart on this question.

In 1890 the fiery oilman charged that Delamater had first supported and then opposed the Billingsley bill. The Senator replied that he had always opposed it as unconstitutional and unwise. He was supported in this version by Captain J. T. Jones and George W. Darr, who had worked for the bill. Jones recalled that he had talked with Delamater at the time. "I told him," Jones said, "that I did not indorse all its provisions, but the situation was such we needed relief. If the bill was not all we could ask, it seemed to be all we could get just then, and any relief, however small, would be appreciated."[44]

Darr said that he had been in a delegation lobbying for the Billingsley bill and that the group had differed widely on the rates which should be specified. He declared that Emery had told them that his interests and those of his Philadelphia refinery had to be protected and had insisted on the lowest rate under consideration.[45]

This explanation of the motivation behind the bill provides an interesting supplement to the arguments for it presented in the *Petroleum Age* of March, 1887. There it was said that the National Transit "exacts from all alike, double what would be a reasonable compensation for its services, and pays the inordinate profits to the Standard Oil Company in the form of dividends . . . with this advantage to themselves, that nobody is indictable for conspiracy as they were under the contracts of 1872." [46] On the other hand, the *Age* contained appeals to the pride and self-interest of Pennsylvanians. They were reminded that the National Transit Company transported oil out of the state for refining and refused to deliver oil where its patrons wanted. Also, since oil delivered in the state would be transported under regulated rates whereas interstate shipments would not be subject to the law, it was hopefully suggested that New York refiners would be forced to move their works to Pennsylvania in order to enjoy the benefits of low-cost crude oil transportation.[47]

Except for the narrow view taken of Pennsylvania's economic interests, these were arguments well adapted to a demand for federal pipeline regulation. Yet there appears to have been no demand for that.

Following the peppery exchanges between Emery and his attackers, the Billingsley bill was defeated April 28, 1887, by a vote of 25 nays to 18 yeas. The affirmative votes were equally divided between Republicans and Democrats. Twenty Republicans, seven of them from Philadelphia, voted against the bill, as did five Democrats. Angry producers charged that bribery and pressure on the legislators by Standard Oil had accomplished this result, but available evidence suggests that the producers were not above using these weapons themselves.[48]

National Transit in March, 1887, had offered to make concessions. Although the offer to reduce storage rates was rejected by the Emery faction, and two members of the committee that negotiated the agreement were hung in effigy, the rate was reduced from 40 to 25 cents per 1,000 barrels per day when the price of oil was one dollar or less. The standard deduction for evaporation and sediment was also reduced from 3 to 2 per cent.[49] These concessions represented the one tangible result of the agitation for the ill-fated measure.

The New York *World*, in a front-page story several weeks after the defeat of the Billingsley bill, devoted considerable space to the pipeline problem and accurately reported that at existing quotations the charges for delivering oil to railroad stations or trunk pipeline stations still constituted 40 per cent of the value of the oil at the wells. "This is what the late Artemus Ward would call a 'jeenyal monop- perly,'" the paper said.[50]

The Producers' Protective Association

The one hundred and fifty producers who had milled about the lobbies, aisles, and galleries of the Capitol on the day of the Billings- ley bill's defeat saw nothing "jeenyal" about Standard Oil. They were in an angry mood that evening as they assembled at the Leland House to discuss the next steps to be taken. They adopted resolutions upholding the principle of the measure which, they said, "established the fact that the Legislature of the State has the power to regulate, control, and if necessary for the public good, destroy this monster corporation." [51] The arguments that had filled the legislative cham- bers on behalf of the bill and vehement attacks on a pipeline com- pany that was supposed to make annually a profit equal to the value of its entire property filled the air.

Since it had been shown once again that in a test of strength at Harrisburg, Standard Oil was not to be bested, attention was turned to the problem of re-establishing an effective producers' organization. A committee composed of David Kirk, Thomas W. Phillips, William Hasson, S. P. Boyer, and W. C. Kennedy was appointed to consider the matter, and a meeting was called to take place at Oil City, May 5. This gathering was followed by others from which emerged the Producers' Protective Association, with Phillips as president. A secret order whose membership requirements specifically excluded indi- viduals connected with Standard Oil, the Association proposed "to defend the industry against the aggregations of monopolistic trans- porters, refiners, buyers and sellers" by handling its own oil.[52] Here was apparent recognition of the fact that challenging Standard Oil involved adoption of its pattern of operations. This concept was carried to the point that in August it was suggested that local assemblies of the Association ratify a proposal to duplicate the entire pipeline network of the National Transit Company, including lines to New York, Buffalo, Cleveland, Pittsburgh, and Philadelphia.[53]

There was, however, a growing conviction among leading members of the Association that something had to be done about overproduction of oil—and quickly. Accordingly, they accompanied the pipeline proposal with one for a shutdown of production. At the same time, reflecting their animus toward Standard Oil, they canvassed the idea of collecting evidence for a new conspiracy suit against their perennial foe.[54]

The last two proposals were inconsistent, as Thomas W. Phillips, president of the association, pointed out. To stop drilling and close down wells without an understanding with Standard Oil would only aid the Trust, which owned a large percentage of the oil already in storage. While producers withheld production, Phillips observed, Standard Oil could release this oil, obtained at depressed prices, for a handsome profit. He therefore refused to participate in the scheme unless Standard Oil were brought into it.

What producers were most interested in was higher prices for crude, and they were willing to co-operate with the late enemy to this end. They found Standard Oil receptive to their plan. John D. Archbold told a committee of the New York State Senate in 1888:

The inducement was for the purpose of accomplishing a harmonious feeling as between the interests of the Standard Oil Trust and the producers of petroleum . . . and we felt it to be in the interests of the American oil industry that a reasonable price should be had by the producer for the crude material, and we wanted to cooperate to that end.[55]

When his questioner suggested that co-operation would advance not only crude prices but also those of domestic refined products, Archbold told the committee that Standard Oil had actually suffered a hardship as a result of the agreement, since it had to sacrifice profit abroad in order to compete with Russian oil.[56]

The agreement itself provided that the Producers' Protective Association would obtain a reduction of 17,500 barrels per day below the figures of July–August, 1887, both by shutdown of wells and

by cessation of drilling. To compensate the producers for this curtail-
ment of production Standard Oil agreed to sell them 5,000,000 barrels
of crude at 62 cents a barrel, plus the usual storage charges and
assessments. If, at the end of three months, the producers could
show the agreed-upon reduction, the oil was to be delivered as fast
as it could be sold for a price in excess of 62 cents a barrel. The profits
were to be held in trust until the end of the first year of the agreement.
If the producers could then show that they had fulfilled its terms,
they were to receive the money. If not, it was to go to Standard Oil.
Upon Phillips' suggestion, the profits from the sale of 2,000,000 barrels
of oil, half provided by Standard Oil and half by the association,
were to go to the workmen who would suffer from the shutdown.[57]

The agreement was ratified by the association meeting at Bradford
on October 18, 1887, and was to go into effect November 1. It was
estimated then that 80 per cent of the producers were ready to co-
operate.[58] Moreover, the shutdown proved effective. Pipeline reports
for November showed a decrease of about 1,000,000 barrels in net
stocks of oil and the lowest average pipeline runs in ten years. The
results appeared in the price of oil, which reached 90 cents a barrel
in December and gave every indication of going higher.[59] The effect
on domestic refined prices seemed minimal, for two-thirds of the oil
was exported, and an advance of four cents a barrel on crude was
reflected by only one-eighth of a cent per gallon rise in the cost of
refined.[60]

These arrangements, following close on the heels of the abortive
Billingsley bill, indicate that the producers' interest in pipeline
legislation was primarily a function of their economic situation rather
than a concern for the public. The benefits to be derived from co-
operation with Standard Oil in controlling the industry were, even to
militants such as Phillips, a pleasing contrast to the barren fruits of
opposing it in legislative halls. Archbold was quite right when he
observed that the distress in the oil country in the first half of 1887
was reflected in an outcry that "our interest was getting a return,
that theirs was not in the business." [61]

The fact that pipeline regulation was bound up with the producers'
self-interest is not to say that it was not also a matter of importance
to the public. Rockefeller admitted in 1888 that Standard Oil did
about 75 per cent of the nation's refining,[62] and this was probably a

somewhat conservative estimate. Unquestionably the Trust's pipeline power was a major bulwark of its predominance in refining, both profitwise and as a weapon against competition.[63] But the significance of pipelines, which were, after all, a comparatively new and specialized mode of transportation, was not recognized by the public generally. Furthermore, the producers were not always reliable guides as to how the public interest in equitable conditions of competition should be protected. Their advocacy of a punitive state policy toward pipelines, their combination with Standard Oil to increase crude prices, and their failure to push for federal legislation on railroad-pipeline pooling indicate their shortcomings as champions of this interest.

The Interstate Commerce Act and Pipelines

Although the construction of trunk pipelines had given the problem of pipeline regulation an interstate character by 1880, Congress was just getting around to dealing with railroad discriminations. These discriminations were indeed a widely felt and popularly recognized evil, whose remedy the oil interest had been promoting since the early seventies. The Reagan bill of 1878, it will be recalled, was directly influenced by complaints from the Oil Regions.

This fact was brought up in House discussion of the measure in 1885. Representative William W. Rice of Massachusetts angrily denounced its origin. "This bill," he said, "born of local passion and strife, discarded in the Legislature of the State where it had its origin, adopted by the gentleman from Texas and corrected and improved by his skillful hand, has worked its way into the national Congress, and seeks sway over the whole country." The Massachusetts Congressman concluded, "It would cramp the commerce of the nation into the straight-jacket designed for the petroleum traffic of Pennsylvania." [64] Nevertheless, the bill managed to pass the House only to fail in the Senate.

The latter event was followed by the appointment in March, 1885, of a select committee, headed by Senator Shelby M. Cullom of Illinois, to investigate the problem of regulating interstate transportation of passengers and freight by rail and water routes. The committee submitted its report the following January and supported such proposals of the Reagan bill as the posting of rates, public notice of changes in rates, prohibition of long haul–short haul discriminations, drawbacks, and rebates. Unlike the original Reagan measure, enforcement was to be lodged in a commission rather than state or federal courts. Meantime, the Supreme Court's decision in the *Wabash* case made Congressional action imperative. The Cullom Committee's recommendations were enacted into law February 4, 1887, and a prohibition on pools, which was part of the Reagan bill but not recommended by the Cullom Committee, was also included.

The rising tide of criticism of Standard Oil undoubtedly played a role in the enactment of the law. William Z. Ripley, the foremost authority on railroad regulation in his day, wrote in 1912: "Whatever the commercial crimes chargeable to the founder of the Standard Oil Company, he should, at least, be credited with the performance of a great public service in finally crystallizing public opinion in 1887 in favor of railroad legislation for the prevention of rebating." [65] In 1885, President Arthur T. Hadley of Yale, who was friendly to many aspects of Standard Oil's operations, noted:

The company, besides the power obtained by controlling an enormous capital, had come into such relations with the railroads and the pipe-lines that no independent refiner had any chance whatever. These contracts [providing rebates], more discreditable to the railroads than to the Standard Oil Company, were what attracted public attention to its doings.[66]

While Hadley exaggerated the situation of the independent refiner to some extent, the remainder of his observation was unquestionably accurate.

Even astute observers of the oil transportation situation in the mid-eighties failed to comprehend the full importance of Standard's pipeline power. Among this group was James F. Hudson who contributed to the growing demand for federal railroad legislation through his book, *The Railways and the Republic*. In a chapter entitled "The History of a Commercial Crime," Hudson declared, "The Standard Oil Company, indeed, embodies the commercial crimes of the past decade." [67] Obviously Ripley got some of the inspiration for his comments on Standard Oil from this source, and so did members of Congress, for both Hadley and Hudson were "often quoted in debate" on the interstate commerce bill.[68] The fact remains that Hudson did not properly assess the role of pipelines in contributing to railroad discriminations. Although he cited efforts in Pennsylvania and Ohio to open pipeline transportation to competition, observed that Standard Oil's possession of pipelines gave it an advantage over outside refiners, and recounted the story of the Columbia Conduit, he mistakenly maintained that Standard Oil's "entire profits were comprised within the discriminations made in its favor by the railways."

The *Petroleum Age*, on the other hand, did note that the Interstate Commerce Act had failed to touch an element of the oil combination's "illicit strength"—its seaboard pipelines. "Whilst these pipe-lines are essentially common carriers," the oil journal declared, "they carry no oil except for firms or corporations belonging to the trust." [69] This situation, it pointed out, was a striking contrast to that in Russia, where government conditions for the construction of a pipeline from Baku to Batoum had stipulated that it must carry for the public and that its owners could not engage in other branches of the petroleum industry. [70]

Although no effort had been made to include pipelines in the Interstate Commerce Act, regulation of their rates and practices was considered and rejected in Ohio as well as in Pennsylvania in 1887. The Ohio measure was an exact copy of the Billingsley bill. Introduced near the end of the legislative session, it passed the Senate on March 18, 1887, but the legislature adjourned before the House voted on it. That the motive behind the proposal was the same as in Pennsylvania seems apparent from the *Cleveland Plain-Dealer's* comment. "It is a notorious fact," the paper said, "that there is no money in the Ohio oil fields because the Standard oil company has a complete monopoly of the pipe lines, and storage tanks. It charges such enormous rates for storage that there is no profit in pumping oil." The paper attributed the death of the bill to "Republican agents" of Standard Oil. [71]

Evidence that dissatisfied producers were definitely not thinking in terms of federal pipeline legislation is obvious from their testimony before a House committee in 1888. When questioned as to whether he had ever given any thought to placing pipelines under the jurisdiction of the Interstate Commerce Commission, I. E. "Farmer" Dean, a producer from Toledo, replied that he had not. Although he bitterly resented his inability to compete with the Standard Oil on equal terms, he reasoned that since there was no apparent discrimination in pipeline rates as to localities or individuals, there was no need to regulate them.[72] Another oilman, David Kirk, who had experience with pipelines dating back to Pithole days, told the same committee that the producers had been "suckers" to think that the Pennsylvania legislature could open Standard Oil's pipes to them. "I think one thing you should do," he said, "is to apply the principles of the interstate commerce law to pipe lines, the transportation of oil by pipes, making them common carriers and subject to regulation." [73] Despite a plethora of testimony taken by the committee, however, these were the only expressions of opinion on a federal public policy toward pipelines.

Meantime, the leading advocate of the Billingsley bill, Lewis Emery, Jr., had sold his Greenwich Point refinery to Standard Oil. Claiming that the refinery was suffering from railroad discriminations, Emery's firm instituted a suit for treble damages against the Pennsylvania Railroad in October, 1887.[74] The property was sold to Standard Oil in the following month for $300,000, and the suit against the railroad was eventually settled out of court.[75] Emery's enemies, who had charged that he had backed the Billingsley bill to aid the sale of his refinery, could claim that their charges had now been substantiated; his supporters could point anew to railroad discriminations as a means of eliminating Standard Oil's competitors.

George Rice was the most active of the latter group in taking advantage of the new Interstate Commerce Act. By October, 1887, he had filed thirteen complaints with the commission alleging railroad discriminations in favor of the Trust.[76] In one of these actions he claimed that the Louisville and Nashville Railroad's charges for barrel oil shipments were excessive and unreasonable.[77] The commission appeared to acquiesce in the railroad's charges for transporting the barrels as well as the oil, though subsequently it declared that "the logic of the discussion and the whole tenor of the reasoning [in that case] are against the practice of charging for the weight of barrels by carriers that employ the two modes of transportation in tanks and in barrels." [78]

The railroads naturally interpreted the Louisville and Nashville decision in their favor. In September, 1888, railroad rates on barrel shipments from Titusville to Perth Amboy, New Jersey, were advanced from 52 to 66 cents, including the charge for the barrels of which Rice had complained.[79] This move caused consternation in the Oil Regions, where independent refineries had sprung up, partly as a result of Standard Oil's increasing concentration on refining in areas close to larger centers of consumption. While Standard Oil could transport crude oil by pipeline to these refineries, the Regions' refiners had to ship their refined products by rail to seaboard markets. Accordingly, they brought complaints before the Interstate Commerce Commission against the Western New York and Pennsylvania Railroad Company and other roads, charging discrimination in rates against barrel shipments.

As the refiners' counsel, Franklin B. Gowen concentrated on the pooling agreement between the Pennsylvania Railroad and National Transit. He argued that the road was discriminating in favor of Standard Oil as the result of the contract guaranteeing the Pennsylvania 26 per cent of the revenues of the oil traffic to the seaboard. Gowen confronted the railroad's representatives with this charge during hearings at Titusville. While they acknowledged that the contract existed, they refused to produce it on the grounds that they might tend thereby to incriminate themselves.[80]

Gowen attempted to show, nevertheless, that Standard Oil was able to transport oil to its seaboard refineries at a fraction of the cost to competitors represented by the open rail and pipe charges. The Pennsylvania's counsel battled vigorously to prevent an estimate of which placed it at six to ten cents a barrel, were finally revealed.[81] the cost of pipeline transportation, but the terms of the contract, If this figure bore only an approximate relationship to actual costs, it seems obvious that Standard Oil enjoyed a tremendous advantage over competitors in the transportation of crude oil. This advantage could be regarded as the reward for entrepreneurship or the fruits of a legal suppression of competition between rival transportation agencies. The Interstate Commerce Commission inclined to the latter view.

In its decision handed down on November 14, 1892, the commission took note of the relations between the Pennsylvania and the National Transit Company. The commission declared, "If they [Standard Oil] own the pipe line the payment of freight charges would be merely going through the process of 'taking money out of

Henry Harley, pipeline pioneer, president of the first
pipeline combination, and unsuccessful promoter of
the first seaboard pipeline

Lewis Emery, Jr., 1839–1924, oilman, legislator, and indefatigable foe of Standard Oil, who used both enterprise and public policy as his weapons

one pocket and putting it in another'; if they control them, they can, and probably do, dictate terms as to rates." [82] The decision pointed out, however, that "a railroad is not interdicted from pooling with a competing pipe line. This contract, therefore, does not fall within the description of contracts forbidden in the Act." [83] The commission continued: "Although transportation by express companies and pipe lines should doubtless be made subject to the provisions of the Act to regulate commerce, the failure to make them so can be remedied only by Congress." [84]

The commission, however, was proving ineffective in dealing with even the railroad abuses over which it already had jurisdiction. Its decision in favor of the barrel shippers was ignored by the roads, and, although the decision was reaffirmed and damages awarded, the case wound up in the courts where it remained for years.

In failing to concentrate on federal rather than state pipeline legislation in 1887, the producers missed an opportunity to strike at the vitals of Standard Oil's power while this could still be done without jeopardizing their own interests. Since Standard Oil had built its first major trunk pipeline, its pipeline operations had been interstate in character; yet the advocates of governmental intervention in this field offered no suggestions for a federal public policy. In view of the producers' contributions to the Interstate Commerce Act, it must be concluded that for them the strategy of attacking the more obvious railroad abuses took priority. The Billingsley bill and its Ohio counterpart appear to have been temporary expedients designed to shift some of the consequences of overproduction to Standard Oil. The failure of these measures turned the producers to co-operation with the Trust and later to the adoption of its weapons. The intra-industry struggle then entered a new phase with both sides using pipelines in much the same manner.

VII

Pipelines as an Issue in the Antitrust Movement and the Petroleum Industry, 1888-1895

THE pattern of industrial organization set by the Standard Oil Trust in 1882 found many imitators during the following decade. As capital was combined and plants grew larger, public interest in the new form of organization mounted. In 1888 each of the seven political parties offering presidential candidates declared against monopolies, and the four leading parties specifically condemned trusts and industrial combinations.[1] Although trusts were not the major issue of the 1888 presidential campaign, they had definitely arrived on the scene as a matter of national interest and concern. Furthermore, the Standard Oil Trust was regarded as the archetype, and state and federal trust investigations provided fresh materials with which the literature of exposure strengthened this popular conception.

The trust investigations stimulated not only attacks on Standard Oil but also a systematic defense of its position. While the Trust had yet to come to a full realization of the importance of public relations, during the years 1888-1895 its officials developed the arguments with which they brought their defense to the public in the next decade. Significantly, they stressed the Trust's accomplishments in the pipeline field while their opponents concentrated their fire on railroad discriminations.

The role of pipelines in the rise of Standard Oil and in the maintenance of its predominant position in the petroleum industry received considerable notice in the trust investigations and some notice in antitrust literature, but there was no clarion call for legislative action. Although one more attempt at pipeline regulation was made in Pennsylvania, the producers there were even more divided than they had been in the past on such measures. Legislators were apathetic on the question, and the public's attention continued to be centered primarily on railroad discriminations.

Pipelines and Trust Investigations, 1888

The Hepburn Committee's investigation of railroads in New York State in 1879 had given the American public conclusive evidence of Standard Oil's great influence with the railroads and revealed that gathering pipelines had been important competitive weapons in the course of that development. In 1888 a hasty investigation of trusts by a committee of the New York State Senate was to disclose how far Standard Oil had come in developing trunk pipelines during the past decade. A concurrent federal investigation provided fresh evidence of the importance of pipelines to Standard Oil's position in the American petroleum industry.

A resolution asking for an investigation of trusts was introduced in the New York State Senate on February 15, 1888, and adopted the following day.[2] Hearings before the Senate Committee on General Laws opened on February 20 and were concluded on February 29. In this brief interval representatives of "trusts" in industries ranging from milk to furniture were summoned to give testimony. Among them, of course, were the leading figures of Standard Oil, John D. Rockefeller and John D. Archbold.

Samuel Dodd and Joseph H. Choate provided the legal guidance for Standard Oil's witnesses. A *New York Tribune* reporter depicted Choate as "sad-eyed and classical looking," listening to the proceedings "with an air of ill-concealed ennui as though to him it was all a twice-told tale." Dodd, "cheerful, ruddy and bulky," had as an associate former Congressman John H. Camp, "thin, slender and dark-eyed, looking well qualified to play Cassius to Mr. Dodd's

Caesar." Rockefeller, his eyes "sad and dreamy," sometimes mildly reproachful, sometimes "tenderly persuasive," defended the Trust with calm assurance.[3]

There was nothing novel in his defense, and perhaps Choate's "ennui" may be attributed to that fact. That large-scale operations resulted in improved products at lower prices was Rockefeller's theme.[4] The Trust's operations had not hurt domestic competition, he maintained, introducing a list of 111 refiners with which Standard Oil "competed" in the domestic market. Further, he declared, Standard Oil was competing vigorously against Russian oil in the world markets.[5] He admitted that the oil combination controlled 75 per cent of domestic refining, but he denied that his organization was any threat to the producers. He summed up his attitude toward the producing fraternity with a note of bitterness in his voice. "Oh no," he said, "the dear people, if they had produced less oil than they wanted, would have got their full price; no combination in the world could have prevented that, . . . they are a bright and able company of men as ever engaged in any enterprise." [6]

The high point of Rockefeller's testimony came when he was requested to produce the trust agreement of 1882. With little hesitation he acceded to the request, but Choate asked that the document not be made public. The committee, however, ruled against him, and the trust agreement was read into the record. At last the Trust was forced to shed some of its mystery.

Rockefeller, in fact, appeared far less reluctant to discuss Standard Oil's pipeline organization and operations than he had been a year before. Testifying at a trial in Buffalo, New York, on May 10, 1887, he had declared: "The business of the Standard Oil Company is refining oil and incidental manufacturing with refining." When asked whether this incidental activity included ownership of pipelines, he had replied: "No, sir." [7] Technically this answer was legally correct, but it was misleading. The Standard Oil Trust held the stock of both refining and pipeline companies. Rockefeller, however, was following the calculated policy of the Trust up to that time, namely, to reveal publicly as little as possible about its operations.

John C. Welch in his article for the *North American Review* in

1883 had noted this policy. He wrote: "If there was ever anything in this country that was bolted and barred, hedged around, covered over, shielded before and behind, in itself and in all its approaches, with secrecy, that thing is the Standard Oil Company." [8] This animadversion applied as much to pipelines as to other phases of Standard Oil's business, but one investigation and trial after another had forced Standard Oil officials to divulge increasing amounts of information on their activities.

Now, before the New York Senate Committee, Rockefeller revealed that approximately one-third of the nine million trust certificates represented pipeline holdings.[9] He also admitted that Standard Oil owned 5 to 10 per cent of the Tide-Water's stock, though he maintained that that line was in competition with members of the Standard Oil combination.[10] He further declared that Standard Oil's pipelines were open to the public on the basis of uniform rates—apparently his definition of a common carrier's responsibilities. In short, Rockefeller's testimony made it quite clear that Standard Oil wielded great power in the petroleum industry and that pipelines were an important ingredient of that power.

The Senate Committee in its report commented briefly on the threat posed by Standard Oil but recommended no corrective measures. It declared that the Trust had the power to control refined oil prices but found that because of increasing production Standard Oil had made the price of oil so reasonable that it was available to all consumers. The potential exercise of concentrated economic power bothered the committee. "The end, if not the purpose of every combination," it said, "is to destroy competition and leave the people subject to the rule of a monopoly." [11] On the other hand, the committee was forced to admit that not a single witness appeared to substantiate the alleged abuse of Standard Oil's power, but it attributed this fact to the brevity of the hearings.[12] In any event no concrete recommendations for legislative action resulted from the inquiry. Standard Oil had emerged from another investigation unscathed.

Meanwhile, a federal investigation of trusts had gotten under way, with the purpose, so Washington reports said, of making "political capital for the free traders." [13] The House Committee on Manufactures conducted the hearings, and Franklin B. Gowen, Standard Oil's longtime foe, acted as the committee's counsel.

Archbold was the Trust's principal witness before the committee. The essence of his defense of Standard Oil's pre-eminent position is contained in these words:

It survives there by virtue of its better service, its superior service, and on no other basis. It has no presumptive right. It exercises no monopoly of franchise. It occupies no field to the exclusion of any other corporation, individual, or firm. It is as free as air. Any man who has ability and capital can engage in the business.[14]

Gowen was relentless in his effort to disprove these generalizations and centered his attention on matters of transportation. Under Gowen's questioning Archbold declared that Standard Oil had been completely justified in opposing the Empire Transportation Company's engaging in both transportation and refining; yet he could see no objection to Standard Oil's being similarly engaged. "The method of the pipe line," he contended, "is an improvement for carrying the oil to get the rate on transportation on oil at a normal point, at which they have stood now for some time." [15]

Archbold refused to be led by Gowen into an analysis of the reasonableness of rates. The current rate for gathering oil in the field was, and for years had been, 20 cents a barrel. The trunk line rate from Bradford, Pennsylvania, to New York was 45 cents a barrel and 55 cents from the lower producing region. Gowen attempted to force the witness to admit that these rates were far above a reasonable level, and he emphasized the fact that the Pennsylvania Railroad and Standard Oil's trunk piplines maintained the same rates on crude oil.

Archbold, while admitting the existence of the railroad agreement, maintained that trunk pipeline rates were reasonable. A typical exchange between the two able antagonists took the following form:

Q. Now, . . . is it not greatly to your advantage as a transporter of oil through the pipes, that the rates of transportation by railroad and pipe line, assuming that they are to be identical, should not sink to a low point? A. As I have before stated, I think the rates are at a reasonable point, and a point below which the railroads have no incentive to cut them for an increase of their traffic. I believe the Pennsylvania Railroad Company has, as I am informed, at different times during the past two or three years, taken the ground that the traffic, even on this basis, was not a profitable one to them; one that they did not care to have.[16]

This was the same line that Archbold had taken in 1884 when questioned about the effect of transferring the United Pipe Lines to National Transit. Again his remarks suggested that the railroads, if left to compete on equal terms with trunk pipelines, would have been completely out of the picture as crude oil carriers.

Gowen still had to prove, however, that they were kept in the business as a result of pipeline rates that represented the railroads' cost of doing business rather than the cost of pipeline transportation. In this effort he got no help from Standard Oil officials. Archbold, pointing to the newness of the business and the risks involved in constructing pipelines in fields of uncertain production, claimed that he did not know what pipeline transportation actually cost.[17] Standard Oil's veteran pipeline builder, Daniel O'Day, also professed ignorance of the relative cost advantages of pipelines as compared with tank cars.[18]

At least two producers were ready to give their views. Lewis Emery, Jr., who had built a short pipeline to avoid dependence on United Pipe Lines, estimated that it cost him one and a half cents a barrel to move oil from his wells in contrast to the United's 20-cent charge. He admitted, however, that no pumping was involved in his operation.[19] David Kirk of the Producers' Protective Association maintained that five cents a barrel would yield fair compensation for local pipeline transportation, but he did not indicate the basis for this calculation.[20]

Kirk stated that in his view state ownership of pipelines "would be a great benefit," [21] and Gowen later used this proposition to set a trap for Archbold. Taking Archbold's argument that Standard Oil paid the same rates as other pipeline patrons and enjoyed no undue advantage from its ownership of the lines, Gowen asked whether Standard Oil would object to having the State of Pennsylvania take over its pipes upon fair compensation and with the assurance that they would be available to all comers on an equal basis. Archbold, obviously angry, at first objected to the question, then admitted that pipelines were a business separate from refining, and finally declared that Standard Oil would not be injured as a refiner.[22]

The Trust's opponents took a different view. Emery testified that his pipeline had given him a profit of two hundred dollars a day and thus enabled him to take losses in the refining end of his business.[23] Kirk declared that Standard Oil's pipeline system had been paid for from its own earnings. "The first line was bought on tick," he asserted, "and they paid for it before they had to buy more pipe." [24] Where he got this information, he did not say. Another producer said: "No question about it; 7 cents a barrel is better business for piping oil than $1 is for the producing of it." [25] He maintained, however, that "Pennsylvania producers are now poor men to look to for money to build a pipe line requiring an expenditure of many million [*sic*] of dollars." He also admitted that he had never given any thought to placing pipelines under the scope of the Interstate Commerce Act.[26]

The long and the short of it was that there seemed to be no way in which to obtain accurate figures on Standard Oil's pipeline profits. Officials of the Trust either did not know or, perhaps more likely, were unwilling to tell what they did know about this aspect of the Trust's operations. Emery, Kirk, and the other producers who testified on the subject could make guesses, but, as long as there was no way to confirm or refute them, their estimates remained in the realm of speculation.

Although witnesses on both sides of the controversy made it clear that the bulk of crude oil transportation was, and for some time had been, in the hands of the Standard Oil pipelines, the greater part of their testimony dealt with the long and familiar story of railroad discriminations. The fight over the Empire Line, the rebates obtained by American Transfer, the producers' appeal to Governor Hartranft and the subsequent legal actions, the Rice case—in fact every major development in the petroleum industry since the South Improvement Company—received attention.

In the face of a staggering amount of information about the Standard Oil and Sugar Trusts, the Committee on Manufactures chose to submit no recommendations for action by Congress. It contented itself with calling attention to the nature of the trust organization. "It is plain," the report said, "that the two combinations . . .

have been intentionally formed so as to avoid, if possible, the charge that the trust, as such, or the trustees, in that capacity, either fixed the price or regulated the production of any article of merchandise or commerce." [27] Thus, as far as policy recommendations were concerned, the committee not only ignored pipelines but even railroad discriminations in relation to Standard Oil's power.

Gowen was distressed by the committee's failure to recommend any concrete measures as the result of its investigation. Reviewing the evidence before the committee in February, 1889, he urged that the Interstate Commerce Act be amended to cover pipelines and that Pennsylvania should be encouraged to take over Standard Oil's pipelines in that state.[28] Nothing came of his proposals, however, and within a year Gowen was dead, a suicide.

The flurry of trust investigations in 1888 had not immediately shaken Standard Oil's power, though it focused public attention on the Trust as a symbol of corporate wrongdoing. Top officials of the organization sensed a need to drop the policy of silence which they had long followed. Their defensive attitude in the area of public relations slowly gave way to a halting offense. Samuel Dodd, Standard Oil's counsel, as a direct result of the New York State Senate investigation, prepared a public defense of combinations on which the Trust thereafter built its case. In this defense the role assigned to pipelines was more prominent than in the counterattack built on the revelations of the trust investigations.

Pipelines in Standard Oil's Public Defense of Combinations

In an effort to "correct" the impressions left by the New York Senate investigation of trusts, Dodd in 1888 prepared a booklet entitled *Combinations: Their Uses and Abuses, With a History of the Standard Oil Trust*. Specifically he set out to refute the committee's charge that "the end, if not the purpose of every combination is to destroy competition and leave the people subject to the rule of a monopoly." His thesis was that combination was necessary to meet America's industrial needs. He quoted with approval from William Graham Sumner's *What Social Classes Owe to Each Other* that "aggregated capital will be more and more essential to the performance of our social needs. . . . This tendency is in the public interest." [29] Dodd declared emphatically:

I repeat again, because it is a principle that seems to be lost sight of, that the right of association must be free, that the magnitude of associations must correspond with the magnitude of the business to be done, that business cannot be localized, that it cannot be confined by State lines, that when the problem is to open and to keep open the markets of the world, it is sheer madness to attempt to restrict the business as that of a local manufacturer may be restricted.[30]

Dodd turned to Social Darwinism for a philosophical justification of his opposition to legislation on economic matters. He wrote:

The Inter-State Commerce Commission has lately decided that every pound of oil is entitled, whether carried in barrels or in bulk, to reach the market at equal rates. This is founded on the modern idea that enterprise, energy and capital are not entitled to advantages in competition. The race is not to the swift, nor the battle to the strong. Controlled by such ideas, competition is of no benefit to the public. All are placed upon a dead level. The unfittest as well as the fittest survive.[31]

Against this conceptual background Dodd defended the Standard Oil Trust. One of the prime purposes of the combination, he declared, was to cheapen transportation. He pointed out that this had involved a thirty million dollar investment in pipelines and storage facilities. In 1872, he argued, the pipeline system was in its infancy; the lines were inefficient and expensive. There were no uniform rates, but it cost 50 cents to transport a barrel of oil ten miles. "The united refiners undertook to unite and systematize this business," he declared. "They purchased and consolidated the various little companies in what was known as the United Pipe Line System." Under United Pipe Lines, rates were reduced from 30 to 20 cents a barrel, and the certificate system, on which the trade depended, in turn depended on the strength of Standard Oil.[32] "Without the pipe line system, the cheap transportation, and the improvements in manufacture which I have narrated," he wrote, "the markets of Europe and Asia could not be held against Russia for a single year." [33] And finally, "Although the [pipeline] business was built up and owned by those who built up and own the Standard Oil Company, the business is done for the public." [34] Dodd thus appeared to reaffirm the statements of other Standard officials that their pipelines were common carriers in the sense that they did not own the oil they transported and that shippers other than Standard Oil were welcome to use these facilities upon payment of uniform charges.

In the September, 1888, issue of the *Political Science Quarterly*, George Gunton continued Dodd's favorable interpretation of Standard Oil's pipeline endeavors. After reviewing the development of the trunk pipelines, Gunton wrote: "This was an undertaking absolutely impracticable for any of the smaller corporations. The result is a saving of 66⅔ per cent on the cost of transportation alone. In 1872 it cost $1.50 to transport a barrel of oil to New York; to-day it costs only 50 cents." [35] Gunton ignored the fact that Standard Oil had paid $1.25 or less on refined shipments during most of 1872 as well as the fact that the current crude oil rate was the same by rail as by pipe.[36]

Gunton gave an answer to the question as to who benefited by the "cheapening" of transportation. He maintained: "Through the economies introduced into the production and transportation of petroleum since 1871, the price of refined oil has been reduced 17.49 cents per gallon, or 72 per cent, being a saving to the consumers of 998,953,011 gallons of refined oil [used] last year alone of $174,716,881." [37] He thus ignored the contributions of Standard Oil to the reduction of refined oil prices except through transportation economies. Similarly, he overlooked the fact that the average price of crude at the wells had dropped from over four dollars in 1871 to less than a dollar in 1888 and in the interim had consistently tended toward the latter figure.[38]

Half-truths were indeed common, whether used by opponents or supporters of the Trust. Richard T. Ely, a pioneer in reformed Darwinian economics, was no exception to this rule when he offered an answer to Gunton and Dodd in his *Problems of Today*, published in 1888. He wrote: "Newspaper organs of monopoly tell us to admire the magnanimity of the Standard Oil people, who have reduced prices. This is a false statement. Prices have fallen in spite of their most strenuous efforts to keep them up." [39] Broad generalizations of this kind were the product of underlying assumptions not susceptible to statistical analysis.

E. Benjamin Andrews in the *Quarterly Journal of Economics* for January, 1889, however, attempted such an analysis. He pointed out that in the years 1861–1872 the net average annual percentage decrease in the price of refining oil and carrying it to the seaboard worked out to 10.4332. From 1873 to 1881, when the Trust was in its formative period, the figure was 7.3897. From 1882 to 1887, the years of the Trust's full reign, it was 2.2879.[40] Andrews pointed out that through the railroads' shortsightedness, Standard Oil had been able to eliminate other possible shippers and then had transferred its oil to its own pipelines. He concluded, therefore, that despite Standard's claims to have reduced the cost of refining and transporting oil, the public had not reaped the benefits. Whether this conclusion was "true" again depended on unstated assumptions, which attackers of the Trust seldom made explicit.

While scholars were offering rebuttals to his claims, Samuel Dodd carried his message to businessmen. Speaking before the Merchants' Association of Boston on January 8, 1889, for example, he stated that without the Standard Oil combination, Russia would dominate the oil markets of the world. Furthermore, Standard Oil had reduced the price of refined oil, cheapened transportation, and otherwise promoted an increase in the consumption of petroleum.[41]

A little more than a year later Rockefeller himself broke years of self-imposed silence to grant an interview to a reporter for the New York *World*. He prefaced his remarks with the observation:

My practice throughout life has been to mind my own business, and I have found that if a man does that in an efficient manner he supplies himself with a sufficiently absorbing occupation. . . . All I ask for the business I represent is unbiased judgment of its aims and merits, and fair criticism of its acts.[42]

His only reason for granting the interview, Rockefeller said, was to show that the oil trade would never have reached its existing magnitude without a combination of capital, which, in the case of Standard Oil, then amounted to ninety million dollars. He stressed the point that transportation was "the most serious problem" in the industry, and he pointed with pride to the fact that Standard Oil had thirty million dollars invested in pipelines. He defended past actions of the Trust and maintained that O'Day had acted without the knowledge of Standard Oil's head office when he forced Receiver Phineas Pease of the Cleveland and Marietta to grant rebates on George Rice's shipments. He refused to be drawn into a discussion of the merits of trusts or their connection with political issues.[43] The fact that Rockefeller granted the interview in the first place, however, indicates that these political issues had placed the Trust on the defensive. Nor must it be overlooked that the Sherman anti-trust bill was then before Congress, destined to become law within four months.

The tide was turning against Standard Oil. Convinced by evidence secured in the New York State and federal trust investigations that Standard Oil of Ohio had been violating its charter, David E. Watson, the Ohio Attorney General, filed a quo warranto petition against the company in May, 1890. The court found for the state on March 2, 1892. It held that The Standard Oil Company (Ohio) was controlled indirectly but effectively by the Trust and that the latter had violated common law by seeking to establish a monopoly and to control prices. In the wake of this decision Dodd announced on March 10, 1892, that the Trust would be dissolved.

Although the Ohio decision was hailed by antimonopolists of the country as a smashing victory, there were more sober evaluations of its significance. The *Yale Review* was only one of many publications which recognized that "the dissolution of the Standard Oil Trust marks the end of a certain form of combination rather than a check to the process of combination itself." The *Review* likewise predicted that dissolution of the Trust would not change appreciably the common management of the Standard Oil companies, and this indeed proved to be the case.

Following the unfavorable Ohio decision, which indicated that the trust form of control was not legally impregnable, Dodd again took up the Trust's defense in a national magazine. Writing in *Forum* in 1892, he declared that the real question concerning trusts "is whether the evils incident to large associations for business purposes are such as to render these associations contrary to public policy." [44] In his view the Standard Oil Trust had justified itself by decreasing the price of its products. His argument, however, rested on a reduction in manufacturing costs rather than in price reductions to consumers. For example, although he pointed out that the pipelines had reduced the costs of crude oil transportation, which was true, he failed to make clear specifically how this economy was passed on to the American consumer.

Roger Sherman, who had been the producers' counsel in their suits against Standard Oil and the railroads in 1878–1879, focused his attention on Dodd's claims in an article appearing in the July, 1892, issue of *Forum*. He denied that the Standard Oil combination had been necessary to develop the pipeline network. He pointed out that local or gathering pipelines had been developed by initiative other than Standard Oil's. Similarly, the Tide-Water had shown the way in the construction of long-distance trunk pipelines. He maintained that the price of oil to the consumer had been reduced only to destroy competition and that when this was accomplished it was raised again. His view of Standard Oil was succinctly stated in the title of his article, "The Standard Oil Trust: The Gospel of Greed." [45] Nevertheless, Sherman offered only a general indictment of the combination rather than specific panaceas for the evils he attributed to it.

The recognition which Standard Oil's pipeline power received from the Trust's attackers was in the form of rebuttals to that portion of the Trust's defense which rested on the need for combination to obtain the economies of pipeline transportation. These accounts, however, were generally longer on assertions than on documented facts, better calculated to sway public opinion uncritically than to serve as the basis for the framing of intelligent public policy.

Wealth against Commonwealth

In 1894, Henry Demarest Lloyd, who had called attention to Standard Oil as a "Great Monopoly" in 1881, developed the story more fully in his book *Wealth against Commonwealth*. Although the *Nation* charged in its review of this work that the author demonstrated on occasion "incoherency of thought," "intemperance of speech," and "violence of passion," [46] Lloyd unquestionably put his finger squarely on the importance of pipelines in the development of Standard Oil.

Lloyd declared that the failure of the railroads to recognize the importance of pipelines had played into the hands of Rockefeller and his associates. He wrote:

These oil men saw what the railroad men had not the wit to see—or else lacked the virtue to live up to—that the pipe line is an oil railway. It requires no cars and no locomotives; it moves oil without risk of fire or loss; it is very much cheaper than the ordinary railway, for this freight moves itself after being lifted up by pumps. The pipe line was the sure competitor of the railway, fated to be either its servant or master, as the railroad chose to use it or lose it. The railways sentimentally helped the trust to gather these rival transportation lines into its hands; then the trust, with the real genius of conquest, threw the railroads to one side. . . . At the expense of their own employers, the owners of the railroads, these freight agents and general managers presented to the monopoly, out of the freight earnings of the oil business, the money with which to build the pipe lines that would destroy that branch of the business of the roads.[47]

While it is obvious that the railroads' attitude toward Standard Oil was not "sentimentally" determined, this passage is indisputably a concise summary of what had happened in their relations, though Lloyd failed to mention here that Standard Oil cushioned the shock of this development by pipeline-railroad pooling. By late 1879 railroad journals and even a railroad president, William H. Vanderbilt, had conceded that the railroads' days as crude oil carriers were numbered. But in 1894, when Lloyd was writing, these predictions, which had long since been confirmed in practice, were still unappreciated by the general public.

Lloyd was on solid ground when he wrote that "the pipe lines are the largest single item in the property of the oil combination. Here its control has been the most complete; and here the reduction of price has been least." [48] On the other hand, it is questionable whether his conclusion that this was "a telltale fact, soon told and soon understood" was equally correct. The producers had failed to impress either legislators or the public with the importance of Standard Oil's pipeline power—partly because they had underestimated it themselves and partly because it was not a subject as well adapted to popular understanding as railroad discriminations. Lloyd undertook the task of enlightening the public with obvious enthusiasm.

The fiery antimonopolist proved himself an able propagandist. When he wrote of the United Pipe Lines' acquisition of the Columbia Conduit, he cleverly but inaccurately combined the words of Dodd and Cassatt and threw them back at the authors. He wrote: "When its [Columbia Conduit's] independent pipe line was 'united and systematized' by being torn up and converted into 'old iron,' as the Vice-President of the Pennsylvania Railroad had told its projectors it would be, the rates of transportation for oil went up." [49]

Like his predecessors in this field, Lloyd attacked Standard Oil's claim of having developed the pipelines. "They did not devise the pipe line," he declared, "and they did all they could to prevent the building of the first pipe line to the seaboard, and to cripple the successful experiment of piping refined oil." [50] He pointed out:

It was the Tidewater that proved the feasibility of trunk pipe lines. The trunk lines the combination has built were in imitation. Extraordinary pains have been taken to sophisticate public opinion with regard to all these matters—for the ignorance of the public is the real capital of monopoly—and with great success. [51]

Tracing the failure of efforts at pipeline legislation, Lloyd declared that Standard Oil had done everything with the Pennsylvania legislature "except refine it."

Phraseology such as this made an impression; yet there is no evidence to show that Lloyd heightened the public's appreciation of the importance of Standard Oil's pipelines or generated a demand for action by a public agency. The growing public awareness of the economic basis of politics, which *Wealth against Commonwealth* undoubtedly stimulated, still did not extend to an appreciation of the complicated mechanics of intra-industry structure.

As the *Nation* noted in its review of Lloyd's book, the evidence produced in the Hepburn investigation of 1879 and in the subsequent state and federal investigations already constituted "a most damaging indictment" of Standard Oil. While attacking the manner in which Lloyd drew that indictment, the review declared: "No episode in economic history better deserves treatment by a competent investigator, and no situation more requires calm and dispassionate consideration." [52] This verdict echoed John D. Rockefeller's plea to the public in 1890 that Standard Oil receive "unbiased judgment of its aims and merits, and fair criticism of its acts." But this plea came late. The Trust, by its very secrecy, the evasiveness of its representatives when brought before investigating committees, and damaging admissions about past practices, had forfeited a claim to "unbiased judgment," and opened the way for attacks like Lloyd's.

While he recognized the important role of Standard Oil's pipelines, Lloyd was more interested in "exposing" than in the means of correcting abuses of economic power. As a result he only added to the public indignation, which Dodd explained in these terms:

What then are the causes which have led to the popular opinion that the Standard Oil Trust is a gigantic monopoly which must be crushed? (1) The principal reason is at present that there is in the air a socialistic prejudice against capital. (2) On account of its aggregation of large capital the Standard serves as a type, in the public estimation, of a monopoly crushing out all competition.[53]

Lloyd added to the latter caricature. In the words of Louis Filler, "*Wealth against Commonwealth* can be regarded as the first muckraking book. . . . It is, moreover, one of the few books that gave permanent expression to the strong feeling unleashed by the Populists in the Nineties." [54] As Filler observes, "It was premature." But Lloyd himself declared as he closed his book: "The first step to a remedy is that the people care. If they know, they will care."

John M. Bonham in a book entitled *Railway Secrecy and Trusts*, published in 1890, had offered a remedy. Using Standard Oil as an example of a trust that exercised arbitrary control over the market for its products, he declared: "Nothing less than the secret control of transportation, the participation in that transportation, and the suppression of competition could have brought about such an aggregation under one ownership." [55] He did not indulge in moral judgments on this situation. Rather he maintained that Standard Oil had taken the system as it existed and had made the most of it. This system had involved railroad rebates and secrecy, and Standard Oil had manipulated them to its advantage. The independent refiner was the victim, but it was the system, not Standard Oil, which was at fault. Accordingly Bonham proposed:

If the secrecy of the quasi-public corporation, therefore, be the source from which the dangerous trusts spring, this secrecy is the point to which legislation should be directed. When the railways and the pipe-lines are brought within such governmental inspection as will lay bare their secrets, the dangerous trusts which owe their being to these secrets must of necessity fall, and when they fall, their weak imitators . . . will fall also.[56]

Oversimple though this solution may have been, it was a reasonable proposal aimed at one of the major problems in assessing the merits of large-scale enterprise—the lack of accurate information about costs, profits, corporate relationships, and power over the market. The *Petroleum Age,* commenting on the Billingsley bill in April, 1887, had remarked on the need for such publicity in connection with pipelines:

At the present time anything concerning pipe lines is of interest to the oil world. Inside and bed rock information, pertaining to the business of piping oil is at a premium. The earnings of pipe lines are easily ascertained through the official monthly statements, but the cost of construction, maintenance and managing of them are points more difficult to determine.[57]

This observation was still appropriate in 1895, despite trust investigations, Interstate Commerce Commission hearings, and the flood of literature on the Standard Oil Trust. In the interim, public opinion had been inflamed against the archetype of trusts, but there were few such specific proposals for dealing with its power as that offered by Bonham.

Standard Oil and New Producing and Pipeline Ventures

While the public controversy over the Trust mounted in intensity, Standard Oil entered on the production of oil and expanded its pipeline operations. In Pennsylvania the independent Western and Atlantic Pipe Line, which had threatened Standard Oil in the Washington County field in 1888, was sold to the combination in November, 1889.[58] Several Pittsburgh refineries which the line had served also succumbed. In Ohio, West Virginia, and Pennsylvania, Standard Oil began its first major venture in oil production.

The center of the new producing area in Ohio was near Lima, in the northwestern part of the state. In this district, which extended into northeastern Indiana, Standard Oil gambled on its ability to transform sulphur-laden crude into marketable refined products. Firmly committed in 1886 to meeting the challenge, Standard Oil men moved with typical efficiency and aggressiveness. While the technical problem of making the Lima oil acceptable for existing uses was being studied, pipelines and storage facilities were constructed and new markets were found for the "sour" crude.[59] By 1891 Standard's Ohio Oil Company was producing 55.95 per cent of the Lima oil as contrasted with the production of 8.91 per cent of Pennsylvania oil by other Standard-affiliated concerns.[60]

The growth of Standard Oil's pipeline network in connection with these developments verified David Kirk's prediction to the House Committee on Manufactures in 1888 that it would become increasingly a matter of interstate commerce. The Buckeye Pipe Line Company, organized in 1886, built and operated an extensive gathering system in the Lima-Indiana district as well as part of the trunk line system in Ohio. The Indiana Pipe Line Company, organized in 1891, carried Lima crude to the great Whiting, Indiana, refinery. The Buckeye and Indiana trunk line systems were linked by the appropriately named Connecting Pipe Line Company. The Cygnet Pipe Line Company joined these lines to the old National Transit system, whose pipes, carrying Lima crude through Pennsylvania to the seaboard, were organized in 1889 under the Northern Pipe Line Company. The Eureka Pipe Line, which stretched from the northern border of Tennessee to Pennsylvania, and the Southern Pipe Line, which carried oil from the West Virginia fields to tidewater, were organized in 1890.

The gamble in Lima oil paid off, and the pipeline investment that accompanied it paid handsome dividends. Flagler reported to Rockefeller in August, 1891, that the five Standard Oil pipelines carrying Lima crude had made profits of nearly $2,500,000 for the first six months of that year, representing an annual return of 53.66 per cent on the investment. Actually, final figures for the year averaged a little better than 57 per cent. These "profits" have to be measured against the costs of rendering the "sour" Lima crude marketable and also depended on finding a market for the oil. Standard Oil's over-all return of 13.419 per cent for 1891 on its $32,000,000 investment in the Lima-Indiana field shows that pipeline profits were a cushion against losses in other areas of the new operation.[61]

Meanwhile, Standard Oil's increased interest in oil production gave the Producers' Protective Association a temporary setback. The association had not abandoned the idea, advanced after the defeat of the Billingsley bill, of entering the transportation, refining, and marketing phases of the industry. A special committee headed by

Hascal L. Taylor had been studying the problem during 1888–1889, while the shut-down agreement with the Standard was still in effect. When it was revealed in June, 1890, that Taylor's firm, the Union Oil Company, had been sold to Standard Oil along with three other producing companies, Taylor and his partners were read out of the association. President Thomas W. Phillips added to the producers' consternation by selling extensive producing property in Butler County to Standard Oil for a reported three-quarters of a million dollars. In the face of these reverses, opposition to Trust demanded redoubled activity.[62]

The Burdick Bill

With Standard Oil steadily increasing its power, Pennsylvania producers made one more attempt to check it by legislation. Efforts to regulate pipeline charges and practices had been made in Pennsylvania in 1875 and 1887, and a final venture in this field was undertaken in 1891. On January 22 of the latter year Representative William Burdick introduced a bill in the Pennsylvania House entitled "An Act to regulate the transportation and storage of petroleum by means of pipe lines and tanks, to limit the charge therefor, to regulate deductions for sediment, water, shrinkage and other losses, and to prohibit the removal of pipe lines running from producing petroleum fields to the seaboard from this to any other State, and imposing penalties for the violation of the same." [63]

The Burdick bill was reminiscent of the Billingsley proposal of 1887. It provided that the pipeline companies should deliver oil in the quality and kind desired to the place specified by the shipper. It set the maximum local pipage charges at twelve cents a barrel per mile for the first fifty miles, and three cents per mile for each fifty miles thereafter. Storage charges were to be reduced, and the shrinkage allowance deducted by the pipeline companies was to be set at 2 per cent. Any pipeline engaged in transporting and storing petroleum was to forfeit its charter and franchises if it took up or discontinued its lines from the producing fields to the seaboard. Violations were also to be punishable by a fine of not more than five thousand dollars and imprisonment for two years.

On February 26, 1891, the Senate sponsor of the bill told his colleagues that when he had introduced the bill in that chamber he had believed that it was almost unanimously desired by the oil producers, but time had proved him wrong. He had been deluged with telegrams, letters, and petitions against it, he said. Furthermore, the newspapers indicated a diversity of opinion in the oil country and opposition throughout the state. Consequently, he opposed placing the bill on the calendar.

With these admissions from the bill's sponsor, the Senate's disposition of the measure was not in doubt. Although it was objected that, since the bill had not yet been printed, two-thirds of the senators did not know its provisions in sufficient detail to vote intelligently, the resolution to place it on the calendar was voted down 27 to 15 on February 26, with every Republican but one voting against the resolution.[64]

Meanwhile, in the Pennsylvania House the Burdick bill had been reported with a negative recommendation by the Committee on Corporations. House members had also received remonstrances against the measure, and this fact plus the Senate's action led to a demand on February 27 that the bill be given no further consideration. Taking into account the possibility that the expressions of public opinion against it might have been inspired by Standard Oil, the House voted to postpone consideration of the measure until a later date.[65]

When House debate took place on March 2, Burdick was ready with an arsenal of arguments in support of his bill. His basic premise was that Standard Oil's pipeline companies were the sole buyers and shippers of crude oil and thus determined its price. He estimated that the National Transit Company, charging 20 cents a barrel for collecting oil, made $4,777,593 in 1890. Figuring the cost of local pipeline transportation at five cents a barrel, and allowing the proposed rate of 12 cents, he maintained that the company could have realized $1,672,156 in net profits on local transportation alone. Since the cost of pipeline transportation to the seaboard had been placed at about six cents a barrel in testimony before the Interstate Commerce Commission, Burdick maintained that even under his proposal, which allowed three cents per mile for each fifty miles after the first fifty, the National Transit Company could have cleared over three million dollars from its various pipeline operations in 1890. He argued that this was a very adequate return for the company, whose paid-up capital in 1889 was reported to be $25,455,200.[66]

Burdick's argument had a certain amount of logic, but it was subject to many qualifications. While Standard Oil was the largest purchaser of crude oil, it was far from the sole buyer. Authors of the latest history of the combination maintain that it could not have controlled the price of crude during this period.[67] Their work also shows that it is virtually impossible to arrive at a figure for the National Transit's pipeline operations which would meet the economists' definition of "pure profit." [68] Nevertheless, the size of Standard Oil's investment in pipelines, the obvious importance attributed to them by Standard officials, and their efforts to maintain dominance in this field suggest that there was a substantial basis for Burdick's attack, although he was clearly using statistics for the purpose of swaying fellow legislators.

As Burdick himself pointed out, a large portion of National Transit's lines were now outside Pennsylvania. Consequently, if the transportation company was making monopoly profits, the problem was properly one for federal rather than state action.

Although Burdick showed how he thought that his bill would affect Standard Oil, he seemed to be at a loss to explain exactly how it would help independent producers and refiners. The chairman of the Committee on Corporations drew his attention to this fact, asking why the producers were so concerned about the cost of pipage when they did not pay for it. The legislator reported that when representatives of National Transit challenged a friend of the bill to cite an instance when oil was not delivered as requested by the shipper, only one minor example was offered to his committee.[69] He also pointed out that the 2 per cent allowance for shrinkage called for in the bill was the current practice and that pipelines already had to buy over 1,000,000 barrels a year to make it good. Furthermore, he declared, not one consumer in the state of Pennsylvania had raised his voice for or against the bill.[70]

F. W. Hays, a representative from Venango County in the oil country, continued the attack on the bill. He stated that since Standard Oil had joined with the producers in the shutdown movement of 1887, the relations of his constituents with the combination had been good. He had received no complaints about Standard Oil in three years, and none of his constituents had expressed an interest in the passage of the Burdick bill.[71] Although it had been previously claimed that the Knights of Labor supported the bill, Hays reported that the Knights in Titusville and Oil City were not in favor of it. He read a letter from independent producers at Emlenton in which they stated that they had suspended plans for piping oil and refining it until they knew whether it would be profitable. If the bill passed, they wrote, they would abandon the project. He produced another letter from an Oil City producer who maintained that the bill was unworkable and would be of no aid to the producers.[72]

Hays was followed by H. F. James of Franklin, who contended that the bill had been drawn up by McKean County parties who did not have the support of all the assemblies of the Producers' Association. He declared that the measure would not benefit the consumer and asked for its defeat in these words:

This bill was begat in sin, born in sin, and in the other chamber died in sin, and we come to you in the name and with the prayers of thousands of workingmen, Knights of Labor and kindred organizations, producers, refiners, etc., all over our section of the State and ask that you bury it so far down in hades so that the stench from its burning carcass will not reach the surface.[73]

A defender of the bill returned to the argument that if pipelines were forced to deliver oil where shippers wanted it, refineries would spring up and Standard Oil would no longer be able to fix crude prices. Again, no proof was offered that the lines refused to deliver oil where it was wanted or that the Trust actually fixed either crude or refined oil prices.

On the other hand, this advocate of pipeline legislation had a stronger case for his thesis that Standard Oil was inspiring opposition to the measure. He pointed out that telegrams opposing the bill were identically worded and that the words were the same as those being circulated among Standard Oil employees, who were probably responsible for the messages.[74]

Burdick took the floor again to present new arguments, but they did little to further his cause. He maintained that the 1883 free pipe bill was inadequate, especially when it came to crossing strips of land purchased to bar a right of way to new pipelines, and that his bill was necessary if capital was to be attracted into the pipeline business.[75] The latter argument flew in the face of entrepreneurial incentives which had motivated both Standard Oil and its opponents since the earliest days of their conflict, and this point had already been noted.

In letters to the Senate committee considering the bill, both Standard Oil's Jacob J. Vandergrift and Tide-Water's David McKelvy had attacked the idea that pipeline legislation could attract new capital into the business. Vandergrift said that if the aim was to promote pipeline competition, rates should be raised rather than lowered. "It seems a little incongruous," he wrote, "in this era, when every effort seems to be directed against combinations, for a bill to receive any consideration whatever which can only in its effect destroy competition." [76] McKelvy backed this stand, declaring that the Tide-Water, which he denied had any longer a pooling agreement with Standard Oil, found it cheaper in 1890 to pay the National Transit Company for collecting its oil than to engage in that part of the business itself. In the light of past developments, this explanation might have been subject to further explanation, but McKelvy singled out an important point when he stated that the Tide-Water's business was interstate in character and therefore its regulation was a matter for Congress alone.[77]

Representative J. N. Thompson summed up the position of the bill's proponents. Standard Oil was a monopoly. It had the exclusive right of transportation in the state. It was the sole purchaser of petroleum. Therefore, he concluded, the Burdick bill should be passed to make the combination's pipelines act as common carriers. By inference this meant that they should carry for all shippers at rates regulated by the state, collecting and delivering oil as shippers directed. This statement of the case was not strong enough to get the bill placed on the calendar, and the motion to this effect was defeated, 97 to 84.

The failure of the Burdick bill is susceptible to several explanations, all of which have a familiar ring when compared with events in the past relationship of Standard Oil to the producers. In this instance the Trust was aided by the good will engendered by its participation in the plan of the Producers' Protective Association for limiting production. The arrangement had reduced the yearly carry-over of oil stocks in 1888 to 18,600,000 and in 1889 to 10,900,-

000 barrels. When the last of the producers' 5,000,000 barrels was sold to Standard Oil in June, 1889, the association reaped a sizable profit, and the well drillers, for whom the profits on 2,000,000 barrels had been put aside, also benefited.[78] As the debate over the Burdick bill showed, this amicable settlement of a mutual problem had helped to divide sentiment in the Oil Regions toward Standard Oil.

There was also a familiar geographical division of opinion in the Regions. A prominent producer in an interview at Harrisburg late in February said that McKean County producers were attempting to protect themselves against the decline of the Bradford field by means of the bill. Since they were two hundred miles closer to the seaboard than operators in Allegheny, Washington, and Green counties and the Turkeyfoot district of West Virginia, the provisions of the bill would work to their advantage.[79]

Representative James of Franklin confirmed this view. In a letter to the *Franklin News*, February 17, 1891, he declared that a man who was with Lewis Emery, Jr., and James W. Lee when the Burdick bill was conceived told him: "The Standard Oil Company is a —— —— nuisance and ought to be driven out of the State and this bill will do it." James said that he had endorsed the attack on Standard Oil, but in reading the bill he had discovered that "in their zeal to strike a death-blow at the 'Great Octopus,' their weapon was an immense boomerang, and would strike a death-blow to the industries of the section of the country which I have the honor to represent. . . ."[80] Within a few days of the publication of this letter, seven hundred Franklin citizens had signed a petition against the bill, undoubtedly influenced by their fear of its effect on Standard Oil's local refineries.

As already noted, Standard Oil officials opposed the Burdick bill. John D. Archbold told the legislators that Standard Oil had $35,000,-000 invested in pipelines, that profits from their operations were less than 10 per cent, and that passage of the bill would hurt many of Standard Oil's employees in the state. The *Oil City Derrick* reported: "He said the Standard are not wicked people. As its representatives came through Philadelphia last night the first oil in the new pipe line from West Virginia was flowing through. In any other place this fact would have been received with a brass band."[81]

Perhaps Standard Oil's managers were right in thinking that their efforts should have met with greater public appreciation, but the fact was that they had begun too late to counteract the work of their detractors. Archbold himself in 1888 had refused to be drawn into a discussion of pipeline profits. Now he maintained that they were less than 10 per cent, but he did not explain just what he meant. A few months later Flagler was reporting to Rockefeller that the Lima lines were netting over 50 per cent on their cost in a half year of operation. The latter figure approached the estimates of the more articulate producers. If their estimates were gross exaggerations of National Transit's profits, it should have been easy to refute them. The Trust's policy of silence, however, died hard, and the task of educating the public in the intricacies of large-scale enterprise must have looked forbidding.

The producers, on the other hand, did little to aid the public. As usual, they seemed unable to agree among themselves on the significance of Standard Oil's pipeline power. The shower of protests against the Burdick bill, though probably at least in part inspired by Standard Oil, indicated that many independent oilmen feared the impact of the legislation on their own economic welfare. The *Parker Phoenix* summed up the situation with considerable accuracy when it observed:

It seems to a fellow up a tree, that the producers are not united on any particular measure, and as yet are still blinded by the immense success attained by the transportation company; namely, the Standard. Whenever the producers shall become blind to outside interests and will pursue unitedly their own business, then, and then only, will the desired end be attained.[82]

In the years since the defeat of the Billingsley bill the Standard Oil Trust had imposed a pattern of operation on the petroleum industry so firmly that its disruption was becoming distasteful to the elements which had traditionally opposed the combination. Those who led the attack on Standard Oil from within the industry had difficulty in pinpointing the abuses which they attacked in general terms. On the other hand, Standard Oil officials did not do an effective job of refuting even these broad allegations.

Meantime, the obvious size and success of the Trust made it a logical target for writers who sensed the growing uneasiness throughout the country about the aggregation of wealth being concentrated in a few hands. The attack on the Trust and its defense were both presented with broad brush strokes. Although a federal antitrust statute was placed on the books, there appeared to be no disposition to apply it to Standard Oil, which seemingly had more to fear from similar state laws. There was certainly no popular demand for pipeline legislation; yet, as Standard Oil spokesmen proudly stated, pipelines had contributed significantly to the Trust's success. Initiative in this area, then, still lay with members of the petroleum industry who increasingly saw rewards to be gained from private enterprise rather than public policy.

VIII

Pipeline Enterprise and
Intra-industry Controversy,
1891-1901

ALTHOUGH the antitrust movement, which gained momentum in the nineties, focused national attention on Standard Oil, none of the Trust's attackers had a concrete program for a public policy dealing with its pipeline power. Instead of relying on public policy, independent producers and refiners joined forces and with the aid of pipelines, one of which was the first refined oil trunk line, offered a challenge which Standard Oil and its railroad allies could not eliminate.

The nature of the resulting intra-industry conflict was revealed to the public in hearings before the United States Industrial Commission in 1899. The commission heard a parade of witnesses from the oil industry. Some offered indictments of Standard Oil. Others provided rebuttals. Both sides stressed the importance of pipelines, but the independents, having adopted pipelines as competitive weapons as well as having followed Standard Oil's pattern of integrated operations, offered no suggestions for a public policy toward these oil carriers.

Pipelines and the Emergence of a Rival to Standard Oil

While there was a lack of unity in the producers' support for the Burdick bill, there was remarkable enthusiasm for a new pipeline venture which was launched contemporaneously. The Producers' Oil Company, Limited, was organized in early 1891 to dispose of the producers' oil to independent refiners. Capitalized at $600,000, the company shortly had well over a thousand subscribers to its stock among producers throughout the Oil Regions of Pennsylvania.[1] Tanks were built at Coraopolis, Pennsylvania, with the expectation of shipping crude by rail to the independent refinery and export terminal of the Columbia Oil Company at Bayonne, New Jersey. A local gathering line was constructed in the booming McDonald field, whence it was hoped to serve by rail the independent refineries of Titusville and Oil City.[2] Despite pleas to the Interstate Commerce Commission, however, railroad discriminations hampered execution of both these plans.[3]

Once again the oilmen turned to crude oil pipelines as a remedy, and a line was laid from the McDonald field to Titusville and Oil City. Producers and refiners pooled their resources for the project, which was undertaken by the Producers' and Refiners' Oil Company, Limited. This concern, organized in 1892, had a capital of $250,000 to which the Producers' Oil Company, Limited, subscribed $160,000.[4]

A leading figure in these moves was Standard Oil's old enemy, Lewis Emery, Jr., who was convinced that the only way to compete with Standard Oil was to beat it at its own game. Although Standard Oil had extended and systematized both gathering and trunk crude oil pipelines, it had never attempted the piping of refined oil over long distances. Its early decision to locate refineries near centers of consumption and to serve them with crude oil pipelines had made this experiment unnecessary. Emery saw that the geographical disadvantage of the independents' inland refineries might be overcome if pipelines could be used to transport refined as well as crude oil. The feasibility of such a plan had been partially demonstrated as early as 1865 when John Warren and Brothers Company had successfully operated a refined oil pipeline over a distance of three miles from the Osceola refinery at Plumer to McMahon's Run near Oleopolis.[5]

The first problem in executing Emery's plan was to obtain a right of way. In late 1890, according to his own testimony, Emery had put twenty expert right-of-way men into the field to investigate a route to the seaboard. Since he knew that it would be impossible to reach the coast immediately, he approached the president of the Reading Railroad with a proposal that the pipeline be built to Williamsport and that the railroad complete the link to tidewater. Although initial conversations were satisfactory, they were broken off when the railroad officials decided that they could not afford to jeopardize their relations with Standard Oil.[6]

Disappointed in obtaining this route, Emery turned to another alternative. With the approval of the Columbia Oil Company, he agreed to try to reach New York by running the pipeline to Hancock, New York, where it could connect with the New York, Ontario and Western Railroad. Eventually the route to New York was to be completed by boat down the Hudson River. The railroad agreed to the proposal and gave the pipeline permission to use its right of way to the Hudson in return for a royalty of two cents a barrel. Emery also received assurances from the Erie Railroad that it would co-operate in allowing the pipeline to cross its property and to effect a connection with the New York, Ontario and Western, whose tracks lay a mile north of the Erie's at Hancock.[7]

In the fall of 1892, the United States Pipe Line Company was organized to undertake this project. Immediately it ran into opposition. County records were carefully searched and mortgages against property through which Emery had purchased a right of way were bought. Emery told the United States Industrial Commission that he "knew the men that were there taking up these rights of way to have been in the employ of the Standard Oil Company. I knew the men personally, and my men knew them." [8] Standard Oil's purchase of strips of land from a mile to a mile and half long across Emery's route in Pennsylvania forced him into court.

Despite the Erie's promise of co-operation, it too offered opposition to the pipeline. When Emery's crews attempted to lay pipe through the railroad's switchyard in Bradford, Pennsylvania, they met resistance. Enjoined by the McKean County Court of Common

Pleas from continuing construction there, Emery found that there was trouble at Hancock. With the ends of the pipe separated by only 120 feet, the Erie took action to halt completion of the line. Two locomotives, two derricks, a flatcar freighted with lumber, a small brass cannon, and a car carrying about seventy-five men appeared on the scene. The railroaders ousted the pipeline men, built fires at the ends of the pipes, and prepared for a long siege. The lumber was unloaded, and shanties were built on each side of the tracks and manned by guards armed with rifles. The New York, Ontario and Western added to the impasse by renouncing its contract with the pipeline—thus effectively closing the Hancock route to tidewater.[9]

Undaunted but more than seventy thousand dollars out of pocket as a result of the Erie's opposition at Hancock, Emery turned to yet another route. An agreement was reached with the Central of New Jersey to transport oil from Wilkes-Barre, Pennsylvania, to the seaboard. While keeping a force of men standing guard over the pipe at Hancock and thus diverting the attention of his opponents, Emery secured a right of way to Wilkes-Barre and by June, 1893, had completed two lines to that point. One brought crude oil from the Bradford field, 180 miles away; the other carried refined oil from the independents' plants at Titusville, Oil City, Warren, and Bradford.

Despite predictions to the contrary, the refined oil pipeline was a success. In the words of Ida Tarbell, "A new advance had been made in the oil industry—the most substantial and revolutionary since the day the Tidewater demonstrated that crude oil could be pumped over the mountains." [10] The combined efforts of independent producers and refiners in the face of apparently strenuous opposition from Standard Oil and its railroad allies had wrought a major innovation in pipeline transportation, and with it came the opportunity to challenge the great refining combination.

Meantime, Standard Oil had encountered a new threat to its predominance. In November, 1892, oil had commenced to flow through the five-inch pipe of the Crescent Pipe Line Company from Gregg's Station in the McDonald field to the seaboard.

This enterprise was the work of a Pittsburgh group led by William Larrimer Mellon. Mellon had become interested in oil in 1889 and had rapidly expanded his operations as the result of successful penetration of the European market. At first the oil had been carried to the seaboard by tank car, but the Pennsylvania's sudden increase in rates, perhaps in response to pressure from Standard Oil, made some alternative method of transportation essential. Mellon turned to the Reading Railroad, but the Reading official responsible for the contract with the Mellon firm was dismissed and his successor would not honor the commitment. As a result, Mellon undertook to complete a pipeline from Carlisle, Pennsylvania, to the seaboard. He met opposition from the Pennsylvania Railroad, but it was finally overcome.[11] A refinery and docks were constructed at Marcus Hook, Pennsylvania, and together with the W. L. Mellon Pipe Lines, which extended into West Virginia as well as into the McDonald field, they represented a sizable enterprise.[12]

In view of these developments it seems more than a coincidence that a bill was introduced in the 1893 session of the Pennsylvania legislature to repeal the act of a decade before forbidding consolidation of competing pipelines. Apparently that act had never been put to use, but during that decade Standard Oil had had no seaboard pipeline competitors. Now there were two.

The repeal bill managed to pass the legislature, but it was vetoed by Governor Robert E. Pattison, who had signed the 1883 bill into law. In his veto message Pattison said:

The inevitable effect would be to drive competing lines into consolidation or to put the shippers of this important product at the mercy of the great monopolies which might be able to secure and hold the controlling interest in the stock or bonds of competing lines. When the Commonwealth conferred upon these companies its high prerogative of eminent domain, enabling them to take private property for what, in contemplation of the law, were public uses, it was upon the implied contract that the public should have all the advantages of the competition thus created and promoted.

He maintained that the proposed legislation was unsound and added that the number of protests against the bill which he had received increased his unwillingness to sign it.[13]

While there is no direct evidence that Standard Oil was behind this measure, the combination stood to profit from passage of the bill. The Mellons, surveying conditions in the panic year of 1893, had decided to dispose of most of their petroleum interests. The Pennsylvania law of 1883, however, prevented the direct sale of the

Mellon pipelines to National Transit. When the repeal bill was finally passed in 1895, this transfer, involving the Mellon Pipe Line of
Pittsburgh, a gathering system in Allegheny and Washington counties, and the Crescent Pipe Line, soon followed.[14] This fact seems to
corroborate James W. Lee's testimony before the United States Industrial Commission that Standard Oil had obtained the repeal of
the 1883 law.[15]

Governor Daniel H. Hastings, who signed the 1895 bill, felt im-
pelled to explain his reasons to the legislature. He reported that
there was "widespread public interest" in the measure and that expressions of opinion from the Oil Regions were divided on the subject. He personally objected to the provisions of the law of 1883
which absolutely forbade consolidation of competing pipelines
"under penalty of the loss of the entire property by escheat to the
Commonwealth." Since stockholders and bondholders as well as
holders of liens and mortgages against a pipeline would suffer
through no fault of their own, he argued, the 1883 law had authorized confiscation of property. Furthermore, he saw no advantages
in it for the petroleum industry. He declared:

I am convinced, after a hearing of both sides of this controversy, and upon
the fullest investigation, that the effect of the act of 1883 is directly the
reverse of its ostensible object. Instead of encouraging competition and
fostering the building of pipe lines to compete with each other, the fact
that, when the property becomes unprofitable, the owners are prohibited
by law from selling it, must necessarily discourage investors in such enterprises.[16]

It would be interesting to know what evidence Hastings heard
on this question. The existence of the 1883 law had not prevented
Emery from pushing through his pipeline project, nor had it dis-
couraged Mellon in his undertaking. Apparently the only thing that
the repeal of the law accomplished was to clear the way for Standard Oil to take over these competitors, which it did in the case of
the Mellon lines.

Standard Oil was not able to dispose of the competition of the
Producers' and Refiners' Pipe Line or the United States Pipe Line
as it had the Crescent, but it tried. The first approach was an effort
to buy into the Producers' and Refiners' line. James W. Lee, a leader

in the independents' enterprise, told the Industrial Commission that in Standard Oil's attempt to purchase stock in the Producers' Oil Company, Limited, which controlled the pipeline, the managers of the combination had "a bank cashier working for them in nearly every town throughout the whole region where the stock was owned, and they had agents in the field." [17] If this was indeed the case, the effort did not prove completely successful.

An effort was made to use this stock when a merger of the Producers' and Refiners' line with the United States Pipe Line was under consideration in early 1894. The proposed merger met opposition from John J. Carter, president of The Carter Oil Company, a recent producing affiliate of Standard Oil. Carter held three hundred shares of stock in the Producers' Oil Company, Limited, and had been elected a member in accordance with the limited partnership law that governed the right to vote in the company's affairs. On March 15, 1894, he filed a bill in equity in the Crawford County Court to prevent the consolidation of the pipelines. In the course of the hearings the fact emerged that one of the companies of the Standard Oil group owned 60 per cent of The Carter Oil Company.

At the meeting of the Producers' Oil Company, Limited, on April 11, 1894, Carter appeared with not 300 shares but 13,013 more. It turned out that these additional shares had come from Standard Oil and that they had been "loaned" to Carter for the occasion.[18] Even with the support of small shareholders, however, Carter could not muster enough votes in the meeting to overcome the group favoring union of the pipelines. He was more successful in court, and an injunction was issued forbidding the sale of the Producers' Oil Company's plant to the United States Pipe Line.[19]

Meanwhile, the pressures for capitulating to Standard Oil grew as oil prices fell in the train of the general depression of 1893 and of rising production from the Ohio and Indiana fields. The squeeze became so tight that three independent refiners, two at Titusville and one at Reno, sold their property to Standard Oil.[20] The refineries themselves were of little consequence to the combination in comparison to the stock that these concerns held in the United States Pipe Line and the Producers' and Refiners' Oil Company, Limited. The loss of the refineries, however, hurt the producers' pipelines directly by reducing their patronage. Theodore B. Westgate, who weathered the storm of 1893–1895, told the United States Industrial Commission that Standard Oil had offered to buy out all the other independent refiners if they would include their pipeline stock in the deal.[21]

If, as the New York *World* charged, Standard Oil had deliberately maintained a close margin between crude and refined oil prices to discourage the independents during this period,[22] by January, 1895, the combination had adopted a different strategy. Beginning in that month Joseph Seep, Standard's crude oil purchasing agent, commenced buying oil at posted prices. In the past, certificates for credit balances of oil had been issued to producers, and the value of the certificates had rested largely on oil exchange transactions. Now credit balances were purchased by Seep at a posted price to be "as high as the markets of the world will justify." Under this procedure the price of Appalachian crude rose, mollifying the producers and increasing the costs of Standard Oil's new competitors whose resources were strained to absorb the increase.[23]

In January, 1895, the independents also took a significant step. They were in desperate need of a marketing and financing agency if they were to survive. With enthusiasm and hope built up by Lewis Emery, Jr., James W. Lee, and David Kirk, a mass meeting of producers and refiners at Butler, Pennsylvania, on January 24, 1895, endorsed a proposal to establish a company with a capital of one million dollars to promote their joint interests. The enterprise was significantly called the Pure Oil Company. Its purpose was well summarized in a letter from a member of the Producers' Oil Company, Limited, which was read at that meeting. He stated:

It is within our power to retire the oil, withhold sales to a certain extent from the Standard or sell only to our independent lines, the effect of which would be to rapidly advance the price of crude, and put it easily within our means to finish our seaboard pipe line, assist refiners or build our own refineries, if necessary, and secure our business at every point and establish it on a solid, impregnable footing.[24]

Producers and refiners eagerly contributed to the cause of the new company, which sought to bar Standard Oil influence in its affairs. The prospectus indicated that voting power of one-half the stock of the Pure Oil Company was to be vested in five men. They were pledged by terms of a permanent trust bond to maintain the company's independence "so that no sales of interest will carry with them any power to jeopardize the policy or existence of the company or the investments of its remaining members." [25]

The Pure Oil Company was incorporated in accordance with this plan on November 8, 1895, with David Kirk as president and James W. Lee as vice-president. The capital stock of the company was two million dollars, of which $1,200,000 was paid up.

The success of this new challenge depended on the independents retaining control of the United States Pipe Line, whose stock Standard Oil had been purchasing. By the summer of 1895 Standard Oil had obtained over 2,500 shares. Archbold later explained the purchases in these words:

Our ownership in the United States Pipe Line was bought at a time when we thought that the business ought to become profitable. It was bought as an investment and with a view to having such knowledge as we could have rightfully through such ownership, as we should acquire in the progress of the affair. [26]

While the United States Pipe Line was fighting Standard Oil's effort to gain access to its management, it was also experiencing familiar difficulties with the railroads. Shipments over the New Jersey Central from Wilkes-Barre had been a temporary measure until the pipeline could be extended to the seaboard, but this construction project encountered hostility from the Pennsylvania and the Delaware, Lackawanna and Western railroads. The pipeline had secured a right of way to a point about thirty miles above Easton, Pennsylvania, and proposed to carry construction forward through New Jersey, which had no free pipe law, to the coast. On crossing the New Jersey line, however, opposition was met in laying the pipe under the tracks of the Belvidere Railroad, which was part of the Pennsylvania system. This difficulty was only overcome after a year in the courts. [27]

Within the borough limits of Washington, New Jersey, new trouble developed, this time with the Delaware, Lackawanna and Western. The pipeline bought what it believed to be the title in fee simple to land over which the Lackawanna had an easement. Repulsed by the railroad early in 1895, a new effort was made to lay the pipe on the night of October 26 and 27, 1895. The pipeline's headquarters at Belvidere, New Jersey, reportedly had been watched for some time by a Standard Oil detective, and Emery's men used elaborate tactics to throw him off guard.[28] Consequently, no resistance was encountered when the pipeliners took possession of the chosen site in the early morning hours of October 27. By nine o'clock they had completed the job of connecting the pipes under the tracks and had built houses on either side of them, prepared to resist attack. What happened next is best told in Emery's own words:

About 12 o'clock some men came along and said: "You get out of here," and came down with their picks and bars. I was there in the pit myself and he said, "You will not get out?" And I said, "No; we belong here. It is our line and we will not disturb the railroad." He said, "You will get out; come along, boys." I said, "Don't be hasty;" but he was a little hasty and I told the boys to take the men by the shoulders and the seat of the pants and take them out and lay them down carefully, which they did.[29]

This first skirmish, which ended successfully for Emery's crew, was shortly followed by another. Two locomotives appeared on the scene, and Emery rushed from his dinner at a near-by hotel to find the railroaders pouring hot water and steam on his men in the pit, accompanied by volleys of hot coals and stones. Rallying his crew, he drove off the attackers and prepared for a siege, borrowing muskets from the Grand Army of the Republic and sending to New York for Springfield rifles.[30]

Violence in pursuit of private ends had become a commonplace, and this dramatic episode attracted only limited public interest. The *New York Tribune* observed:

We do not know that there was any thing really novel about this affair. Such proceedings are quite familiar and present the same general features. Perhaps the most singular fact in connection with them is that they attract scarcely any attention outside the immediate neighborhood which furnishes spectators.[31]

As usual, the dispute between the pipeline and the railroad went to the courts, where it remained for four years. Finally, a verdict was handed down in favor of the railroad. Meanwhile, the pipeline was extended to Hampton Junction, New Jersey, fifty miles from New York, with the Jersey Central completing oil shipments to tidewater.

The pipeline's difficulties with the Lackawanna demonstrated anew that the lack of a free pipe law in New Jersey hampered competition with Standard Oil. Accordingly, a free pipe bill was introduced in the New Jersey legislature in February, 1896, and the leading figures associated with the United States Pipe Line appeared on its behalf. At first, hopes of its passage were high, but as the session neared its end, opposition began to mount. According to Ida Tarbell, on the morning that the measure was to be presented in the Senate, the senator having it in charge failed to appear. The legislature adjourned four days later without taking action on the bill.[32] The legislation might have failed in any event, as its predecessors had, but its demise may also have been speeded by familiar forces. At least an official of Standard Oil later told Miss Tarbell: "We asked our friends on the railroad and in the New Jersey Legislature to look after our interests, of course. . . . That was our right." [33]

Standard Oil had not given up hope of influencing the affairs of the Producers' Oil Company, Limited. In January, 1896, J. J. Carter appeared at Standard Oil's New York office with an offer to purchase the combination's holdings of the Producers' Company's stock, which, together with his own three hundred shares, would give him a majority of it. Carter reportedly told Archbold and his associates that if he gained control of the Producers' Pipe Line, he did not propose to discriminate against either the independents or Standard Oil.[34] The officials of the latter organization were sufficiently convinced of Carter's friendship toward them to part with the stock for less than what they thought it was worth.[35] The secretary of the Producers' Oil Company, Limited, however, refused to transfer the shares, and the question of Carter's relation to the concern was taken to the courts.

Standard Oil's attempt to gain a voice in the affairs of the independents' pipelines was now the subject of two legal actions. The first concerned the right of Standard Oil's representative, J. C. McDowell, to be recognized as a director of the United States Pipe Line. The second involved the recognition of Carter as the majority stockholder of the Producers' Oil Company, Limited. Standard Oil won the first case, for the United States Pipe Line was organized as a corporation and McDowell held the amount of stock necessary to be recognized.[36] On the other hand, the Producers' Oil Company was a limited partnership, and on this basis the independents convinced the lower courts and finally the Pennsylvania Supreme Court that Carter was not entitled to vote his shares in the company. As a result, Carter's stock was of no value for influencing the firm's policies, and it was bought in by the Producers' Company.[37]

In the same year, 1897, the Pure Oil Company was reorganized under New Jersey law, and its authorized capital was increased to ten million dollars. The independent producers and refiners now lacked only the formal integration of their facilities, which for the time being were linked by common ownership.[38] The Producers' Oil Company, Limited, the Producers' and Refiners' Oil Company, Limited, and the United States Pipe Line worked closely with the Pure Oil Company, which was a financial and marketing organization. According to Emery, the refineries acted independently, selling oil to others, including Standard Oil.[39]

By 1900, Pure Oil was a firmly established competitor of Standard Oil. In that year the control and operations of Pure Oil's three subordinate companies were formally integrated. Eventually the unfavorable decision against the United States Pipe Line in its litigation with the Lackawanna Railroad caused its withdrawal from New Jersey. Taking advantage of the Pennsylvania free pipe law, the line was completed from Wilkes-Barre to Marcus Hook, Pennsylvania. On May 2, 1901, the first refined oil to be piped all the way from the Oil Regions to the seaboard reached its destination.[40] Despite the obstacles put in their way, the independents had at last successfully challenged Standard Oil.

A New Attack on Standard Oil's Pipeline Power

The creation of Standard Oil's new rival coincided with a period marked by a growing animus against the concentrated economic power of which Standard Oil was a symbol. Opponents of the Trust in the petroleum industry contributed to the mounting attack on it by making the courts and investigating bodies a sounding board for familiar charges, which were essentially the same as those aired at intervals for the past two decades. In Ohio, however, a more threatening attack was launched on Standard Oil by the state's attorney general,

Following the 1892 decision to disband the Trust, its affairs had been placed in the hands of liquidating trustees, but management continued to be centralized in a small group of men.[41] Standard Oil had a large share of the production in the Lima-Indiana field, which increased in importance during the nineties as Pennsylvania production waned. Young, crusading Frank S. Monnett, who was elected attorney general of Ohio in 1896, saw an opportunity to capitalize on the apparent failure of the various Standard Oil companies operating in Ohio to sever their connections with the Trust. He was encouraged in his design by George Rice, who had acquired a small number of shares in the Trust in 1892 and was using them to harass his long-time enemy.[42]

In the fall of 1897, Monnett informed the Ohio Supreme Court that Standard Oil of Ohio was acting in contempt of the court order of 1892 to end its affiliation with the Standard Oil Trust. Shortly thereafter separate actions were instituted against The Standard Oil Company (Ohio), The Solar Refining Company, The Ohio Oil Company, and The Buckeye Pipe Line Company, all of which were alleged to be constituent parts of the Trust.

The quo warranto proceedings against the Buckeye represented a major part of Monnett's self-appointed mission of ridding the state of Standard Oil's influence. The pipeline company was charged with violation of the state's Valentine-Stewart Antitrust Act, confederating with the other companies to evade the decree of 1892, and, later, with violating the terms of its charter by taking telegraph messages for hire and moving its offices to Oil City, Pennsylvania.[43]

In the course of the proceedings it was charged that the Buckeye purchased 95 per cent of the crude oil produced in Ohio. A deposition submitted by one producer declared: "We are at the mercy of the pipe line; they can control the market. They can put the oil down to twenty-five cents or they can put it up to two dollars, and we have to take it." [44] Another producer deposed that the price of oil was telegraphed from Oil City, Pennsylvania, and that producers' balances of oil were recorded at Oil City or Pittsburgh. The offices of Standard Oil's Seep Purchasing Agency, he said, were next door to those of the Buckeye. The implication as to their relationship was clear, but Daniel O'Day, general superintendent of the line, repeated a story made familiar in the Rice case when he declared that he did not know that the Buckeye was a member of the Standard Oil Trust.[45]

Monnett attached great importance to the Buckeye proceedings. In a special communication published in the New York *World*, March 18, 1899, he declared: "If we can present evidence to the Ohio courts which will result in the revocation of the charter of the Buckeye Pipe Line we will have taken away the very life-blood of the trust, for without it the trust will be helpless in Ohio." The case suffered a setback, however, when two independent refiners failed to appear to testify. One of them, tracked down by the *World*, declared that he could not afford to testify. "The railroads would put me back on the old basis of rates in a minute," he said.[46]

Testimony in the contempt proceedings against Standard Oil of Ohio added to its unfavorable publicity. Hearings were held in New York in October, 1898, and March, 1899. On the latter occasion the New York *World* made the most of a vigorous exchange of epithets between Archbold and George Rice. Archbold, it reported, declared that Rice was attempting to secure the sale of his business by blackmailing Standard Oil with threats of litigation. He denounced Rice with, "There is nothing to you but weight and wind." "I don't want any of your money," Rice replied. "You have only got dirty money obtained by robbing the people." [47] Much to the delight of the *World*, Archbold also became embroiled with Monnett's assistant.

In Ohio Standard Oil had taken steps to influence public opinion more favorably. In late 1898 news items complimentary to Standard Oil and critical of Monnett began to appear in the press there. Upon investigation the attorney general uncovered the fact that some of them had been provided by the Jennings Publishing Advertising Agency. Jennings was summoned to testify in the Buckeye proceedings and admitted that he had a contract to place articles about Standard Oil which were not to appear as advertisements. He defended this type of agreement as a common practice and denied that editorial matter had been furnished. The provision for placing the reading matter on the editorial page, he explained, was to keep country newspapers from burying his contributions in the miscellaneous section.[48]

Monnett's attack produced publicity but no legal results. His campaign for re-election failed, and the antitrust cases were dropped after he left office in December, 1899. A year later the Ohio Supreme Court ruled against the state in the contempt proceedings against Standard Oil of Ohio. Apparently Monnett had overplayed his chosen role as defender of the public interest.

Intra-industry Conflict before the U.S. Industrial Commission

The independent oilmen's chance to bring Standard Oil even more into the public spotlight than it had been was offered by the United States Industrial Commission's hearings on the trust problem in 1899. The hearings themselves became a forum for a bitter intra-industry contest to influence public opinion for and against Standard Oil.

Thomas W. Phillips, president of the Producers' Protective Association during the years 1887–1890, introduced the bill leading to the establishment of the Industrial Commission. A member of the House of Representatives in the Fifty-third and Fifty-fourth Congresses, he offered a bill in July, 1894, "authorizing the appointment of a nonpartisan commission to collect information and to consider and recommend legislation to meet the problems presented by labor, agriculture, and capital." [49] The bill failed to pass in that session or in the next two. In 1897 it passed both the House and the Senate but arrived on President Cleveland's desk just before he was to leave office. Cleveland refused to sign it without the benefit of careful scrutiny. The measure was, therefore, reintroduced in the Fifty-fifth Congress and became law June 18, 1898.

The commission was to be composed of five members of the House, five members of the Senate, and nine other persons appointed by the President. Senator James H. Kyle of South Dakota was named chairman of the commission and Phillips, now a private citizen, was made vice-chairman. Because of Kyle's frequent absences, Phillips presided over most of the hearings involving Standard Oil.

Standard Oil thus found itself in the unusual position of being summoned before a federal body presided over by one substantially interested in its new rival, the Pure Oil Company. To make sure that the record would not suffer thereby, Standard Oil employed a stenographer to take down in full the testimony affecting it. His report was subsequently made the basis of a book published by the *Oil City Derrick* in an effort to show that the editing of the commission's report had substantially distorted the real tenor of the testimony.

The Commission heard much testimony on pipelines but few suggestions for dealing with Standard Oil's pipeline power through public policy. James W. Lee, who had been closely allied with Phillips in the developments leading to the formation of the Pure Oil Company and was then its president, was the first witness in the investigation. He placed great emphasis on the possession of pipelines as a source of Standard Oil's power and as a *sine qua non* for challenging that power. Referring to the repulse of attempts by Standard Oil to purchase the independents' refineries and pipelines, Lee said:

We believe that the price of that oil is largely dependent upon having an open competitive market for refined oil. Their [independents'] pipe lines will give them an open competitive market, and therefore they would not give them up. They had rather have them wiped out, if they must be.[50]

Although in 1891 he had been a leading advocate of the Burdick bill to regulate pipeline rates, Lee now had no suggestions to make when questioned as to whether the Interstate Commerce Commission could be utilized to check Standard Oil.[51] Participation in pipeline enterprise obviously had made members of Pure Oil less enthusiastic about governmental regulation of pipelines.

Attorney General Frank Monnett of Ohio, the next witness, had some general views on the importance of pipelines. After summarizing the charges against the Standard Oil companies in Ohio, he remarked:

If you examine the freight charges in cases where a competing pipe line has been constructed along a railroad, that formerly had a fixed rate, you will find that instead of the competitive pipe line which parallels the railroad lowering the price, it has absolutely raised it, showing that the independent shipper is discriminated against.[52]

Monnett told the commission:

In gaining control of the transportation department, you will find, gentlemen, lies the secret of the maintenance of discrimination in favor of commercial trusts.[53]

His remedy was for the "Government to maintain competition," but he outlined no specific public policy which would accomplish this end other than seizing the charters of pipeline companies which charged excessive rates.[54] This, of course, was what he was then attempting to do in Ohio in the case of the Buckeye Pipe Line.

Patrick C. Boyle, publisher of the *Oil City Derrick*, appeared at his own request to give the history of the industry and Standard Oil's role in it. The *Derrick* was reputed to be a Standard Oil paper, and Phillips attempted to bring this out. Boyle denied that there were any special ties with the oil combination. When Phillips asked whether the *Derrick* had criticized Standard Oil, Boyle said that it had. He continued: "Oh, I can not recall any particular time. Within the last 10 years there has been no occasion for adverse criticism of the Standard Oil Company. There unquestionably would have been [criticism] if there had been any occasion for it." [55]

Boyle said that his paper took the position that independent pipe-lines were not justified if there were lines already serving a field efficiently and at the same cost. He maintained that the construction of the Producers' Oil Company line in the McDonald field in 1891 was useless to the producers because of its limited capacity in comparison with the herculean efforts of the National Transit Company to serve the field.[56] This observation led to a very interesting and germane exchange:

Q. There might have been a free pipe-line law in Pennsylvania, which was opposed by the Standard Oil Company for years, and finally granted. Do you not think that there would have been pipe lines of sufficient capacity to have taken care of the oil, if the producers had had the right to build them in our State, if they had had the right of eminent domain. Is it fair, therefore, to instance the capacity of a single pipe line, just starting up, to care of the whole field?—

A. To begin with, we will have to assume that the producers, or the persons engaged in constructing the pipe lines, under a free pipe-line law, previous to 1877, would have been willing and satisfied to form a compact organization, to put in sufficient capital, and to continue to act as a unit, as the persons owning the existing pipe-line interests there have done. If all these things could have been brought about, then I believe it would have been possible to have had enough lines there, but the constant cooperation of all the parties interested would have been necessary. They would necessarily have been obliged to be united on every proposition, and that was something that was never accomplished before; nor has it been since.

Q. Do you not believe that the pipe-line industry would have held out just such inducements as the railroad industry has to the country, that there would have been two or three large competing lines in the field, and that the burden of taking care of that oil would not have been self-imposed by the Standard Oil Company?—

A. All we can judge is by what did occur at the time, when there were a great many competing organizations. There were one or two strong pipe lines, and they were owned by one or two strong railroad companies, and managed, in part or in whole, either openly or by agreement.

Q. It was then a growing industry—away back before it was monopolized?—

A. It was not a growing industry. It was over-production. There was no pipe line in the business previous to the organization of the pipe lines in 1877 that had made a dollar.[57]

When questioning was pressed along the line that Standard Oil had been responsible for obstructions to the construction of competing pipelines, Boyle denied that he knew of any such instances. On the other hand, he declared that George Rice had attempted to obstruct the National Transit's Macksburg pipeline.[58]

Toward the end of his testimony Boyle came out forthrightly for Standard Oil. He declared: "Darwin's theory of the survival of the fittest was never better illustrated than in the organization of the Standard Oil Company; it represents the best element in all branches of the trade." [59] When questioned as to whether Standard Oil could exist without the pipeline system, Boyle replied: "Oh, no; but it is only one of the means of their success. Their great success is due to their capacity to find markets." [60] He maintained that Standard Oil's greatness was due to the organization of capital, intellect, and industry. "Brains come in more than anything else," he exclaimed. "That is what I mean to say. The Standard Oil Company was unknown when the pipe lines were organized; they came as strangers into the business." [61] Nowhere in the testimony before the commission was there a more succinct summary of the conditions that favored the development of Standard Oil's pipeline power nor a more determined refusal to admit that the combination had attempted to bar the same road to others.

John D. Archbold took the stand on September 8, 1899, and iminediately called the commission's attention to the fact that both the Pure Oil Company and the United States Pipe Line embodied voting trusts. Although Lee had denied that the appellation of "trust" could be properly applied to Pure Oil, Archbold made the most of it. "I make this statement, gentlemen, not as a criticism," he said, "but as rather a striking evidence of the irresistible tendency toward combination." [62] He then denied Lee's charge that Standard Oil had opposed the free pipe law in Pennsylvania. "We were entering the pipe-line business," he declared, "fully understanding its great importance to the future of the petroleum trade, and it is not likely that we would be prejudiced by any such action as Mr. Lee claims." [63]

In his testimony Archbold dealt with familiar charges against Standard Oil. He denied that it had offered obstructions to the United States Pipe Line other "than would attach to any competitor in a line of business engaging against another." [64] He came out firmly for the Interstate Commerce Act, maintained that Standard Oil had received no rebates since enactment of the law, and claimed that the United States Pipe Line received lower freight rates over the Central of New Jersey than Standard Oil had ever received for an equal distance. [65] He charged that representatives of the independents had approached him with propositions to divide the business and to co-operate in marketing oil and all that pertained to it. [66] He also accused Rice of attempting to blackmail Standard Oil into purchasing his properties. [67]

Questioning then turned to price policies. Archbold left no doubt about Standard Oil's power over refined oil prices and its use against competitors.

Q. So far as an organization of the size of the Standard Oil Company is concerned, if you put prices down to cost you can afford to hold them there, of course, very much longer than a smaller rival could?— A. I think so.

Q. And I presume you are in the habit of doing that to get rid of a competitor at times?— A. We are in the habit of fighting vigorously to hold our trade and advance it.

Q. To the extent of holding prices down to cost until the rivals give way?— A. Yes.

Q. Now, the general result then is this: By virtue of your greater power you are enabled to secure prices that on the whole could be considered steadily somewhat above competitive rates?— A. Well, I hope so. I think we have better merchandizing facilities, better marketing facilities, better distributing facilities, and better talent than a competitor can have.[68]

Henry H. Rogers followed Archbold and was subjected to minute questioning on Standard Oil's pipeline operations. He estimated that the National Transit Company had 35,000 miles of pipe, or more, and stated that its charter was practically the same as that under which the Pennsylvania Railroad owned stocks of rail lines west of Pittsburgh.[69] Although he admitted that in the past competition had forced the payment of premium prices for crude, he denied that such payments were now being made for purposes other than obtaining superior oil. He maintained that these premiums could not be considered as a rebate to producers since pipeline charges were paid by the party transporting the oil, in most cases, oil exporters.[70] In view of the risks involved in pipeline construction, he maintained that rates were reasonable.[71] Rogers declared that he could not estimate the cost of collecting oil, "but I could probably say and be confirmed by you that we are not in business for our health, but are out for the dollars; what that profit is I could not say." [72]

Phillips then stepped out of his position of vice-chairman of the commission to become a witness. He testified as to the efforts of Standard Oil to obtain access to the Producers' Oil Company, Limited, and to the United States Pipe Line. The oilman stated that the putting of half the stock of the Pure Oil Company into a voting trust was for the purpose of protecting the company against such inroads. Accordingly, he did not classify it a "trust" in the sense that Standard Oil was one. Rather, he said, its purpose was to maintain competition.[73] He testified that the independents' approaches to Standard Oil were "to secure the right to deliver in New York, without their [Standard's] opposition, the capacity of the then existing [pipe] lines, which would not exceed seven or eight thousand barrels of oil per day." [74] Phillips testified that the independents believed Standard Oil to be the source of opposition to the laying of the United States Pipe Line across New Jersey, and he maintained that the only offers made by Standard Oil were to purchase the pipeline or the independents' producing properties.[75]

Phillips stressed the importance of pipelines. In reply to a question about the benefits of the independents' pipelines, he replied:

If it were not for these pipe lines none of these independent refiners would be living to-day. It is for mutual protection that these people have united. We believe we have received much better prices for oil; the last year the refiners have given much better prices than they would have given if there had not been this independent movement.[76]

Phillips estimated on the basis of the experience of the United States Pipe Line that the transportation of crude to the seaboard cost five cents or less per barrel, depending on the amount carried, and he placed the cost of collecting oil at three to five cents a barrel.[77] Although Phillips stated that the United States Pipe Line did have a favorable rate from the Jersey Central, he maintained that it was an open one. He admitted that pipelines might have sold oil to independent refiners "at special rates" in times of stress.[78]

Lewis Emery, Jr., appeared before the commission on September 11, 1899, and prefaced his remarks with the comment that he held no animosity toward Standard Oil. As he put it, "They believe in their method of doing business, and I believe in mine." [79] Thereupon he proceeded to read a prepared statement dealing with the development of pipelines, which showed little sympathy for "their method." He declared that Standard Oil, by a "corrupt bargain" with the railroads, had forced all but one of the eighteen lines built under the provisions of the Pennsylvania pipeline law of 1872 "into bankruptcy, and practically, sale to itself." [80] "The railroads of this country are responsible to-day for the existence of these trusts," he went on to declare, "because they gave the favored shippers such drawbacks and rebates that finally the Standard Oil Company, with its privileges, drove the entire oil industry into its own hands." [81]

Up to 1872, Emery said, the oil industry was open to all, but the South Improvement scheme changed this situation. He introduced the contract between the Pennsylvania Railroad and the South Improvement Company. Pointing out that it had also been in the records of the congressional investigations of 1872 and 1888, as well as of the Hepburn Committee, he exclaimed, "It seems to me that investigations don't amount to a cent." [82] Still, he appeared determined to exploit fully the current opportunity to air his grievances against Standard Oil.

Emery attributed the "fading" of the industry after 1872 to a continuation of the principles of the South Improvement scheme. He explained his view in these words:

Would it have been possible for you to go into the business and possess an equal amount of oil, equal facilities, equal refineries, unless you had behind you a railroad combination itself? It was impossible, absolutely impossible, for any set of men to go out and get equal contracts, because they had got all of the roads then leading to the Atlantic coast and into the western country. There was no chance whatever for a man with a single pipe line. . . . I was one of the hundreds that went to the wall under that contract, although it is said by witnesses and everybody else that it was repealed and went out of existence.[83]

He maintained that it was easier to compete with Standard Oil in Europe than in the domestic market, especially in Germany, where there was legislation against "unfair trading." He was not quite sure, however, of the exact provisions of that law. In the United States, he pointed out, the independents of the oil business had fought monopoly since 1872, but now the popular demand that something be done by legislation was rising. "I wish," he said, "to help you in every possible way to remodel our laws so we can all live, and if you don't the results are going to be very serious." [84]

Emery charged that Standard Oil had neither cheapened nor improved oil products:

They have got nothing better in any of their works than I have got in mine, except it be, perhaps, in their fine laboratories, in the manufacture of residuums or the by-products. . . . The whole question is the question of transportation. If you will force the railroads of this country to obey the law, you will have cured this evil.[85]

The Pennsylvania Railroad became the target of Emery's wide-ranging attack. He maintained that in his suit against the railroad, commenced shortly before the sale of his Greenwich Point refinery to Standard Oil, he had proof that the road was paying rebates to B. B. Campbell and others of eight to twenty-eight cents a barrel. He admitted, however, that he had accepted thirty-five thousand dollars and costs to settle his own case against the road.[86]

Emery pointed out that the New York free pipe law of 1878 had been a good one and that the Pennsylvania law of 1883 had been copied from it. He recounted alleged steps taken by Standard Oil to bar the enactment of the Pennsylvania law, citing instances of his own experience.[87] He also intimated that bribery had halted the passage of the free pipe law in New Jersey when it was essential for the United States Pipe Line to have its benefits.[88]

The witness introduced the contracts between the Pennsylvania Railroad and the National Transit Company dividing the oil traffic to the seaboard and asserted that he believed them to be still in force. In support of this claim he cited an alleged incident which took place two years before. He charged that at that time the Buffalo, Rochester, and Pittsburgh Railroad had been brought into the agreement to prevent its disturbing the existing arrangements.[89] In later testimony Howard Page of Standard's Union Tank Line Company seemed to confirm the continued operation of these contracts, for he stated that the crude oil rates of Standard Oil's seaboard pipelines and of the Pennsylvania Railroad had been unchanged for the last ten years.[90]

Emery concluded that the remedy for the problems which had afflicted and still confronted the petroleum industry lay primarily in the rebate and drawback practices of the railroads. He asserted that no remedy was to be found in the Pennsylvania legislature, nor in the courts, nor by appeal to state or national law enforcement officers. Accordingly, he declared: "I say Government ownership of railroads would be my remedy unless we can get Attorneys-General of the United States and of the several States that will enforce laws." [91] This was a surprising and certainly a weak conclusion from one who was himself an entrepreneur par excellence.

George Rice appeared and told his story in a vein similar to Emery's. He testified that Standard Oil had issued a pamphlet similar to the one that he had put out under the title of "Black Death." He complained bitterly to the commission that the Standard Oil version contained sentiments such as these: "If George Rice's goods are no better than his pamphlet, you don't want them"; "His pamphlet boiled down simply means 'sour grapes'"; "Such missionaries as George Rice work mostly for George Rice." [92] Rice denied efforts to blackmail Standard Oil into purchasing his property and, like Emery, came out squarely for government ownership of the railroads,[93]

Archbold saw a need to counteract Rice's testimony, and through Senator Boies Penrose he arranged for Howard Page of the Union Tank Line Company to appear and to deny Rice's charges of freight discriminations. Page told the commission that in the period since he had become vice-president of the company in 1889 it had received no "rebates or concessions from tariff rates contrary to either the letter or spirit of the interstate-commerce law." [94]

John D. Rockefeller submitted a statement to the commission in which he admitted that rebates had been received prior to 1887 but maintained that since that date, to his knowledge, the Standard Oil Company had received no financial favors from any railroad.[95] He attributed the success of Standard Oil "to its consistent policy to make the volume of its business large through the merit and cheapness of its products." [96]

Rockefeller gave special credit to the role of the pipelines in this development. His statement indicated how dependent Standard Oil was on these crude oil carriers:

We soon discovered as the business grew that the primary method of transporting oil in barrels could not last. The package often cost more than the contents, and the forests of the country were not sufficient to supply the necessary material for an extended length of time. Hence we devoted attention to other methods of transportation, adopted the pipe-line system, and found capital for pipe-line construction equal to the necessities of the business.

To operate pipe lines required franchises from the States in which they were located, and consequently corporations in those States, just as railroads running through different States, are forced to operate under separate State charters. To perfect the pipe-line system of transportation required in the neighborhood of fifty millions of capital. This could not be obtained or maintained without industrial combination. The entire oil business is dependent upon this pipe-line system. Without it every well would shut down and every foreign market would be closed to us.[97]

Rockefeller thus underlined the importance of pipelines as a source of Standard Oil's power and a reason for its combination of capital. The opponents of Standard Oil had fully documented how the combination had acquired and used its pipelines; yet they still attributed the combination's predominant position to railroad discriminations.

Rockefeller laid the failure of legislation concerning combinations to the fact that it had attempted to destroy rather than to control them. He suggested, therefore, that federal laws be enacted to create corporations and to regulate them. Failing that, he recommended "State legislation as nearly uniform as possible encouraging combinations of persons and capital for the purpose of carrying on industries, but permitting State supervision, not of a character to hamper industries, but sufficient to prevent frauds upon the public." [98]

Other Standard Oil officials took a similar position. Archbold favored a national corporation law subject to the supervision of a commission or some other government authority. Commenting on recommendations of the Industrial Commission in a letter to Senator Boies Penrose on January 5, 1900, Archbold indicated how close he believed federal supervision of corporations should be. "Private corporations," he wrote, "should not be required to make public items of receipts and expenditures, profits and losses. A statement of assets and liabilities is all that can benefit the public. Items of receipts and expenditures, profits and losses, can only benefit the competitors." [99] Henry H. Rogers also advocated a federal incorporation law. He declared: "The advantage would be, in my judgment, the power to do business in the several States under the Federal law, subject only to such laws of the States as pertain to taxes and the police regulations that govern in our States." [100]

Undoubtedly Monnett's current attack on Standard Oil in Ohio was uppermost in the minds of the Standard Oil representatives as they gave this testimony, and steps had already been taken to lessen the possibilities of similar onslaughts by crusading public officials. In June, 1899, Standard Oil had taken advantage of the liberal New Jersey incorporation law to meet this threat. The charter of the Standard Oil Company (New Jersey) had been amended to facilitate ownership of stocks of the different Standard Oil corporations, and its authorized capital stock was increased from ten million to one hundred and ten million dollars. The stock of this holding company was to be exchanged for the outstanding certificates of the Standard Oil Trust and for the stock of nineteen sister companies. [101] When questioned about the New Jersey law during his appearance before the Industrial Commission, Rogers commented: "Of course the laws of New Jersey have recently been followed by Delaware in liberality, and all the bad will naturally go to New Jersey and Delaware for incorporation. I think a Federal charter would do away with that evil." [102]

The arguments on behalf of combinations, if not those for federal incorporation, apparently struck fertile ground with the commission. Its preliminary report found that combinations were a permanent fixture of the business scene and that the problem was to "destroy" their power for evil while maintaining their "means for good." As initial steps, the commission recommended publicity for the financial affairs of corporations and trusts, including an annual statement of assets and liabilities, with profit and loss. It also recommended that the Interstate Commerce Commission be authorized to prescribe the methods for keeping the accounts of the railroads, that the commission's decisions should be effective until reversed by the courts on appeal, and that it be authorized to prescribe classifications of freight articles and to make rules and regulations for freight transportation in the United States.

Standard Oil had not been without friends on the commission, nor was it dissatisfied with the commission's preliminary report. Returning the document to Boies Penrose, Archbold wrote on February 21, 1900: "We think the report so fair that we will not undertake to suggest any changes." [103] One source of his satisfaction might have been the fact that the commission, despite lengthy testimony which showed the importance of Standard Oil's pipeline power, did not even mention this subject in its recommendations.

The Industrial Commission continued in existence for two more years, and Archbold kept a wary eye on it. Its chairman, Senator Kyle, died on July 1, 1901, and two days later Archbold wrote Penrose that he hoped that he would become chairman.[104] He also wrote to Matthew S. Quay, the other Pennsylvania senator, asking his support to this end.[105] When Penrose declined to seek the post, Archbold enlisted his support and that of Mark Hanna to win the place for Colonel Albert Clarke. Clarke was chosen for the job and remained in it until the commission was terminated in 1902. But there were few additions to the record concerning Standard Oil during this period. The case for and against the combination was made while Kyle had been chairman and Phillips was in the chair.

The complete record of the hearings on Standard Oil as taken down by its stenographer and published by the *Oil City Derrick* is illuminating. It shows that Phillips framed many questions in the form of arguments and took care to label the friends of Standard Oil as such, while giving its opponents the maximum opportunity to state their case. On the other hand, other members of the commission, and especially John M. Farquhar, did not fail to check the vice-chairman, note weaknesses in the independents' case, and to catch them in half-truths.

The fact that the commission was a forum for an intra-industry contest emerges from the full record. A typical instance occurred when Phillips was attempting to demonstrate Boyle's connection with Standard Oil. Although Boyle made no objection, members of the commission, including Farquhar, asked that he be allowed to make his statement uninterrupted.

Vice-Chairman PHILLIPS. All right; I simply wanted to get Mr. Boyle's status before the commission before he proceeded with his testimony. This is not for the reporters, and I may have asked questions that I did not design to ask—

Mr. FARQUHAR. Well, Mr. Phillips, the newspapers will take all you say; you need not be afraid of that.[106]

Toward the end of Boyle's testimony Phillips made an attempt to get Boyle's conviction on libel charges into the record. Farquhar again objected:

I am beginning to learn a good deal about this. If they have any quarrels to settle on this oil question let them settle it outside. This commission will not lumber its records with anything at all about the character of Mr. Boyle unless specific charges are brought here in that regard. The attempt was made at the beginning of his examination to do it, and I objected to it then and I object to it now.[107]

On another occasion Phillips prefaced a question with the statement that the National Transit Company had opposed the granting of the right of eminent domain. He then asked Boyle whether or not it had been impossible for a number of years to secure a right of way to the seaboard after the National Transit had obtained its route.[108] Several members of the commission objected to the form and nature of the question. Phillips defended it, and it remained in the record.

Later, in a passage stricken from the official version, he said, "This
is very pertinent to this investigation, this pipe line system, because
this is the controlling power in the oil field." [109] Neither Phillips
nor the independent oilmen, however, succeeded in impressing this
point on the public.

In the decade 1891–1901 pipeline enterprise helped to create a
new rival to Standard Oil. Freed from the combination's grasp on oil
transportation, Pennsylvania producers and independent refiners
were able to compete with Standard Oil in the domestic and export
markets. Their competition, however, did not reduce the Trust's
control of the oil industry appreciably. On the other hand, in order
to sustain their challenge the independents adopted an organization
and integrated their operations in the pattern that Standard Oil
had fixed on the industry. The success of the Pure Oil Company
ended the pleas for governmental intervention in the pipeline field
by formerly ardent advocates of pipeline regulation.

The changing picture was brought into sharp focus by the hearings on the oil industry before the United States Industrial Commission. The independents concentrated their fire on Standard Oil
as an iniquitous example of monopoly and repeated the story of its
rise to power in terms made familiar by their testimony in previous
investigations. Although pipelines figured prominently in this testimony, when it came to making recommendations for dealing with
Standard Oil, the independents preferred to concentrate on remedies for railroad discriminations.

Standard Oil's representatives offered an array of arguments on
behalf of pipeline monopoly. They also declared that they were in-
nocent of any violations of the Interstate Commerce Act and seemed
quite willing to see its provisions against railroad discriminations
strengthened. Perhaps Standard Oil's pipeline power, which railroad legislation and its enforcement would not touch, was partially
responsible for this attitude. Although Rockefeller himself stressed
the vital contribution of the pipeline system to the Trust's success,
neither the members of the commission nor the independents appeared interested in using this fact as a springboard for public policy
recommendations.

Standard Oil and the independents were clearly interested in influencing public opinion by means of their testimony before the Industrial Commission, but the intricacies of the pipeline business were not well adapted to this end. While the *New York Tribune,* for example, reported the controversy between Henry H. Rogers and Thomas W. Phillips over reasonable pipeline rates, the details of the Dreyfus case, the Transvaal question, and the death of Cornelius Vanderbilt received far more space and provided more interesting reading fare for the general public. Nevertheless, there was a high level of public interest in the trust problem, and the Industrial Commission hearings provided a wealth of material with which able writers could appeal to this interest. Although pipeline enterprise silenced one group which had advocated pipeline regulation, the public's hostility to Standard Oil, carefully nurtured by members of Pure Oil, created an atmosphere favorable to increasingly severe attacks on the combination. Federal pipeline legislation came in their wake.

IX

Politics, Pipelines, and the Mounting Attack on Standard Oil, 1902-1906

IN THE years 1902–1905 popular antagonism toward the country's great industrial combinations was on the increase, and the political scene reflected this fact. The Industrial Commission had recommended measures to help differentiate the "good" combinations from the "bad" and urged that the Interstate Commerce Act be strengthened. President Theodore Roosevelt's program for obtaining legislation in line with these recommendations was aided by the public's hostility to Standard Oil and heightened by writers who probed the origins of its power and focused attention on its social consequences.

While Standard Oil's predominant position in the petroleum industry was becoming a national political issue of the first magnitude, little public attention was paid to the role of pipelines in sustaining that position. As in the past, the complexities of intra-industry structure did not seem well adapted for the purposes popular writers had in mind. Moreover, since the establishment of the Pure Oil Company, complaints against the exercise of Standard Oil's pipeline power in the Appalachian field had subsided to a murmur; nor were there expressions of major grievances in the Lima-Indiana field. The call for legislative action, state and federal, came suddenly from a new quarter—Kansas.

Theodore Roosevelt and Standard Oil

The public image of Standard Oil as a grasping "octopus" preying on competitors and the public alike had by 1903 become a useful political weapon, and Theodore Roosevelt made the most of it. In that year a bill for the establishment of a Department of Commerce and Labor, including provision for a Bureau of Corporations to perform the investigative function recommended by the Industrial Commission, was before Congress. There was also a measure, sponsored by Senator Stephen Elkins of West Virginia, to strengthen the Interstate Commerce Act.

Standard Oil's position on these proposals was stated in a telegram sent by John D. Rockefeller, Jr., to Senators William Allison, Henry Cabot Lodge, Eugene Hale, and Henry Teller on February 6, 1903. "Our people are opposed to all the proposed trust legislation except the Elkins Anti-Discrimination Bill," young Rockefeller said. "Mr. Archbold, with our counsel, goes to Washington this afternoon. Am very anxious they should see you at once and shall much appreciate any assistance you can render them." [1] A telegram substantially in the same vein from Archbold to Matthew Quay was published in the *New York American* on the same day.

Roosevelt was quick to seize on this opportunity to promote passage of the Department of Commerce and Labor bill. On February 7, 1903, the President told correspondents that unless the bill were passed, he would call Congress into special session. He then told them that six senators had received telegrams from John D. Rockefeller to the effect that the legislation must be stopped. Riding the wave of public reaction to this announcement, the bill passed the House on February 10 by a vote of 252 to 10 and cleared the Senate without difficulty the following day. The political potentialities in exploiting public animus against Standard Oil had been confirmed. Roosevelt later told a Senate investigating committee: "All I know is that I got through the bill, and it was largely the publication I gave to these telegrams that enabled me thus to get it through." [2]

The Elkins Act became law shortly after the Department of Commerce and Labor bill. Under its provisions, shippers as well as carriers were made liable to prosecution for rebating, and railroad corporations as well as individuals were made subject to the law. Published rates became the standard of lawfulness; the criminal provisions of the 1889 amendment to the Interstate Commerce Act were removed; and the Interstate Commerce Commission was permitted to apply for injunctions when it believed that carriers were departing from published tariffs.

These changes were along the lines of the recommendations of the Industrial Commission, and just as that body's conclusions had been silent on pipelines so was the new law. The underground carriers seemed to be as remote from federal regulation as they had ever been.

As the elections of 1904 approached, Standard Oil officials sought to ingratiate themselves with Roosevelt. Standard Oil men had swelled the Republican campaign chest in 1896 and in 1900 with liberal contributions, and, according to Archbold's later testimony, they contributed one hundred thousand dollars to the 1904 campaign through Cornelius Bliss, national Republican treasurer, and twenty-five thousand through Senator Boies Penrose.[3] Archbold recalled that in making the contribution to Bliss he had said: "We do not want to make this contribution unless it is thoroughly acceptable and will be thoroughly appreciated by Mr. Roosevelt."[4] Bliss appeared to accept these conditions, and Rogers and Archbold were strengthened in their belief that the "Republican side was the safest." Subsequently Bliss seems to have asked for further aid from Archbold, who refused it despite Bliss's intimation that Standard Oil was following an unwise course thereby.[5]

Meanwhile, the newspaper barrage of criticism against Standard Oil had reached a high pitch. Foremost among the attackers was Joseph Pulitzer's New York *World*, which connected the Republican administration with Standard Oil. On October 1, 1904, Pulitzer in an open letter to Roosevelt asked: "Does the public know any less about the internal workings of the Standard Oil Company, for example, than it does about the internal workings of this Bureau of Corporations?" In the 583 days of the Bureau's existence, Pulitzer charged, it had provided the public with no information about the trusts. The publisher asked how it happened that George Cortelyou, national Republican chairman, was soliciting campaign con-

tributions from the malefactors of great wealth. "Is not your personal
political agent secretly levying and collecting a franchise tax for your
Presidential campaign?" he asked. Roosevelt was busy with efforts to
pin the Standard Oil label on the Democrats,[6] and for the time being
he ignored this attack.

Standard Oil, however, attempted to refute the charges that it
was actively engaged in promoting the Republican cause. Samuel
Dodd released a statement which denied that "Mr. John D. Rockefeller or any officer of the Standard Oil Company has taken part in
securing the nomination of any of the candidates for office, as is so
positively stated." [7] On the day that this statement appeared, October 26, 1904, Roosevelt ordered Cortelyou to return Standard Oil's
contribution—if there had been one. Confirming this directive in a
letter the following day, Roosevelt wrote: "In view of the open and
pronounced opposition of the Standard Oil Co. to the establishment
of the Bureau of Corporations, one of the most important accomplishments of my administration, I do not feel willing to accept its
aid." [8] Apparently Pulitzer's thrusts at the President had sunk deeper
than at first had appeared.

Archbold's view that the Republican side was the "safest" failed
to be substantiated by events after 1904. "Darkest Abyssinia," he
later told a Senate committee, "never saw anything like the course
of treatment which we experienced at the hands of the administration following Mr. Roosevelt's election in 1904." [9] He charged that
the Bureau of Corporations was deliberately used as a weapon
against Standard Oil. "It came to be more than a coincidence,"
Archbold declared, "that whenever any question of ours which was
before the courts was approaching a decision, or when there was
some question of legislation pending here, there was sure to be a
report." [10]

Roosevelt maintained that his treatment of Standard Oil had
never been anything but fair. He told the senators investigating the
campaign contributions of 1904:

I never changed my attitude toward the Standard Oil Co. in any shape
or way. It antagonized me before my election, when I was getting through
the Bureau of Corporations bill, and I then promptly threw down the
gauntlet to it. . . . I never suggested to any governmental official to
investigate it rather than any other trust. The Bureau of Corporations and

the Department of Justice both investigated it on their own accounts, and I acted on their reports and recommendations precisely as I acted in all other cases.[11]

The fact was that the popular pressures for action against concentrated economic power had become greater than Standard Oil could cope with in its own field. Moreover, the pressures were being intensified by writers like Ida M. Tarbell.

Muckraking Standard Oil

On one occasion Roosevelt told Miss Tarbell: "I don't object to the facts, but you and [Ray Stannard] Baker are not *practical*." [12] These two muckrakers did indeed have a passion for facts which a successful politician might deem impractical, but it made Ida Tarbell's *The History of the Standard Oil Company* an enduring classic of the muckraking period and an influential work at a critical period in that organization's affairs.

Miss Tarbell had close connections with the development of the petroleum industry. She had been brought up in the Oil Regions, where her father was a pioneer in oil tank construction. Her brother, who was connected with the Pure Oil Company, had fought Standard Oil with an independent pipeline and as a member of the Producers' Protective Association. Ida had followed her bent for writing and was studying in Paris when she was discovered by Samuel S. McClure, the publisher of *McClure's Magazine*, one of the new, mass-circulation magazines that became the mainstay of the muckraking movement. It was natural, then, that as the public furor over trusts rose, Miss Tarbell should suggest a series of articles on Standard Oil and that McClure should approve.

She set about the task systematically, attempting to compile the documentary record as fully as possible. She drew on the records of state and federal investigations as well as court cases involving Standard Oil. Her writing technique was to simplify the complexities of the story, to let the record speak, and seemingly to leave the reader to draw his own conclusions. Her view of her work as well as its point of departure is well summarized in the following words. "We were neither apologists nor critics," she later wrote, "only journalists intent on discovering what had gone into the making of this most perfect of all monopolies." [13]

For a time Standard Oil officials, hoping to keep the record straight, provided Miss Tarbell with information. In January, 1902, through Mark Twain, she had met Henry H. Rogers, who proved to be a surprisingly willing informant. "We've changed our policy," he told her. "We are giving out information." [14] In view of the difficulty she had experienced in digging out the written record, this was indeed a refreshing change, and she agreed to use material he furnished, reserving the right to make her own judgments on it. The interviews continued even after the publication of the first installment of *The History of the Standard Oil Company* in the November, 1902, issue of *McClure's*. They stopped abruptly, however, after the publication of her indictment of Standard Oil for its alleged tactics against independent oil shipments. Daniel O'Day had furnished information about the early development of pipelines, but his assistance was the subject of criticism by other Standard Oil officials who soon became convinced that Miss Tarbell was not being influenced by material favorable to the company. [15]

In 1904 *The History* appeared in book form. The two volumes carried few footnote references, but the copious appendices contained lengthy excerpts from the trials and investigations in which Standard Oil had been involved. Items pertinent to pipeline history, such as the full text of the Billingsley bill, were included.

In Ida Tarbell's view, pipelines played a subordinate role in the rise of Standard Oil, but she left no doubt about their importance in maintaining the combination's hold over the petroleum industry. She stated emphatically:

As a matter of fact, the Standard's ability to cut off crude supplies from the outside refiners is much greater than in the days before the Interstate Commerce Bill, when it depended on its alliance with the railroads to prevent its rival getting oil. It goes without saying that this is an absurd power to allow in the hands of any manufacturer of a great necessity of life. [16]

Miss Tarbell praised the efficiency of Standard Oil, which she thought shone to its best advantage in its pipeline system, but she had no sympathy for the methods by which its power was attained and then utilized. They were, she observed, only the most obvious examples of what could be and was being done by businessmen throughout the country. Her interpretation of the current industrial situation was best summarized in these few words: "At all events, until the transportation matter is settled, and settled right, the monopolistic trust will be with us, a leech on our pockets, a barrier to our free efforts." Her remedy was equally brief: "That our first task is to secure free and equal transportation privileges by rail, pipe and waterway is evident." [17]

Despite the documentation provided in the book, the reviewer for *The Nation* did not feel that this work fulfilled the need for an objective study of Standard Oil which another reviewer for the same magazine had recommended after reading *Wealth against Commonwealth*. *The Nation's* appraisal of the Tarbell effort, therefore, was scarcely less critical than that of Lloyd's volume a decade before.[18] Although this review was not typical of the book's general reception, Standard Oil, for obvious reasons, had it reprinted and distributed widely throughout the country.[19]

The answer to many of Miss Tarbell's charges was ably handled by a young economist, Gilbert Holland Montague, whose book *The Rise and Progress of the Standard Oil Company* had appeared in 1903. Although the publication of the volume was financed by Standard Oil, Montague apparently arrived at his conclusions independently. He maintained that, given the railway and economic conditions of the period, Standard Oil had attained and maintained its position of supremacy through the sheer superiority of its organization. Although he attributed Standard Oil's rise to its transportation advantages, he justified them in these words: "If the Standard Oil Company were not the strongest refiner, its most powerful rival would certainly have seized the same control over transportation that the Standard Oil Company in fact secured. In the last analysis, monopoly by the Standard Oil Company was, under existing conditions, inevitable, simply because it was most efficiently organized." [20] He agreed with Paul de Rousiers that discriminations, "though important in the beginning, went into the background with the absorption of pipe-lines, and, though very helpful in the creation of the trust, were not indispensable to its continuance." [21]

Montague attributed the combination of the pipelines under Standard Oil to the over-capacity, over-competition, and doubtful solvency of the early pipelines. The net effect of the maneuverings of 1874 "was particularly to build up the larger pipe-line and the larger refiner at the expense of the smaller. For this reason the economies in transportation by rail and pipe-line effected in 1874 tended greatly to increase the predominance of the United Pipe-Line Company and the Standard 'alliance.' " [22]

The young author saw no reason to fear Standard Oil's power, which was only such as "naturally accrues to so large an aggregation of capital." [23] He argued that "in the ever-present possibility of competition which meets the Standard Oil Company in the direction of every part of its policy, lie the safeguards of this great power." [24] Standard Oil officials were sufficiently impressed with Montague's thesis not only to pay for its publication but also to arrange for the distribution of a number of volumes.[25]

The attempt to influence public opinion for and against Standard Oil was no new development, but the attackers and their audience were. In the past, oilmen had been in the forefront of campaigns to shackle the tentacles of the "octopus," but they were conspicuously absent in this new movement. Whereas their primary target had been the legislatures of oil-producing states and the urban areas that carried weight in those bodies, the muckrakers sought to arouse the nation. Where independent oilmen had had some specific legislative proposals, frequently faulty as they were, the muckrakers had none. But the new generation of critics succeeded in gaining their objective whereas members of the petroleum industry had shifted theirs to a remedy through private enterprise rather than public policy. Even though the results of this new strategy had not seriously undermined Standard Oil's position, independent oilmen for the most part seemed satisfied.

Pipelines in the Lima-Indiana and Appalachian Fields

Since the 1880's Standard Oil had developed a magnificent pipeline system in the eastern fields. The Lima-Indiana fields were connected to the seaboard pipelines and to the Whiting, Indiana, refinery. An extensive system of gathering lines, operated in conjunction with the trunk lines, permitted oil to be shifted between the various Standard Oil refineries as production and refining demanded. In 1899 the combination made its only important acquisition of a competitor in the Lima-Indiana field, the Manhattan Oil Company.

Thereafter this firm was used to discourage the entrance of additional independent·lines there.[26] Reportedly there were only three of them in 1905, and together they accounted for less than 10 per cent of the pipeline runs.[27]

The rise of Pure Oil did not appreciably diminish the flow of oil through Standard Oil pipelines in the Appalachian field,[28] and many producers appeared content with the *status quo*. As a result, Pure Oil in 1902 commenced the production of crude and gradually expanded its operations into West Virginia and Ohio, following the westward shift of oil production.

A trunk line was built by Pure Oil interests from Browns Mill, Ohio, to Coraopolis, Pennsylvania, to accommodate this new traffic. At the latter point a connection was made with the crude oil line of the United States Pipe Line, which until 1904 handled crude chiefly for the Columbia Oil Company of New York. Because of the obstacles to completing the pipeline to tidewater, the oil was carried across New Jersey by rail. In 1904, however, Pure Oil opened a refinery at Marcus Hook, Pennsylvania, and the bulk of the United States Pipe Line's crude deliveries was shifted there.[29] Most of the refined oil delivered to that point by pipe was exported, the inland refineries associated with Pure Oil selling their products largely in the domestic market.

The continuing silence of erstwhile proponents of governmental regulation of pipelines seems to have stemmed from their venture in pipeline operation. Subsequent to the termination of its contract with the Columbia Oil Company in 1903, the Pure Oil Company declined to transport crude from the Columbia's West Virginia properties. When this decision was protested, it was pointed out that the Producers' and Refiners' Pipe Line, which formed part of the route, had never acted as a common carrier. Officers of Pure Oil had a ready explanation for this fact. First, they maintained that it was not a common carrier under the laws of Pennsylvania, since it was not a corporation nor had it exercised the right of eminent domain. Second, they feared that to operate it as a common carrier would be equivalent to inviting Standard Oil to divert oil from the independent refineries and to block operation of the line by insisting on thirty days' storage as provided by law. Finally, they declared that the line was sufficiently occupied with supplying the needs of the refineries with which it was associated. Consequently, they insisted upon sale of the oil to the pipeline as a condition of carriage.[30] The arguments were cogent, but they indicated that as the owner of pipelines, Standard Oil's chief rival took just as proprietary a view of them as did the Standard Oil combination.

But the "octopus" came in for its share of familiar criticism, too. Independent refiners now purchased most of their oil directly from Standard Oil rather than buying pipeline certificates prior to having the oil run into the pipe. Some refiners complained that the combination's refusal to sell oil to them was an unfair competitive tactic. However, when this form of pressure was brought to bear on the National Refining Company, which was competing with Standard Oil's Buckeye Pipe Line for wells near Findlay, Ohio, the independent concern built its own pipelines, and Standard Oil was neither able to purchase nor force it out of business.[31] Another complaint came to the United States Bureau of Corporations from the Union Petroleum Company of Philadelphia. It alleged that "on one or more occasions" prior to 1902 Standard Oil's purchasing agency had bought from it certificates representing a claim to pipeline transportation and at the same time sold the company an equivalent amount of crude oil. In the Union Company's view, this transaction represented an effort to "avoid acknowledging the legal requirement to transport the oil for others." [32] Whether this conclusion necessarily followed is doubtful since the Standard Oil pipelines in the East apparently had always offered to carry for other shippers, albeit under conditions and at rates already discussed.

A key factor in the behavior of Standard Oil in the Appalachian field at this time was the declining production there. Standard Oil's management put great emphasis on the need for protecting the "pipeline interest." [33] Undoubtedly some producers benefited from this policy, which on occasion meant that premiums would be placed on regular crude oil to keep it out of the hands of competitors. On the other hand, it involved restrictions on the sale of oil to outsiders and also pressure on producers who considered selling to independent pipelines.

Actually many producers were reluctant to sell their oil to independent interests without a premium price. They feared that, if this outlet failed, the Standard Oil pipelines might be unwilling to re-connect. Standard Oil pipeliners made the most of this consideration. At least, one producer reported that a representative of the Buckeye Pipe Line, which was engaged in its war with the National Refining Company, told him: "If you give your oil to the National, when they are gone I don't know whether the Standard will take your oil." [34] Obviously pipelines were still important weapons to both Standard Oil and a growing number of competitors. Both groups in the Appalachian and Lima-Indiana fields, however, preferred to play the game without governmental intervention.

Kansas and Standard Oil

Up to 1900 virtually all crude oil production had been centered in the Appalachian and Lima-Indiana fields, but the situation changed rapidly after that. In 1901 Texas commenced its rise as an oil-producing state, followed the next year by major development of the Kansas oil fields. Before another two years had passed, Oklahoma and Indian Territory were contributing to the production of the Mid-Continent field. By 1905 California was producing more oil than any other state in the Union. As a result of these rapid shifts in the centers of oil production, more than 60 per cent of the nation's crude in 1905 was coming from fields outside those in which pipeline development to 1900 had taken place.[35] From the Mid-Continent field came a flood of new protests against pipeline practices which operators in the eastern fields had long since given up trying to remedy by legislation.

Standard Oil gave more attention to developments in the Mid-Continent field and in California than in Texas, where the legal climate was unfriendly and production prospects at first seemed less promising.[36] In 1895 the Standard's Forest Oil Company acquired the interests of James M. Guffey and John Galey, who the year before had found oil while seeking natural gas near Neodesha in the southeastern part of Kansas.[37] Two years later the Neodesha refinery of The Standard Oil Company (Kansas) commenced operations. To provide for greater expansion than seemed possible under the Forest Oil Company's charter, that concern's property was transferred in 1901 to a company which in the following year was renamed The Prairie Oil and Gas Company.[38]

The Prairie purchased crude and constructed and operated pipelines as well as provided tankage for Standard Oil in the southwest. As production boomed in Kansas, Oklahoma, and Indian Territory during 1904, the company undertook construction of a pipeline to link Humboldt, Kansas, with Griffith, Indiana. From the latter point Standard Oil would be able to supply its great Whiting, Indiana, refinery with mid-continent crude or transfer the oil to the seaboard pipelines for delivery to the east coast. A branch line supplied the new refinery that Standard Oil had constructed at Sugar Creek, Missouri, close to Kansas City. Only oil purchased or produced by the Prairie was run through this system, which took every precaution to keep from being classified as a common carrier.[39]

Until March, 1904, the Prairie purchased Kansas crude on a basis equating it with oil from the Lima, Ohio, field. Early in that year Kansas crude brought a maximum of $1.31 a barrel, and this price attracted many speculative elements into the trade, resulting in a veritable craze for oil prospecting. Kansas production shot up from 1,017,015 barrels in 1903 to 5,559,054 barrels in 1904, but the increase in production was accompanied by a phenomenon familiar to Pennsylvania producers—a drop in price. From its peak in February, 1904, the price of crude skidded to 88 cents a barrel in July and to 80 cents in December.[40]

Standard Oil received the blame for this development. In the interim the basis for purchasing oil had been changed, and prices posted by the Prairie reflected the specific gravity of the oil.[41] Under this system the price of Kansas crude sank steadily in comparison with that of the Lima field. Since Kansas producers could not see that the quality of their oil had changed, they attributed the cut to Standard Oil's power over transportation and corresponding near-monopoly of purchases. Those lured into prospecting by the high price of crude were now convinced that Standard Oil had deliberately manipulated the price to get them to do its work.[42]

Standard Oil pipeliners were themselves critical of the new price policy for fear of its effect on their relationship with the producers, and their misgivings, discounted by Standard Oil's managers, proved justified. By July, 1904, the Kansans' anger at Standard Oil was running high. Mass meetings were held at Chanute and Independence, and from them emerged a proposition to launch a company, modeled on the Pure Oil Company, to engage in all phases of the petroleum industry and to run Standard Oil out of the state. The promoters, however, soon had to face the fact that raising the fifty million dollars' capital for the project would not be easy. In making their proposal they had ignored the fact that Pure Oil had been the end product of a decade of hard effort, financial reverses, and constant harassment. As had been the case with Pennsylvania producers, the Kansans found it easier to turn to the state.

The circumstances were propitious for successful legislative action. Although the price of Kansas crude oil had dropped steadily, the price of refined oil in the state had remained constant. With many of the state's citizens hard-hit by speculative ventures in oil, the discrepancy was a glaring one. While producers were still discussing the formation of a company to compete with Standard Oil, Samuel M. Porter of Caney, who had just been nominated for state senator, hit on the idea of the state's constructing and operating a refinery with prison labor. There was a precedent for such a step in the fact that the state was already producing twine for the Kansas wheat crop in a successful challenge to the "twine trust." [43] Nevertheless, the new proposal gained relatively few proponents at first, though there was an "oil plank" in the Republican state platform of 1904, and the refinery idea was injected into the campaign.

Edward W. Hoch, the successful candidate for governor, adopted the refinery plan somewhat reluctantly. In his message to the new legislature on January 10, 1905, he gave the scheme his qualified blessing:

Rather, therefore, than permit the great monopolies to rob us of the benefits of the vast reservoirs of oil which have been stored by the Creator beneath our soil, I am inclined to waive my objection to the socialistic phase of this subject and recommend the establishment of an oil refinery of our own in our state for the preservation of our wealth and the protection of our people.[44]

With this encouragement a large group of the oilmen organized to promote the bill, which was a device to rally popular support for their cause rather than to supply refined oil on a large scale. Both the producers and their legislative agent, Senator W. J. Fitzpatrick, had to overcome their own reluctance to see the state enter the refining business. Nevertheless, they became convinced that the state refinery would be a "measuring stick" for the effectiveness of laws which they hoped would promote competition in the industry.

Pennsylvania experience was embodied in the proposed legislation, for it was drawn up with the aid of Marcus L. Lockwood, who had taken a hand in such matters at Harrisburg. The refinery bill, a measure declaring pipelines to be common carriers, and other bills on price discrimination and railroad rates were first introduced in the State Senate.[45] Governor Hoch revealed his position on these measures when he issued a statement, February 6, 1905, in which he suggested that a sum of twenty-five to fifty thousand dollars would be sufficient for the state refinery if the transportation legislation were passed.[46] The Senate responded, however, with an authorization of four hundred thousand dollars for the refinery and ten thousand more for housing the convict-labor involved. The bill declaring pipelines to be common carriers passed easily by a vote of 29 to 8.[47]

Meantime, Standard Oil had taken steps which divided its opponents. Work was stopped on the Prairie's pipeline and on storage tank construction in the Mid-Continent field, a boycott was placed on the transportation of Kansas oil not already contracted for, and the price of refined oil was dropped throughout the state.[48] Reactions to these moves were mixed. Disgruntled work crews added to the agitation for legislative action, and the cut in refined prices seemed to confirm the charges of Standard Oil monopoly in this area. On the other hand, frightened oil operators began to bring pressure on the Speaker of the House to have that body go slow on the oil legislation.

The Kansas Oil Producers' Association was doing its best to fan popular resentment against Standard Oil. It obtained the name of every town trustee in the state and combed the files of the state's Department of Agriculture for the names of farmers to whom it could send letters outlining the nature of Standard Oil's threat to the general welfare.[49] Although Standard Oil, through the press and through contacts with influential citizens, attempted to stem the flood of criticism, the effort was useless.

A combination of circumstances, then, insured passage of the Kansas oil legislation. The House approved the refinery bill on February 15 by a vote of 90 to 30, and the other measures were passed in rapid succession. In the space of a few months Kansas producers had obtained all the legislation that their Pennsylvania counterparts had striven for decades to obtain with indifferent results.

The refinery bill, regarded by the oilmen as a side issue, assumed the greatest importance in the eyes of the legislators and the public. The Topeka *Capital* regarded the refinery as necessary but at the same time was disturbed by its socialistic implications. The Kansas City *Journal* likened the refinery plan to an effort to bail out Lake Superior with a hand scoop. It went on:

There is just one way in which the Standard oil monopoly may be broken. That is by establishing conditions under which cut-throat practices must be abolished and fairness in transportation established all over the country. There are millions of capital ready to go into the oil business when such conditions are assured. They can be assured in only one way and that is through the intelligent action of Congress. . . . For Kansas can not have anything to say about interstate commerce.[50]

The Kansas producers, however, were determined to follow every avenue that promised relief. With the assistance of Frank Monnett, who had failed in his campaign against Standard Oil in Ohio, the Kansans instituted antitrust proceedings against the Santa Fe Railroad. The Kansas Attorney General followed with a similar suit against The Prairie Oil and Gas Company.

The attitude of other states toward Standard Oil was revealed in their reaction to the Kansas oil legislation. The Illinois legislature offered Kansas a loan of one hundred thousand dollars for the refinery project. A pipeline bill was introduced in the Texas legislature, and a movement for a state refinery was reported under way there. By March, 1905, similar measures were also said to be under consideration in four other states.[51]

The uproar in Kansas had repercussions in Washington. On February 15, 1905, Congressman Philip Campbell of Kansas introduced a resolution which directed the Secretary of Commerce and Labor to investigate the low price of crude oil, the wide margin between crude and refined oil prices, and the possibility that contracts or combinations in restraint of trade were responsible for the situation in Kansas.[52] The resolution passed the House unanimously, and

President Roosevelt enthusiastically endorsed it. According to *The Independent,* he gave his assurance that "all the power of his Administration that should be needed . . . would be used, and his aim would be to secure fair treatment for small producers, for dealers and for consumers, without doing injustice to the great company." [53] The President may already have seen in this investigation a potential weapon to be used in furthering a project close to his heart—railroad rate regulation.

The Administration and the Railroads

In December, 1904, Roosevelt had urged Congress to extend the Interstate Commerce Commission's powers. Specifically, he suggested giving the commission authority to render a decision on the reasonableness of challenged railroad rates, to decide on a reasonable rate, and to have that rate go into effect at once and remain in effect subject to judicial review. These proposals were embodied in the Esch-Townsend bill introduced early in 1905.

In view of this proposed legislation and events in Kansas there was political capital now to be made by advocating federal supervision of interstate pipelines. At least this motive may be inferred from the fact that Congressman William Randolph Hearst of New York introduced a measure on February 20, 1905, to declare pipelines common carriers and to place them under the jurisdiction of the Interstate Commerce Commission. Two days later Congressman Charles F. Scott of Kansas, for more obvious reasons, offered a similar bill.

Neither the railroad nor the pipeline bills passed Congress in 1905, but Roosevelt was determined that his proposals for railroad rate regulation should be enacted into law. Writing Joseph B. Bishop shortly after the end of the session, the President outlined his strategy for the coming Congress. "I feel that we can get the issue so clearly drawn that the Senate will have to give in," he said. "On that issue I shall have a number of my own party against me. . . . I much prefer moderate action; but the ultra-conservatives may make it necessary to adopt what is radical." [54]

The President's legislative program as laid down in his annual message to Congress on December 5, 1905, emphasized his concern with the role of transportation in the development of industrial power. He declared that "the revolution in transportation which has taken place during the last half-century has been the most important factor in the growth of the new industrial conditions." He urged that "some competent administrative body" be given power to decide whether a given rate, upon complaint brought under the existing tariff schedule, was just and reasonable and, if necessary, to establish a maximum rate in its place. The new rate, he said, ought to go into effect after a reasonable time and be subject to judicial review. He also recommended that all "private-car lines, industrial roads, refrigerator charges and the like" should be brought under the jurisdiction of the Interstate Commerce Commission, where their rates were concerned.[55] Although this statement may be interpreted to include pipelines, there was no specific mention of them in the message.

A bill embodying Roosevelt's recommendations was introduced in the House of Representatives by William P. Hepburn of Iowa on January 24, 1906. It passed that body on February 8 by an overwhelming majority, 346 to 7. In the Senate where, as Roosevelt had predicted, a large number of his own party were against him, the opposition was intense and powerful.

Nelson Aldrich, Rockefeller's son-in-law, skillfully maneuvered the Hepburn bill onto the Senate floor in the care of Benjamin R. Tillman of South Carolina, a long-time opponent of the President. Ironically, a Democrat on bad terms with Roosevelt now managed the bill which carried the administration's hopes. The situation was further complicated by the introduction on February 18, 1906, of an amendment to the bill which, by permitting judicial reinterpretation of the facts in each case, would in effect nullify the power of the Interstate Commerce Commission to decide on rate questions and to enforce its decisions. This issue of "broad" judicial review as contrasted with the "narrow" type, limited to procedural questions, became the chief battleground between Roosevelt and Aldrich supporters.[56] It was against this background that proposals for federal pipeline legislation again came before Congress.

The events of 1904–1905 indicated that major areas of privately controlled economic power were going to receive increasing political attention on the national scene. The Republican administration was already firmly committed to strengthening existing railroad legislation. Standard Oil was an obvious target in this connection both because of its past relations with the roads and because writers like Ida Tarbell had raised public antagonism toward it to a new, high level. The outcry against Standard Oil in Kansas, where remedies derived from Pennsylvania experience brought no relief, set in motion a federal investigation whose findings tied in closely with the strategy for obtaining passage of the Hepburn bill.

X

The Pipeline Amendment
to the Hepburn Act

FEDERAL pipeline legislation came out of the struggle to obtain the passage of the Hepburn bill. The Roosevelt administration deliberately inflamed public opinion against Standard Oil and the railroads, and the desired results were obtained in Congress. Protests from the petroleum industry against any step that would imperil existing relationships in production and transportation mitigated the severity of the pipeline legislation. The resulting law, however, met continuing opposition from other integrated concerns besides Standard Oil, and eventually the United States Supreme Court had to decide on its constitutionality. The issue hinged on the relationship of private enterprise to public policy in the development and operation of American petroleum pipelines.

The Lodge Amendment

Proposals to declare pipelines to be common carriers subject to the Interstate Commerce Act were renewed without fanfare in early 1906. William Randolph Hearst reintroduced his bill in the House, and Congressman Joseph L. Rhinock of Kentucky offered a similar proposal on February 22. Both measures were buried in obscurity when suddenly on March 28 Senator Henry Cabot Lodge proposed an amendment to the Hepburn bill declaring interstate pipelines to be common carriers and proposing to make them subject to the provisions of the Interstate Commerce Act.

The immediate motive for Lodge's action is not clear, but the available evidence indicates that it was closely related to the strategy for gaining acceptance for the Hepburn bill. Although Lodge had been by no means an enthusiastic supporter of the railroad measure, by the end of February it seemed that he might reluctantly go along with the President. He was certainly one of Roosevelt's intimates and was undoubtedly privy to the findings of the Bureau of Corporations, whose investigation of petroleum transportation, commenced the year before, was now fast drawing to a close. It seems logical to assume, therefore, that the Lodge amendment was introduced with the President's concurrence, if not on his initiative.

Roosevelt was clearly intending to use the Bureau's report to strengthen the case for the Hepburn bill. In late February, 1906, a joint congressional resolution had been adopted requesting the Interstate Commerce Commission to investigate and report to Congress from time to time on the relations of oil carriers and oil owners. The President did not want the new investigation to interfere with the completion of the current one, and on March 19, 1906, he advised Chairman Martin A. Knapp of the Commission not to invade the Bureau of Corporations' field until its work was completed. One month later he freed Knapp from this restriction.[1]

Senate debate on the Lodge amendment coincided with a shift in the President's position on the Hepburn bill. In late April he began preparing to abandon his effort to win Democratic support, and on May 4 it was reported that Roosevelt would support the Allison amendment, which treated the judicial review question with sufficient ambiguity to win the approval of Senator Aldrich.[2] On the same day the President submitted a synopsis of the Bureau of Corporations' report on petroleum transportation to the Senate.

The timing of these moves—the introduction of the Lodge amendment, the shift in the President's position on the Hepburn bill, and the submission of a summary of the Bureau of Corporations' report on the same day as Senate debate on the pipeline measure—seems more than coincidental. In any event the Lodge amendment fitted the pattern of the President's strategy perfectly, though there is no

way of determining to what extent—if any—Roosevelt planned it
that way.

The report, summed up in Commissioner James R. Garfield's letter
of submittal, proved to be a sensation. Its main theme was that
Standard Oil had been profiting by secret rates granted by the railroads, but it also called attention to Standard Oil's pipeline power
in this and other connections. Garfield declared that pipelines enabled the oil combination to do its refining in advantageous locations
which high railroad rates and pipeline charges barred to competitors. "The development of the pipe-line system by the Standard Oil
Company was the result of special agreements with railroad companies," he said.[3]

The full report, submitted to Congress on May 17, amplified these
charges. "The principal pipe-line systems, those of the Standard Oil
Company, while thus able to transport oil at figures which would be
ruinous to railroads, nevertheless demand practically the same
charge as the railroad rate from any prospective shipper," the report
stated. "The Standard Oil Company's pipe lines in the East are theoretically common carriers," it continued, "but practically, as a result
of the exorbitant pipage charge and of other causes as well, they are
not available to shippers generally. . . ."[4] The report charged that
the operation of Standard Oil refineries at the seaboard and at
Whiting, Indiana, was made possible by pipelines which carried at
"much less than the cost of rail transportation which the competitors
have for the most part to pay in order to reach the same points."[5]

Both the synopsis and the full report gave their main emphasis to
the charge that Standard Oil had benefited by alleged railroad favoritism. Roosevelt stressed this point in his message of May 4, but
he did not mention pipelines. He did say that "the report is of capital importance in view of the effort now being made to secure such
enlargement of the powers of the Interstate Commerce Commission
as will confer upon the Commission power in some measure ade-
quately to meet the clearly demonstrated needs of the situation."[6]
Whether this statement was intended to cover pipelines or not, the
presidential message and Garfield's abbreviated report clearly eased
the way for adoption of the Lodge amendment.

With the scene so well prepared, Senate consideration of the pipeline legislation was perfunctory. Senator Joseph B. Foraker of Ohio agreed that it was proper to regulate common carriers in interstate commerce. He argued, however, that private pipelines crossing state boundaries should be exempted from regulation by limiting the act's application to those carrying "for the public." [7] Senator Porter J. McCumber of North Dakota took a similar position. If this view had prevailed, the legislation would have scarcely touched Standard Oil's pipeline power. Lodge rejected Foraker's proposal, and the Ohio Senator did not press the matter.

Senators William P. Frye of Maine and Nathan B. Scott of West Virginia declared that they had received protests against the amendment from independent producers. Lodge brushed these objections aside. "The small well owner, to whom there have been pathetic references this morning, has not as yet made his objections known to me," Lodge said. "I heard within twenty-four hours after the introduction of my first amendment, on May [sic] 28, from the Standard Oil Company." He told the Senate that a representative of Standard Oil had protested that the proposed amendment was useless and unjust. On the other hand, he declared that he had received "a great many" letters from independent producers and refiners endorsing the legislation. He made it clear that he had no intention of forcing a reduction in pipeline rates but rather wanted to provide a jurisdiction before which rate complaints could be heard.[8]

The assertion that Pure Oil followed the same pipeline practices as Standard Oil appeared in the course of Lodge's speech. He produced a letter from Hugh King of the Columbia Oil Company, who complained that neither Standard Oil nor Pure Oil would deliver his oil and that he had to sell the oil to them at their own price. King stated that although the National Transit Company was nominally a common carrier, it did not act as such because its initial or receiving lines were private.[9] As previously described, Pure Oil similarly maintained that its Producers' and Refiners' Pipe Line was not a common carrier and therefore refused to make deliveries to the United States Pipe Line for the Columbia Oil company.[10] King had helped promote the latter pipeline and was still a director of the concern; yet his interest no longer seemed to coincide with Pure Oil's any more than with Standard Oil's.

Lodge's personal motive in offering the pipeline amendment may

have appeared in his comment that oil transported partly by pipeline and partly by water or partly by rail should be subject to the
Interstate Commerce Act.[11] Standard Oil utilized all three methods
of transportation in serving the New England market, shipping
crude by pipeline to New Jersey, thence by water to various ports,
where it was distributed by rail. According to the Bureau of Corporations, the advantages inherent in this route were increased by
the refusal of several New England railroads to name through rates
for shippers reaching some points of the territory entirely by rail.[12]
As a result, Standard Oil allegedly enjoyed a favored position in the
northeast. Lodge obviously had this point in mind when he introduced his amendment. Roosevelt also had mentioned it in his message.

Several changes in the Lodge measure were made in the Senate.
Calling attention to the fact that the Union Oil Company of California, a Standard Oil rival, had been granted a revocable license
to lay a pipeline across government land in Panama, Senator John T.
Morgan of Alabama asked that the act be extended to cover such
areas. His suggestion was accepted. Senator Thomas H. Carter of
Montana, fearing that the bill might be applicable to irrigation,
wanted pipelines carrying water specifically exempted. Lodge was
quite agreeable. "All I want to get at is the transportation of oil, for
that is where the great abuse is," he said.[13] Foraker and Scott both
wanted natural gas pipelines of all kinds exempted from the legislation. Senator Albert J. Beveridge of Indiana was opposed to this
proposal, and a major part of the debate revolved about this point.
The objection, however, was not too strenuous, and the amended
Lodge measure passed the Senate by a vote of 75 to 0, with fourteen
senators not voting.[14]

Public Reaction to the Garfield Report

Judging by the comments of the eastern press, Roosevelt's submission of the Garfield report at a crucial time in the progress of the
Hepburn bill was regarded as a master stroke. The *New York
Tribune*, which had been far from unfriendly to Standard Oil, observed that the transactions reported by Garfield seemed to place
"the company in the unenviable attitude of profiting by practices
which Congress had condemned and sought to put an end to." [15] The

New York *Sun* was more cautious and praised the President's message only as it indicated a determination to come to grips with the "most powerful corporation in the United States." [16] The *Pittsburgh Daily Dispatch* praised the President's timing in submitting his message and Garfield's report. "The President's moves," the paper commented editorially, "while sometimes questionable in judgment, have always the merit of hitting something. But he has produced none that hit the mark more notably nor at such an effective moment as this one." [17] The *Boston Evening Transcript* quoted James W. Lee of the Pure Oil Company as saying: "For fifteen years we have been contending for a square deal, and from the President's message it looks as if our labors were to be rewarded at last." The *Transcript* itself declared:

The President's message on the Standard Oil monopoly is mainly significant because of its high source. . . . It is one thing, however, to ignore Ida Tarbell. It is not so easy to ignore the chief magistrate of the United States when he brings against this business an indictment so sharp and direct as that contained in this message which interests the people of the country as few of its predecessors have done.[18]

The Washington *Evening Star* added its voice to this chorus, asserting: "The Rockefeller crowd are not to be trusted when it comes to promises, or matters of fair play, but must be held to the strictest accountability by statutes of the most comprehensive and exact terms." [19]

Comment on the pipeline proposal was limited. The New York *World* quoted Ida Tarbell as saying: "It will be observed that nothing is given out for publication on the pipe line question, which is of great importance, greater in fact, than the rebate and transit side of the case." [20] The Philadelphia *Press* endorsed the Lodge amendment, declaring:

If the Standard Oil has built pipe lines, these must be run as common carriers. They must not be used to gain advantages. Hitherto, with these lines and two of its members on the New York, New Haven and Hartford directory, it was easy to use the pipe lines to put on pressure and prevent prorating. The public will not accept this. It is not just.[21]

The paper predicted that public indignation at railroad abuses revealed in the Garfield report would force passage of the Hepburn bill.

Standard Oil did what it could to stem this tidal wave of criticism. Henry H. Rogers and John D. Archbold issued a statement on May 4 in which they denied charges that Standard Oil had acted illegally or that its pipeline system was the result of special arrangements with the railroads. "What this can mean," they said, "is beyond our comprehension."

In defense of their pipeline operations the Standard Oil officials said: "At enormous cost and in the face of steadfast railway opposition, at an early date the Standard Oil Company adopted the pipe line method for handling crude petroleum." [22] The *Pittsburgh Daily Dispatch*, which had long criticized Standard Oil's pipelines, commented acidly on this part of the statement, suggesting: "To make it state the case correctly it should read that the extension of the pipeline system by the rivals of the Standard was in the face of violent hostility on the part of the railroads, which ceased when the Standard got control of the lines." [23]

Standard Oil spokesmen clearly felt that Garfield's charges were unfair. Answering the assertion that Standard Oil by means of its pipelines was able to obtain low intrastate railroad rates, thus avoiding the letter of the law, they pointed out: "To say that a man in Ohio who had never expended a dollar for a pipe line to Whiting should be able to transport his oil to an inland town in Illinois over an all-rail line at the same rates that we enjoyed by reason of our pipe lines must appear absurd to any one." [24] But the climate of public opinion was such that these arguments fell on deaf ears.

Lewis Emery, Jr., viewed the discomfiture of his adversaries with satisfaction. He had just been in to see the President with Commissioner Garfield when he told a reporter: "There is a tremendously strong feeling in Washington on the subject of the rate bill. The air is charged with anti-trust and anti-corporation sentiment. It is the one theme of conversation in every circle." He also said that he had been assured by Congressman William Sulzer of New York that the Lodge amendment would have no difficulty in passing the House.[25]

Despite a growing interest in Standard Oil's pipelines, the combination's relations with the railroads continued to receive the main focus of the public's and the government's attention. On May 11 the Interstate Commerce Commission opened new hearings on the subject. A by-product of the investigation was information on Standard Oil's use of railroad rights of way for its pipelines.[26] One view might have been found in the public statement of John B. Thayer, fourth vice-president of the Pennsylvania Railroad, denying Garfield's charges of favoritism to the oil concern. Thayer termed the Commissioner's report on this subject an "inexcusable and outrageous perversion of the facts." However, he underlined the potency of the pipeline weapon when he admitted that a special rate of nine cents a barrel had been in effect between Olean and Rochester, New York, as the result of agreements originally made in 1888 to retain traffic which otherwise would have gone to the pipelines.[27] As anyone familiar with Standard Oil's relations with the railroads knew, co-operation between the two interests, even to the extent of providing railroad rights of way for pipelines, had proved more profitable to the railroads than opposition.

On May 16, Charles M. Pratt, secretary of Standard Oil, issued to the company's stockholders a defense against Garfield's assertions. The statement admitted that some explanations had to be made but maintained that nothing illegal or reprehensible had been done. Pratt denied that Standard Oil was a monopoly, stated that it had a "very moderate percentage" of crude oil production and pointed out that there were 125 independent refineries and that 60 per cent of Standard's oil was exported to fight for a place in competitive world markets. He noted that the Commissioner had not shown a single clear-cut instance of Standard Oil's receiving a rebate prohibited by the Interstate Commerce Act.[28] On the following day, however, Garfield replied by reiterating several statements in his report, which was submitted to Congress in full on the same date.

Pipelines and the Commodities Clause

So little attention was paid by the national legislators to the implications of pipeline legislation that it became embarrassingly entangled with a controversial railroad measure. On May 7, Senator Stephen B. Elkins offered an amendment to the Hepburn bill aimed at preventing railroads from transporting commodities that they produced. The wording of this so-called "commodities clause" was such that it would apply to pipelines in the event that they were declared to be common carriers. The Philadelphia *Press* called the Elkins proposal a "staggering blow" to Standard Oil, which, the paper suggested, would have to choose between producing oil and operating pipelines—in addition to refining—if both the Lodge and Elkins amendments were adopted.[29] The full significance of this possibility, however, had seemingly not been recognized in Congress when the Hepburn bill was sent to the conference committee at the end of May.[30]

On May 29, Lodge informed Roosevelt that he had learned from Tillman that the House conferees were preparing to fight the pipeline amendment and Elkins' prohibition on railroads owning coal lands whose product they transported. Lodge declared that they were "two of the best things" in the bill and that to have them eliminated would be "to have Standard Oil flung at us on Every Stump." He therefore suggested that the President express his support for these measures to Hepburn and Sherman in the House and to Elkins or Cullom in the Senate.[31] Roosevelt complied by writing Hepburn the same day: "I do hope you can keep in the Standard Oil and railroad coal-ownership propositions that were put on in the Senate. It seems to me very important from every standpoint that this should be done. I think it is not only important from the standpoint of decency, but that it is important from the standpoint of political expediency." [32] A copy of this note was sent to Lodge, who was given permission to show it to Cullom and Elkins.

The application of the commodities clause to pipelines was definite in the first conference committee report of June 2. The impact of the requirement that no interstate oil pipeline transport its own products to market had serious implications for the petroleum industry. According to the later recollections of Congressman Joseph Sibley, a former official of the Standard-affiliated Galena Signal Oil Company, Standard Oil had about 90,000,000 barrels of oil in storage at that time. He stated that if the combination had become subject to such a provision it would have had to suspend purchases until it got rid of the stored oil. This development would have dealt a harsh blow to producers, who, he said, sent him four to six hundred telegrams protesting the measure.[33] Nevertheless, the provision was unchanged when the bill was returned to the conference committee.

By mid-June the application of the commodities clause to pipelines was receiving more critical attention in Congress, though the pressures for action against Standard Oil, however drastic, were still strong. In the second conference committee, Senator Cullom was beginning to waiver on requiring the separation of oil production and transportation, but reportedly he feared that a change in his position might be attributed to pressure from Standard Oil.[34] A group led by Congressmen James F. Burke and John Dalzell, both of Pittsburgh, were said to be working to quash the entire pipeline section.

Meanwhile, the administration continued its effort to influence public and congressional opinion on Standard Oil to insure passage of the Hepburn bill. On June 22 it was announced that action was being taken against Standard Oil for violating the Elkins Act and also, possibly, the Sherman Act. According to a report from Washington printed in the *Pittsburgh Daily Dispatch,* this was a calculated move by the President to offset the activities of Burke and Dalzell, whom he believed were actually working for Standard Oil.[35]

The fact remained, however, that independent producers had poured in protests against subjecting pipelines to the commodities clause. The President's implied support of this proposal was accordingly condemned by the *Dispatch* writer. "By giving notice that he will not stand for an elimination of pipe lines from the bill," the newspaperman wrote, "it is admitted that he will force Congress to slap the Standard on the wrist while it hits the independents over the head with a sledge hammer." [36]

The conference committee evidently saw merit in the objections to including pipelines under the commodities clause, and its second report, which reached the Senate floor on June 25, recommended changing this provision. Despite his earlier reluctance to approve this step, Cullom signed the report. Tillman, believing the new version was a concession to Standard Oil, did not sign. In fact, he had informed Lodge of the reversal in Cullom's position on this question, and the Massachusetts Senator relayed this news to Roosevelt on June 22. While Lodge stated that he was not sure that Tillman was correct in his view that the change would insure Standard Oil's monopoly, he did observe: "I am certain that it will be a great help to Standard Oil to make the change." [37] Despite the interpretation put on the move to prosecute Standard Oil, as reported in the *Pittsburgh Daily Dispatch,* the President apparently took no further action directly to influence the conference committee's recommendations on pipelines.

The eastern press generally supported the revised pipeline legislation. The New York *Sun* declared that the telegrams from Ohio, Illinois, Kansas, West Virginia, Texas, and other oil-producing regions were genuine expressions of the independent producers' alarm. The paper praised Cullom's stand and observed: "The truth is that in adopting the Lodge amendment the Senate did not regard the consequences to the independent oil men, which would have amounted practically to confiscation. It was considered a good amendment because it smashed the octopus between the eyes—a temper that may be very dangerous to humble vested interests, as the result shows." [38] The Philadelphia *Press* took a similar position. It declared: "But simply because the Standard Oil will profit is no good reason against sound legislation. A railroad can carry anything. A pipe line can carry only oil. No capital except capital in oil will build a pipe line. In the nature of things, the oil well and the pipe line cannot be separated." [39]

Tillman felt very differently on this question. In the Senate debate on the latest conference committee report, the South Carolinian declared: "I shall feel that every man who votes that way will be branded on his forehead with the letters 'S. O.' in the estimation of the people of this country." [40] He questioned the genuineness of the producers' complaints, and Lodge backed him on this score.

Senator Joseph W. Bailey did not question the genuine character of the protests but pointed out that they were probably inspired by the producers' dependence on Standard Oil for the purchase of their oil. He wryly noted that while all the senators appeared to favor the separation of transportation and production of oil, each wanted exceptions to cover the interests of his own constituents.[41]

Senator Cullom offered a case in point. He told the Senate that he had gone along with Tillman on pipeline matters until the Elkins amendment came up. He stated that in the first conference "it was not discussed except to agree generally that whatever would curb the Standard Oil Company we ought to be for." He had suddenly discovered, however, that there was oil production in his state and that the producers there opposed the measure. He concluded, therefore, "I am not willing to vote for an amendment simply for the purpose of punishing the Standard Oil Company if it is going to punish the common people of my own State and other States surrounding much more than it will the Standard Oil Company." [42]

On the following day, June 26, Tillman with the support of Bailey, again led the fight against the committee's report on the commodities clause. Senators Elkins and Scott of West Virginia and Chester I. Long of Kansas led the defense.

Although Elkins had introduced the amendment in question and was a member of the conference committee, he apparently had not anticipated the reaction that it brought from the petroleum industry. He now vigorously attempted to rectify his mistake. He pointed out that West Virginia had brought pipeline rates and practices under regulation in 1879 but that the legislation did not apply to Standard Oil, which carried the bulk of the oil in his state, because it had not used the right of eminent domain and also purchased the oil before transporting it. He stated, however, that he had heard no complaints against the pipelines from producers or shippers. He argued that the inclusion of the lines in the commodities clause would deny independent operators "the right" to transport their own products and that it would "work great injustice, destroy great industries." Elkins maintained that while the measure would hurt independent producers, Standard Oil could negate its effectiveness by organizing both producing and transportation companies. "What we wish to do," he said, "is to improve conditions, stop abuses, prevent monopolies, but not to injure any interest doing business in the country." [43]

Long of Kansas took a similar position. He declared that his state had made pipelines common carriers but that the step had not provided an effective answer to the producers' problems since the pipelines were "not in fact common carriers." "Pipe lines," Long explained, "are not constructed for the purpose of conveying oil for hire, but for the purpose of reaching the field, getting the product, and transporting it to the refinery." Furthermore, the Kansan pointed out,

The Kansas legislature never thought, while making pipe lines common carriers, to prohibit them from transporting their own products through their own pipes, for the legislature was in direct touch with the oil producers—with people who understood the business, and anyone familiar with the production or distribution of oil knows that a provision like this, or like these two provisions when taken together, would absolutely destroy and ruin the oil industry in all the States where it would be operative.

Finally, he maintained that a movement in Kansas to construct a pipeline to the Gulf of Mexico would be wrecked if the commodities clause were applied to such enterprises.[44]

Tillman scoffed at these arguments. He observed that if the proposed Kansas-Gulf pipeline carried only oil that it owned, the producers would remain in the same relation to it as they were to Standard Oil.

Long replied that there was nothing wrong with the existing situation. He cited the example of an independent pipeline from Bartlesville, Indian Territory, to Cherryvale, Kansas, operated in the same manner as Standard Oil's lines, purchasing the oil that it ran. He maintained:

We want an opportunity for more independent refineries and more independent pipe lines to be constructed, and this legislation, which is directed specially against the Standard Oil Company, will go wide of the mark and not injure it, but it will injure the development of the oil industry and prevent the construction of independent refineries and independent pipe lines in the midcontinent field.[45]

The exact meaning of the Lodge amendment was still in question. Long's argument rested implicitly on the assumption that the measure made all interstate oil pipelines common carriers. If this were not the case, the commodities clause would not apply to lines like Standard Oil's which carried only their own oil. Hence his fears would have been groundless. On the other hand, if the Lodge proposal did not touch lines that carried their own oil, it would have been meaningless as far as curbing Standard Oil was concerned.

In the excitement caused by the Garfield report, the Senate debate of May 4 had paid little attention to such questions. On May 17 there had been further discussion of whether the amendment applied to all interstate oil pipelines, and Lodge had reiterated that such was his intention. Now the issue arose again. Senator Alexander S. Clay of Georgia declared that the Lodge amendment would not be applicable to private pipelines carrying their own oil. Long replied that the amendment, as presented by Lodge, definitely applied to all interstate oil pipelines. Bailey, however, challenged this interpretation, declaring that pipelines could not be declared common carriers unless they carried for hire or had used the right of eminent domain. Clapp also upheld this view.[46]

Long maintained that as things stood, the application of the amendment was a matter for the courts to decide. Bailey's colleague from Texas, Charles A. Culberson, took Long's side. When the conference report was returned to committee on June 26 without having had pipelines restored to the commodities clause, the New York *Sun* attributed this fact to the efforts of these two men.

Discussion of the pipeline measures in the House was cursory. On June 26, Joseph Rhinock, who had introduced a bill similar to Lodge's at the beginning of the session, spoke on behalf of the Senator's measure. He received applause when he declared: "I am decidedly in favor of this pipe-line legislation, as are the vast majority of the people of my State and of the country." [47] Two days later there was very limited debate on the final conference report, and only Oscar W. Gillespie of Texas spoke even briefly in favor of retaining pipelines under the commodities clause.[48]

The next day, June 29, the third conference report came before the Senate. The other conferees having insisted on the elimination of pipelines from the commodities clause, Tillman had signed the report under protest. He explained to the Senate that he had no alternative but to sign on the penalty of losing the entire bill. He insisted, however, on restating his position.

The Democrat was bitter over his desertion by the President, which, he said, had taken place under cover of the furor raised by the Garfield report. In an astonishing collection of mixed metaphors he exclaimed:

The big stick and the pitchfork, which had been in alliance, or at least fighting together, then separated. The pitchfork, while on duty on the firing line, to use a military phrase, looking around for the ally, saw the tail of his coat hustling to the rear, and, to use a baseball phrase, the last seen of him he was sliding towards the Allison base, trying like football players, to reach the home base.[49]

Tillman intimated that Roosevelt had compromised with Standard Oil on pipeline legislation. He declared: "But it is a little remarkable that just when he might do something toward thwarting the policy of this gigantic monopoly to control the entire oil industry of the United States . . . he is as mum as a mouse."[50] The disgruntled Senator reported that he had heard that Frank Monnett was about to be discharged by the Interstate Commerce Commission, and he suggested that if the rumor were true, Standard Oil might be responsible for such a development. This charge was vigorously challenged, and Elkins came to the President's defense. The West Virginia Senator declared that "his [Roosevelt's] action, his bold and courageous course in behalf of the people, speaks trumpet-tongued for him. The people are behind the President." He denied Tillman's right to interpret Roosevelt's stand on pipeline legislation when the chief executive had not spoken his mind on it.[51]

Elkins re-emphasized the opposition of the petroleum industry to the application of the commodities clause to pipelines. He introduced a protest by the Eastern Oil Men's Association, backed by the signatures of a number of producers, whose names were headed by that of Judge Nathan Goss, one-time Attorney General of West Virginia. Tillman asked pointedly whether these men were engaged in interstate pipeline operations. If they were not, he pointed out, their protests should not be considered pertinent evidence. Elkins avoided a direct answer and replied: "I submit to the Senator himself, to the Senate, and to the country that these people engaged in this great industry know more about this subject and are better able to speak for themselves than is the Senator from South Carolina to speak for them."[52]

By now the final outcome of the pipeline legislation was no longer in doubt, but several senators made brief speeches for the record. Bailey admitted that he knew little about pipelines, but he declared that he saw merit in making them common carriers and thought that they should also be subject to the commodities clause.[53] Long of Kansas completed his contributions to the pipeline debate by introducing a telegram denouncing the report presented by Senator Moses Clapp of Minnesota that Standard Oil had sponsored the protests from the Mid-Continent field. Robert M. La Follette made a final plea for applying the commodities clause to pipelines and argued that no dire consequences would follow since it was not in the power of Congress to make common carriers out of companies that were not already in that category.[54]

These arguments were rear-guard actions. In effect, the decision had been made on June 26 that pipelines should be declared common carriers but that they were not to be forbidden to carry oil which they owned. No one, not even Tillman, was going to challenge this decision with the fate of the entire Hepburn bill hanging in the balance. The third conference report had already been approved by the House. It was now accepted by the Senate.

With the President's signature that evening, June 29, the Hepburn bill became law. As it related to pipelines the statute read:

That the provisions of this Act shall apply to any corporation or any person or persons engaged in the transportation of oil or other commodity, except water and except natural or artificial gas, by means of pipe lines, or partly by pipe lines and partly by railroad, or partly by pipe lines and partly by water, who shall be considered and held to be common carriers within the meaning of this Act . . . from one State or Territory of the United States, or the District of Columbia, to any other State or Territory of the United States, or the District of Columbia, or from one place in a Territory to another place in the same Territory.[55]

Protests from the petroleum industry had mitigated the severity of federal pipeline legislation, but the question still remained as to what the statute in its final form actually meant. Reporting the passage of the Hepburn bill, the *New York Tribune*'s correspondent declared that "most Senators believed that all which they desired was accomplished by placing all pipe lines under the supervision of the Interstate Commerce Commission."[56] Although Lodge stated specifically on May 4 that he intended his amendment to cover all interstate oil pipelines and reiterated this point subsequently, on the last day of the debate even La Follette indicated that such was not his understanding. Nevertheless, no action was taken to qualify the wording of the amendment to make it clear that it did not apply to lines carrying only oil that they owned.

Most senators, prodded by the President's skillful manipulation of public opinion, certainly intended to curb Standard Oil's pipeline power. Some were not sure of how far they should go in this direction. In response to complaints by members of the petroleum industry, Elkins, Long, and Cullom all shifted ground on the application of the commodities clause to pipelines. Most senators knew little about the complexities of the pipeline business, and in view of the oilmen's complaints and the absence of counter-pressures from the White House or public opinion, they acquiesced in the change demanded by the industry. Nevertheless, it must be concluded that most of the national legislators believed that the Lodge amendment would subject Standard Oil's pipelines to some measure of effective public control.

The Pipeline Amendment in Perspective

The available evidence indicates that the pipeline amendment to the Hepburn Act was primarily a stratagem for furthering the progress of the railroad measure. Standard Oil had been made a symbol of the results of alleged railroad abuses, and the pipeline proposal seems to have been an incidental step aimed at further stressing the combination's iniquities and the need for combating them with every means available. Lodge made no secret of his aim. On May 17 he told the Senate: "My object, I state frankly, in this amendment is to bring the pipelines of the Standard Oil Company within the jurisdiction of the Interstate Commerce Commission." [57] As protests from the industry revealed, however, other oil concerns were as opposed to the bill as was Standard Oil.

Government agencies regarded the pipelines of organizations outside Standard Oil as comparatively unimportant. The Interstate Commerce Commission, reporting to Congress in January, 1907, declared: "The possession of these pipe lines enables the Standard to absolutely control the price of crude petroleum and to determine, therefore, the price which its competitors in a given locality should pay." [58] In the conclusion of this report, the agency said: "More than anything else the pipe line has contributed to the monopoly of the Standard Oil Company, and the supremacy of that company must continue until its rivals enjoy the same facilities of transportation by this means." [59] A few months later the Bureau of Corporations pointed anew to Standard Oil's pipelines as a source of the combination's alleged monopoly power. This time the charges were contained in an extensive report on the petroleum industry with particular emphasis on Standard Oil's position in it. In many respects this report, based largely on private inquiries, seemed to substantiate the findings of the Interstate Commerce Commission, which had examined witnesses under oath and in the presence of counsel.[60]

There was certainly no question about the fact that Standard Oil had resolved to contest the application of the Hepburn Act to its pipelines. Apparently in anticipation of the federal pipeline legislation, Standard Oil prepared in late 1905 to divest its Appalachian trunk lines of the appearance of being interstate common carriers. In July, 1906, just before the Hepburn Act became effective, the New Jersey and Maryland properties of the National Transit and New York Transit were transferred to the Standard Oil Company (New Jersey). According to the Interstate Commerce Commission, this action effectively barred to other refiners the seaboard delivery of crude via Standard Oil's lines, for neither New Jersey nor Maryland had declared pipelines to be common carriers. Thus, although in New York and Pennsylvania the trunk lines held themselves out to be common carriers, outside shippers would have to take delivery of their oil at isolated locations on the borders of New Jersey and Maryland and then find a way to move it to its destination.[61] Subsequently a similar technique was applied to oil shipments via Standard Oil pipelines from Oklahoma to Louisiana. At each state line title to the oil was transferred, simultaneously with the flow of the oil itself, from one Standard-affiliated company to another.[62]

The situation was not as clear-cut as the commission maintained. It was true that in the past Standard Oil had stated that its pipelines in the East were common carriers.[63] National Transit and New York Transit both had charters which carried common carrier status with them.[64] Furthermore, in Pennsylvania pipelines had been held to be common carriers by judicial decision, and West Virginia in 1879 and New York in 1890 had enacted common carrier pipeline laws.[65] In the latter two states, however, there does not seem to have been any major controversy over the performance of common carrier functions by Standard Oil pipelines, and in Pennsylvania the issue had long since subsided. If, as the Commerce Court later declared, the Maryland and New Jersey lines had transported oil only for the parent organization,[66] Standard Oil's seaboard trunk lines may have been common carriers mainly in theory and, at least for a number of years, had not carried oil to tidewater for other shippers. The actions of 1906, in this light, seem to represent an effort to confirm legally a situation which had long existed.

In the newer oil fields Standard Oil pipelines had never held themselves out to be common carriers, and they required the purchase of oil as a condition of moving it. Although Kansas had declared pipelines to be common carriers in 1905, The Prairie Oil and Gas Company had been incorporated before that time, and the law was not enforced against it.[67] On these grounds, then, Standard Oil felt entitled to resist the application of the Hepburn Act to the lines of the Standard Oil Company (New Jersey), The Prairie Oil and Gas Company, the Oklahoma Pipe Line Company, The Ohio Oil Company, and the Standard Oil Company of Louisiana.

Rivals of the combination likewise rejected the application of the law to them. Among those who declined to file tariffs in compliance with the law were the Gulf Pipe Line Company, the Emery Pipe Line, the Producers' and Refiners' Oil Company, Limited, the United States Pipe Line Company, the Pure Oil Company, the Pure Oil Pipe Line Company, the Uncle Sam Oil Company, the Uncle Sam Oil Company of Kansas, and the Tide-Water Pipe Company, Limited.

In June, 1911, the Interstate Commerce Commission instituted proceedings to determine what action might be necessary and appropriate to enforce the Hepburn Act against the companies which denied its application to them. The commission concluded in 1912 that the act applied to all interstate oil pipelines, that segmentation of pipeline operations by interruptions at state lines did not divest the traffic of an interstate character, that the validity of state common carrier laws had no bearing on the case, that use of the right of way of railroads did not impose common carrier status on pipelines any more than the fact that they crossed public highways, and that the facts showed that Standard Oil's actions of 1906 in Maryland and New Jersey constituted "an arrangement whereby a common carrier divested itself of its terminals and turned them over to its principal patron for that patron's sole use."[68] The commission, therefore, ordered the offending companies to file tariffs by September 1, 1912, a deadline which was subsequently extended.

Four Standard Oil companies, the Tide-Water, and the Uncle

Sam Oil Company appealed the decision and brought suit to annul the commission's order. The petitioners maintained that the 1906 act applied only to those lines which were common carriers at the time that it was adopted, or had been subsequently declared so by judicial decision, or had voluntarily adopted that status. They denied that these conditions applied to their companies. They argued that if the law was taken literally it would violate the due process clause of the Fifth Amendment.[69]

The Assistant Attorney General, on the other hand, declared that the act was a valid exercise of the interstate commerce power directed against monopoly. "It does not prohibit the private operation of these pipe lines because they *are* monopolies," he said, "but because such private ownership has proved itself to be the *source* of monopolies, because it contains an *inevitable tendency* toward monopoly." [70] The government's victory over Standard Oil in antitrust proceedings under the Sherman Act was undoubtedly fresh in this official's mind.

The Commerce Court, speaking through Presiding Judge Martin Knapp, whose 1907 report as Chairman of the Interstate Commerce Commission had helped to provide the basis for the government charges, rejected the government's contentions. Although the court agreed with the Interstate Commerce Commission that the act embraced all interstate oil pipelines, it declared that in attempting "by an act of legislation to transmute the agencies of private business into instrumentalities of public service," Congress had violated the Fifth Amendment.[71] The court dealt harshly with the government's monopoly argument, of which it said:

The discussions in the Senate and in the report of the Commissioner [of Corporations] deal with the conditions of unified ownership or control by the Standard Oil Company of a great portion of the pipe lines of the country, including the common carrier pipe lines, and the resulting advantage and power of that company, which were alleged to constitute an unlawful monopoly. But this comes quite short of disclosing how or why a private pipe line used solely in its owner's private business becomes of necessity, or can become while so employed, a facility which he may be forbidden to use, or the use of which he may be compelled to give to the public, because it is claimed to be a monopoly or to have a monopolistic tendency.[72]

The court made several other pertinent observations. With reference to the argument that utilization of a railroad right of way obtained by the exercise of the right of eminent domain was a justification for imposing common carrier status on pipelines, the decision said: "Whether or not a given pipe line company is a common carrier depends upon the business in which it engages and for which its pipe lines were provided, and not upon the character of the route upon which those lines are located." [73] It denied the relevancy to the case of the motive in the transfer of the New York Transit and National Transit lines in New Jersey and Maryland to the Standard Oil Company (New Jersey). It thereupon ordered a preliminary injunction issued in each case.

Justice Julian W. Mack dissented from these findings. He pointed out that a presumption of the constitutionality of legislation was proper unless a reasonable doubt about it existed. He maintained that, given the conditions in the petroleum industry, the act was within the realm of federal authority and was not arbitrary, unreasonable, nor beyond the necessities of the case. "The remedy prescribed by this amendment is far less drastic than that adopted to abate other restraints on interstate commerce," the justice said. [74]

The question of the constitutionality of the pipeline amendment came before the Supreme Court of the United States in its October Term, 1913. Again the pipelines' attorneys maintained that the act did not apply to private lines. Their argument is best summed up in these words:

As construed by the Government, the act makes common carriers of persons and corporations owning and operating private pipe lines used solely for the purpose of transporting the oil of the owners in the conduct of their private business, even though such owners have never held themselves out as common carriers, have never exercised or possessed and do not now possess any right of eminent domain, and derive no powers from state laws under which common carrier corporations are organized. It follows that the act deprives such persons and corporations of their property without due process of law, and takes it for public use without just compensation. [75]

Furthermore, they maintained that there was nothing inherent in the operation of private pipelines that caused a tendency toward monopoly and that the government had failed to substantiate the charge.

The government attorneys declared that the act was a reasonable means to the accomplishment of a legitimate end. Their brief stated: "The object of the pipe line amendment, to regulate interstate commerce in oil by protecting well owners and independent refiners from duress by pipe line owners is one for which the authority of Congress may properly be exercised." [76] Whether private pipelines might be entirely prohibited "in order to give the public adequate protection is a matter of legislative discretion," the government claimed. Denying that the act amounted to a confiscation of private property, the government brief maintained: "The exclusive element is the monopoly element. No compensation need be given for that." [77] It charged that the businesses of the appellees were "quasi-public" in nature and that they provided public markets for oil. The brief stated: "Each appellee is engaged in buying crude oil in the fields of production; they have their business headquarters where oil is bought from producers; the oil is inspected, graded and gauged for sale, by the agents of the appellees and other pipe lines." [78]

Relying almost exclusively on the "public market" argument, the Supreme Court decided for the government. It was held that the pipeline statute did not deprive the owners of interstate pipelines of their property without due process of law, that interstate transportation of oil purchased from producers by pipeline owners was interstate commerce and under the control of Congress, and that while the act did not require such owners to continue in operation "it does require them not to continue to transport oil for others or purchased by themselves except as common carriers." [79] Speaking for the majority, Justice Holmes said: "It not only would be a sacrifice of fact to form, but would empty the act if the carriage to the seaboard of nearly all the oil east of California, were held not to be transportation within its meaning, because by the exercise of their power the carriers imposed as a condition to the carriage a sale to themselves." He concluded that the amendment's "evident purpose was to bring within its scope pipe lines that although not technically common carriers yet were carrying all oil offered, if only the offerers would sell at their price." [80]

One exception was made to this interpretation of the law. The court ruled that the Uncle Sam Oil Company, which supplied its refinery in Kansas with oil transported by pipeline from its own wells in Oklahoma, was not subject to the act. Chief Justice White, in a concurring opinion, pointed out that the distinguishing fact here was that the company purchased no oil.[81] Justice McKenna, in a lone dissent, failed to see the distinction and maintained that the Uncle Sam ruling should have been applied to the other appellees.

McKenna was distressed by the implications of the verdict, for he saw in it a threat to property rights. "The employment of one's wealth to construct or purchase facilities for one's business greater than others possess," he said, "constitutes no monopoly that does not appertain to all property." He pointed out:

There were no prior or present rights in other owners of oil wells to the use of the lines of the appellee companies. They contributed nothing to the construction of the lines and their exclusion from their use is the exclusion resulting from the separate ownership of property as distinguished from rights of community ownership.[82]

Actually, however, the 1914 decision did little to change the mode of pipeline operation. The Federal Trade Commission, for example, found in 1916 that even though the pipelines of the Gulf and Texas companies, which were competitors of Standard Oil, filed tariffs, they apparently did no interstate common carrier business.[83] Fifteen years later a close student of the Interstate Commerce Commission found that "little occasion has arisen for regulating the rates and practices of these [pipeline] carriers, either on complaint or on the Commission's own motion." [84] As late as 1940 the commission itself declared:

Although the respondent pipe lines [the most important east of California] hold themselves out in their tariffs to carry oil for all, and although in the eyes of the law they are common carriers, the record indicates that their facilities are relatively infrequently used by other than the large oil refineries or those with whom they are affiliated.[85]

The pipeline amendment to the Hepburn Act was clearly directed against Standard Oil and was adopted on that basis, though the move fitted in closely with the strategy to obtain railroad rate regulation. Although Standard Oil was the immediate object of the

pipeline legislation, other concerns, which had patterned their operations on those of the combination, opposed the law just as vigorously as Standard Oil itself.

Against the background of pipeline development, the issue was a
familiar one. Since the early days in the Pennsylvania oil fields,
private enterprise in pipeline development had offered challenges
to public policy. At the same time the complexities of intra-industry
structure and conflict had made public policy, like the pipelines
themselves, a weapon in the hands of interested parties. Unlike
previous pipeline legislation in the states, however, the pipeline
amendment to the Hepburn Act was primarily the product of political rather than economic considerations. It was thrown into the
struggle for the railroad bill with little preparation and adopted
with relatively little thought to its specific consequences. Protests
from the petroleum industry against the commodities clause as
applied to pipelines caused this provision to be dropped, but the
requirement that all interstate oil pipelines act as common carriers
was seemingly accepted with little dissent. The resulting pipeline
legislation proved far less effective as a weapon against concentrated economic power in the petroleum industry than other measures of public policy and private enterprise. Although the law was
upheld by the nation's highest tribunal in a decision of far-reaching
implications for private enterprise, the economic basis of existing
pipeline operations had become too firmly established to be changed
in substance by public policy decisions alone.

XI

Conclusions

PIPELINE development in the formative period of the American petroleum industry was complicated and its history is obscure, but therein lies the significance of a study of the evolution of this mode of oil transportation. Because they could transport crude oil more efficiently, cheaply, and safely than other land carriers, pipelines became vital arteries of petroleum transportation. Virtually unnoticed by the public, a vast network of pipes was developed between the oil wells and collecting points and then between producing areas and refining centers. In this process both private enterprise and public policy were involved.

In a free enterprise economy the fact that pipelines were important transportation facilities made them also important competitive weapons. Although the first pipelines were constructed by individual entrepreneurs to carry oil between the wells and railroad depots, the trunk railroads serving the Oil Regions of Pennsylvania soon developed their own feeder pipeline systems to protect their oil traffic from one another.

The initial rewards of pipeline innovation were high, but as the lines multiplied, profits dropped and combination of lines resulted. So it was in other parts of the petroleum industry.

By 1872 overproduction of crude and refined oil and strenuous railroad competition for oil freight had created a situation which was generally unsatisfactory to all branches of the industry. The attempt to remedy it through the railroad-inspired South Improvement Company plan, whose anticipated but unrealized benefits seemed to be reserved for a select group, aroused a storm of protest in the Oil Regions, where pipelines were used to help enforce the boycott against selling oil to members of the railroad-refiners' combination. Public policy toward pipelines quickly became an issue in this controversy.

In Pennsylvania and later in other oil-producing states, public policy toward pipelines was used as a competitive weapon. Seeking to break the control over crude oil transportation exercised by the Pennsylvania Railroad, a group of Pennsylvania producers and refiners had sought since 1868 to have the right of eminent domain granted to pipelines throughout the state. They had hoped thereby to be able to invoke railroad competition for oil traffic and to reach alternative water transportation routes. The Pennsylvania Railroad had successfully used its influence at Harrisburg against such a law. Its opponents, however, created such public indignation at the South Improvement Company that the railroad's privileged position in the state was endangered and some concessions had to be made on the pipeline question. The result was a free pipe law limited in its application to the eight oil-producing counties. For the next eleven years dissatisfied elements of the petroleum industry made the extension of this law to the whole state a major legislative issue whenever they sought relief from economic distress by means of public policy. In 1883 they finally succeeded in having the law made general in its application, but the result did not change the course that pipeline development had taken in the interim.

By dint of astute management a Cleveland firm, which became The Standard Oil Company (Ohio) in 1870, outdistanced its competitors in the Ohio city and extended its influence in Pennsylvania. Exploiting the current railroad practices for obtaining traffic, this oil concern gained an advantage over other shippers. A member of the abortive South Improvement Company scheme, Standard Oil learned the lesson that pipelines could be used as effective weapons against its crude oil supply. On its own and in partnership with the New York Central and the Lake Shore, therefore, the company entered the pipeline business in 1873.

The failure of the 1872 effort to stabilize railroad competition for the oil traffic did not end further attempts to do so, and in 1874 they resulted in railroad and pipeline pools that favored Standard Oil's further growth both in refining and in dominance over the local transportation of crude oil by pipelines. The rapid development of pipeline facilities had resulted in over-capacity and in resulting competitive tactics that resembled the railroads'. The major pipelines were anxious to suppress unprofitable competition, and the lines had become such an integral part of petroleum transportation that the railroads consented to join the pipeline plan to their own. The arrangements gave Cleveland and therefore Standard Oil, whose pipelines were also in the pool, an advantage over Pennsylvania competitors.

Private enterprise in pipeline construction helped to undermine both pools. Despite opposition from the Pennsylvania Railroad, a trunk pipeline was constructed from Butler County to Pittsburgh. The crude oil delivered by this line, the Columbia Conduit, enabled the Pittsburgh refiners outside the pipeline-railroad-refiners' alliance to continue in operation, shipping their products via the Baltimore and Ohio Railroad and the Ohio River. Although the pipeline pool had been calculated to eliminate nonmember lines, the increase in pipeline rates spurred new pipeline construction. The competition of the Baltimore and Ohio caused the Pennsylvania to break the pool in early 1875, and the Erie, after strengthening its ties with Standard Oil, did likewise. The inability of the pipeline pool to maintain its position as the exclusive feeder of the oil traffic was an important factor in the disruption of its railroad counterpart.

The effort to break the transportation pools brought new proposals for pipeline legislation in its wake. Debate on these measures indicated that there was more than the Pennsylvania Railroad standing in the way of their adoption at Harrisburg. The right of eminent domain for pipelines throughout the state was regarded by Philadelphia refiners and exporters as a threat to their business because it might divert business to Baltimore. Pittsburgh refiners, on the other hand, feared that construction of pipelines under such a law would be at their expense whether the lines delivered oil to Philadelphia or Baltimore. The economic interests of the oil producers who sponsored the pipeline legislation clearly did not coincide with those of some influential representatives of urban areas in the state legislature.

The chief beneficiary of the Pennsylvania oilmen's reverses at the hands of the legislature and the railroads was Standard Oil, which worked ceaselessly and efficiently toward its objective of predominance in refining. Some of the objections to the proposed pipeline legislation of 1875 were doubtless inspired by the fact that important Pittsburgh and Philadelphia refiners had decided to cast their lot with the rising concern. These arrangements were formally confirmed in the spring of 1875 when much of the refining power of the country allied itself with Standard Oil. The resulting combination was able to bring increasingly greater pressure to bear on the railroads to grant it favors. As long as the railroads pooled oil freights, the Standard Oil alliance by virtue of its volume of traffic virtually had to be included as an "evener."

The pipelines which had participated in the pool soon became Standard Oil's property. With facilities for gathering oil, a volume of traffic that insured preferential treatment by the railroads, and a rapidly increasing percentage of the nation's refining capacity, the Standard Oil alliance seemed close to stabilizing the petroleum industry through combination. Joseph D. Potts of the Pennsylvania Railroad's affiliate, the Empire Transportation Company, however, saw a danger to his concern in Standard Oil's growing influence over petroleum transportation. He therefore put his fast-freight line into the refining business. By the spring of 1877 the scene was set for a contest between the Standard Oil combination allied with the northern railroads and the Pennsylvania committed to supporting the Empire Line.

Again pipelines were important competitive weapons. The struggle of 1877 was as much a fight between the combination's United Pipe Lines and the Empire's pipes as it was between the northern roads and the Pennsylvania. The possession of pipelines enabled both groups to collect oil in the fields and transport it to railroad depots in competition with one another.

Deprived of Standard Oil's shipments, the Pennsylvania sought desperately to generate traffic from producers and independent refiners. The losses resulting from these arrangements plus the costly railroad riots of that summer persuaded the Pennsylvania of the futility of continuing the struggle. The Empire was forced to surrender, and its pipelines were voluntarily included in the sale of its assets to the combination by the Pennsylvania Railroad. Officials of the New York Central and the Erie, who freely claimed responsibility for initiating the contest, were indifferent to this pipeline transaction, which put the origination of the railroad oil traffic thenceforth irrevocably in the hands of the Standard Oil alliance.

The Empire Line's defeat proved costly to shippers outside the combination. Commencing on the day of the transportation company's sale to Standard Oil, the New York Central and the Erie paid a Standard Oil pipeline company commissions and rebates on all crude oil that they transported, whether it originated with the combination or not. Meanwhile, the Baltimore and Ohio was made entirely dependent on the alliance for its oil shipments by the sale of the Columbia Conduit to the refining group. When confronted with these developments, the Pennsylvania's management also agreed to pay rebates on all crude oil carried by their road.

Alexander J. Cassatt, third vice-president of the Pennsylvania, later indicated that an important consideration in this decision was the oil combination's obvious ability to seek alternative routes by extension of its pipelines. The trunk pipeline that the combination had completed to Pittsburgh in the fall of 1877 was a case in point.

The opponents of Standard Oil, now reduced to the producers and a dwindling number of independent refiners, had both public policy and pipeline enterprise as potential weapons against railroad discriminations in transportation. Attempts to obtain a railroad antidiscrimination law from Congress in 1876 and 1878 were as futile as similar efforts in Pennsylvania. While a general free pipe law continued to be sought at Harrisburg, New York State adopted one in 1878, and a comprehensive common carrier law was adopted by West Virginia in 1879. Despite legal proceedings against Standard Oil, its pipelines and railroad allies, commenced in 1878 and abandoned in 1880, the combination's advantages in

petroleum transportation remained undiminished, though the rebates on competitors' shipments were abandoned.

Public policy had brought Standard Oil's opponents little relief,
but pipeline enterprise did. The legislative efforts of the Pennsylvania producers paralleled attempts to reach the seaboard by
pipeline and thus to break the grip on crude oil transportation
maintained by the oil-carrying railroads. The need for such relief appeared even more urgent as a result of the tremendous production of the Bradford field, where sale of oil at a reduced price
became the condition of moving it for brief periods of time in 1878.
Mismanagement and railroad opposition had wrecked one attempt
to develop a seaboard pipeline in 1876. A combination pipeline-
rail-water route was temporarily successful in 1878. Finally, in 1879,
the Tide-Water Pipe Line in alliance with the Reading Railroad
succeeded in establishing a route to the seaboard in defiance of
the Standard Oil combination and its railroad collaborators.

From this time on, the railroads' economic importance in the
transportation of crude petroleum began to diminish. Although
the trunk railways attempted to challenge the Tide-Water and the
Reading, the economies of pipeline transportation could not be
overcome by the all-rail carriers, who soon had to come to an understanding with the newcomers to the oil traffic. Standard Oil had
no choice but to develop a seaboard trunk pipeline system of its
own in order to maintain its predominant position, and in 1883 the
combination also came to terms with the Tide-Water.

Pipelines offered greater economies in crude oil transportation
than railroad carriers, but the benefits of Standard Oil's trunk pipelines were largely denied to shippers outside the combination. Although these lines held themselves out to be common carriers,
their rates effectively limited their use as such. By agreement with
the Pennsylvania in 1881, renewed in 1884, and effective at least
until 1899, the Standard Oil's seaboard pipeline rates were maintained on a noncompetitive basis with the railroad's. A similar
arrangement of undetermined duration was made with the Erie.
Standard Oil's gathering lines, which performed many services for
producers, maintained a uniform rate throughout this period. Although it is impossible to calculate accurately the extent of pipeline profits, they unquestionably strengthened the combination.

Public attention was increasingly focused on Standard Oil in the eighties, but its opponents in the petroleum industry capitalized on the interest of the public in railroad discriminations and placed their primary emphasis on this problem rather than on proposals for curbing the combination's pipeline power. Although the Standard Oil trunk pipelines were interstate in their operations, no effort was made by oilmen to make them subject to the Interstate Commerce Act in 1887. In the course of a congressional trust investigation in 1888, which revealed anew the importance of the pipelines to Standard Oil's predominant power in the oil industry, only one or two voices were raised in favor of this step. The general public, whose knowledge of oil operations was gained from such investigations, was still indifferent to the whole matter of pipelines.

On the state level proposals for pipeline legislation reflected the economic distress of their proponents. An effort to "punish" Standard Oil through a poorly drawn regulatory measure failed at Harrisburg and at the Ohio capital in 1887. A similar bill revived in the Pennsylvania legislature in 1891 also failed amidst public apathy and oilmen's complaints that it favored Bradford producers over others in the state.

The success of a new pipeline enterprise, which undertook to transport refined as well as crude oil, silenced the group which had most ardently promoted pipeline regulation at Harrisburg in 1887 and 1891. Despite harassment from the railroads in the construction of the lines and attempts by Standard Oil to win a place in the management of the companies involved, the venture was a success. In 1895 its promoters formed the Pure Oil Company, whose organization was, so its defenders claimed, patterned on that of Standard Oil to resist penetration by the combination. The new company became a fully integrated concern in 1900 and a few years thereafter was accused of operating its pipelines in the same manner as Standard Oil's.

In the interim new oil fields had replaced the Appalachian field as the primary oil-producing area, and Standard Oil pipelines became the object of new attacks. Development of the Lima-Indiana field through Standard Oil's enterprise had been accompanied by the dominance of Standard Oil pipelines there. Successful antitrust action against The Standard Oil Company (Ohio) in 1892 brought the decision to abandon the trust form of organization, but the process was drawn-out. A new Ohio Attorney General in 1897 attempted to drive the combination out of the state by further antitrust action, including quo warranto proceedings against the principal Standard Oil pipeline system in Ohio. The effort ended in failure in 1900. A few years later, however, a similar episode was re-enacted in Kansas. The former Ohio Attorney General and a former Pennsylvania oilman aided Kansas producers in challenging the Standard Oil's power in the new Mid-Continent field by the same legislative and legal remedies that had proved ineffective in the East. While they were quickly adopted, they failed to provide effective relief.

The oil controversy in Kansas coincided with two developments which made pipeline operations an object of national political interest. The first was a successful campaign by writers like Ida Tarbell to awaken the nation to the dangers of concentrated economic power, conveniently symbolized in Standard Oil. The second was the determination of President Theodore Roosevelt to extend the powers of the Interstate Commerce Commission. In his campaign to obtain federal regulation of railroad rates by means of the Hepburn bill in 1906, the President deliberately manipulated public and congressional opinion against Standard Oil. In its anxiety to satisfy an aroused public and in its ignorance of the internal structure of the petroleum industry, the Senate at first approved a measure which would have forced the separation of oil production from oil transportation as well as declaring interstate oil pipelines to be common carriers. Deluged with protests from members of the industry, the legislators dropped the more extreme provision. The resulting law, nevertheless, had far-reaching implications, for it appeared to decree that all interstate petroleum pipelines should act as common carriers.

Not only Standard Oil but its rivals rejected this interpretation of the statute. The literal meaning of the law was upheld by the Interstate Commerce Commission, firmly rejected by the Commerce Court, and finally interpreted by the United States Supreme Court to mean that all interstate pipelines which purchased the oil that they carried had to accept common carrier status. The Supreme Court plainly construed the law to be directed against monopoly in oil transportation, but its decision came too late to constitute an important weapon against Standard Oil, which had already fallen prey to the Sherman Antitrust Act. Meanwhile, Standard Oil's pattern of pipeline operations had become so firmly established throughout the petroleum industry that public policy pronouncements could not easily change the existing basis of pipeline transportation.

What then can be finally concluded about the relationship of private enterprise to public policy in the development of American petroleum pipelines? The key factors in this relationship were clearly that pipelines were an innovation in petroleum transportation, they were more efficient than other overland oil carriers, they performed a function with which the general public had no direct contact, and they were developed in a free enterprise economy. The last fact was the controlling one. In the period under consideration the struggle over pipelines, whether in state legislatures, in the oil fields, or along railroad rights of way, was a conflict among businessmen attempting to promote their economic self-interest as they saw it. The other factors influenced the course that specific events took, but from first to last the development of American petroleum pipelines was the product of intra-industry conflict and private enterprise. Public policy proposals affecting pipelines were used as much to sway public opinion against one of the parties to the conflict as to advance the interests of the other. Even this device was abandoned as private enterprise in pipeline construction and emphasis on railroad discriminations, whose remedy would hurt no oilman's pocketbook, promised to pay greater rewards in the competitive struggle. When the pipeline issue appeared on the national scene as a subject for public policy, it was too late to change the place that private enterprise and inadequate public policies on the state level had given pipelines in the petroleum industry.

Notes

Chapter I. The Introduction and Early Development of Petroleum Pipelines

1. The term "Oil Regions" is used throughout this study to designate the area of Pennsylvania where oil production was centered. The boundaries of this area naturally varied from time to time.

2. Sir Samuel Morton Peto, *The Resources and Prospects of America Ascertained during a Visit to the States in the Autumn of 1865* (London and New York, 1866), p. 203.

3. Andrew Cone and Walter R. Johns, *Petrolia: A Brief History of the Pennsylvania Petroleum Region, Its Development, Growth, Resources, etc., from 1859 to 1869* (New York, 1870), p. 101.

4. Paul H. Giddens, *The Birth of the Oil Industry* (New York, 1938), pp. 107–108.

5. *The Derrick's Hand-Book of Petroleum: A Complete Chronological and Statistical Review of Petroleum Developments from 1859 to 1899 [1898]* (2 vols.; Oil City, Penna., 1898–1900), I, 30.

6. *Ibid.,* p. 27.

7. Cone and Johns, *Petrolia,* p. 103.

8. Rolland H. Maybee, *Railroad Competition and the Oil Trade, 1855–1873* (New York, 1940), p. 4.

9. *Ibid.,* p. 45.

10. Giddens, *Birth Oil Industry,* pp. 151–152.

11. John J. McLaurin, *Sketches in Crude-Oil* (Harrisburg, Penna., 1896), p. 262.

12. *Titusville Morning Herald,* July 20, 1865.

13. Cone and Johns, *Petrolia,* p. 104.

14. Peto, *Resources and Prospects,* p. 203.

15. McLaurin, *Sketches in Crude-Oil,* p. 265.

16. *Ibid.,* pp. 139–140.

17. *Laws of the General Assembly of the State of Pennsylvania, Passed at the Session of 1862, in the Eighty-sixth Year of Independence* (Harrisburg, 1862), p. 60. Volumes in this series are hereafter cited by short title and date.

18. *Derrick's Hand-Book,* I, 27.

19. Giddens, *Birth Oil Industry,* p. 142.

20. McLaurin, *Sketches in Crude-Oil,* p. 266.

21. *Titusville Morning Herald,* March 6, 1866.

22. McLaurin, *Sketches in Crude-Oil,* p. 266.

23. Giddens, *Birth Oil Industry,* p. 114.

24. Quoted in Henry D. Lloyd, *Wealth against Commonwealth* (New York, 1894), p. 185.

25. *Derrick's Hand-Book,* I, 35.

26. Alexander von Millern, *All about Petroleum and the Great Oil Districts of Pennsylvania, West Virginia, Ohio, etc.* (New York, 1864), p. 85.

27. Giddens, *Birth Oil Industry,* p. 112, citing *Crawford Democrat,* December 20, 1864; Edmund Morris, *Derrick and Drill, or, an Insight into the Discovery, Development, and Present Condition and Future Prospects of Petroleum, in New York, Pennsylvania, Ohio, West Virginia, etc.* (New York, 1865), p. 31.

28. Giddens, *Birth Oil Industry,* pp. 128, 135.

29. Cone and Johns, *Petrolia,* p. 75.

30. Giddens, *Birth Oil Industry,* p. 132, citing *Business Directory of Pithole City, 1865–66.*

31. Alfred W. Smiley, *A Few Scraps, Oily and Otherwise* (Oil City, Penna., 1907), p. 121.

32. Giddens, *Birth Oil Industry,* p. 147.

33. *Derrick's Hand-Book,* I, 52.

34. *Titusville Morning Herald,* October 9, 1865.

35. *Derrick's Hand-Book,* I, 55.

36. *Ibid.,* p. 52.

37. *Titusville Morning Herald,* December 11, 1865.

38. *Ibid.,* March 6, 1866.

39. *Derrick's Hand-Book,* I, 55.

40. *Ibid.,* p. 668.

41. *Titusville Morning Herald,* March 6, 1866.

42. *Ibid.*

43. McLaurin, *Sketches in Crude-Oil,* p. 267.

44. *Derrick's Hand-Book,* I, 65–66.
45. *Titusville Morning Herald,* April 21, 1866.
46. J. T. Henry, *The Early and Later History of Petroleum with Authentic Facts in Regard to Its Development in Western Pennsylvania* (Philadelphia, 1873), p. 530.
47. *Titusville Morning Herald,* April 21, 1866.
48. Charles A. Seely, "A Week on Oil Creek," *Scientific American,* XV (September 1, 1866), 144.
49. *Derrick's Hand-Book,* I, 83.
50. Cited, *ibid.,* p. 84.
51. Smiley, *Few Scraps,* pp. 137–140.
52. *Ibid.,* p. 133.
53. Cone and Johns, *Petrolia,* p. 112.
54. Testimony of Patrick C. Boyle, publisher of the *Oil City Derrick,* in United States Industrial Commission, "Standard Oil Combination," *Preliminary Reports on Trusts and Industrial Combinations* [*Reports of the Industrial Commission* . . . (19 vols.; Washington, 1900–1902)], I, 424. Hereafter cited as *Industrial Commission Report.*
55. See "Recollections of Charles P. Hatch," *Derrick's Hand-Book,* I, 962–969. Credit for introduction of pipeline oil certificates has also been assigned to John R. Campbell, who became treasurer of the Vandergrift and Forman lines in 1868. See McLaurin, *Sketches in Crude-Oil,* p. 271.
56. "Recollections of Charles P. Hatch," *loc. cit.*
57. Maybee, *Railroad Competition,* pp. 178–179, citing Titusville *Petroleum Reporter,* April 7, 1866.
58. *Derrick's Hand-Book,* I, 74.
59. Henry, *Early Hist. Petroleum,* p. 528.
60. *Penna. Laws, 1867,* pp. 242–243.
61. Henry, *Early Hist. Petroleum,* p. 531.
62. *Penna. Laws, 1868,* p. 116.
63. Chester McA. Destler, "The Standard Oil, Child of the Erie Ring, 1868–1872," *Mississippi Valley Historical Review,* XXXIII (June, 1946), 104–106.
64. Allan Nevins, *John D. Rockefeller: The Heroic Age of American Enterprise* (2 vols.; New York, 1940), I, 209.
65. *Annual Report of the Secretary of Internal Affairs of the Commonwealth of Pennsylvania for 1875–1876,* Part III, "Industrial Statistics" (Harrisburg, 1877), p. 177. Reports in this series are cited hereafter by short title and date.
66. Maybee, *Railroad Competition,* pp. 235–236.
67. Maybee presents a good discussion of these terms and their application (*ibid.,* pp. 308–311).
68. Nevins, *Rockefeller,* I, 257. Destler challenges Nevins' accuracy in citing 1867 as the date of Standard Oil's first rebate arrangement with

the Lake Shore. See his article in *Miss. Valley Hist. Rev.*, XXXIII (June, 1946), 97, n. 19.

69. For the size of crude shipments to the two cities, 1865–1871, see Maybee, *Railroad Competition*, p. 224.

70. Affidavit of James H. Devereux in the case of *Standard Oil Company* v. *William C. Scofield et al.*, Court of Common Pleas, Cuyahoga County, Ohio, in Ida M. Tarbell, *The History of the Standard Oil Company* (2 vols.; New York, 1904), I, 277–279.

71. *Ibid.*

72. *Titusville Morning Herald*, March 19, 1872, citing the *New York Herald*. With his line about to reach Oil City, Devereux wrote to William H. Vanderbilt, "Whilst the oil men have just cause of grievance with the Erie people they must not be allowed to play their cards in forcing a strife between us and the Erie on this traffic!" (letter of March 21, 1870, quoted in Thomas C. Cochran, *Railroad Leaders, 1845–1890: The Business Mind in Action* [Cambridge, Mass., 1953], p. 311).

73. *Proceedings of the Special Committee on Railroads, Appointed under a Resolution of the Assembly to Investigate Alleged Abuses in the Management of Railroads Chartered by the State of New York* (8 vols.; New York, 1879–1880), VII, 537. Hereafter cited as *Hepburn Proceedings*.

74. Henry, *Early Hist. Petroleum*, p. 531.

75. *Ibid.*, pp. 532–533; *Penna. Laws, 1869*, pp. 495–497, 584–585.

76. Testimony of Joseph W. Guppy of the Erie Railroad, *Hepburn Proceedings*, III, 2469.

77. Maybee, *Railroad Competition*, pp. 181, 353.

78. By 1872 the company controlled about 500 miles of pipe (Henry, *Early Hist. Petroleum*, pp. 532–533).

79. This is the date given in legislative debates on a similar bill in 1883. See also *Titusville Morning Herald*, March 19, 1872, citing *New York Herald*.

80. *Derrick's Hand-Book*, I, 127.

81. The South Improvement Company scheme apparently originated with the railroads, more specifically the Pennsylvania. Once committed to it, Rockefeller and his associates supported it with typical wholeheartedness. See Nevins, *Rockefeller*, I, 314–321; Maybee, *Railroad Competition*, pp. 285–307. The commission agency interpretation is advanced for the first time by Ralph W. Hidy and Muriel E. Hidy, *Pioneering in Big Business, 1882–1911* (New York, 1955), p. 16.

82. The contract between the South Improvement Company and the Pennsylvania Railroad is in "The Standard Oil Trust," *Report on Investigation of Trusts* (50th Cong., 1 sess., House Report no. 3112, Washington, 1888), pp. 357–361. Hereafter this report is cited as *House Trust Investigation, 1888*.

83. In effect the scheme would have allowed a member refining firm in

Pittsburgh to transport its oil from the Regions to Pittsburgh to Philadelphia for 85 cents while a nonmember would have paid $2.65 for the same service (Maybee, *Railroad Competition*, p. 305).

84. Quoted in *Derrick's Hand-Book*, I, 168.

85. Austin L. Moore, *John D. Archbold and the Early Development of Standard Oil* (New York, 193[?]), p. 80.

86. *Derrick's Hand-Book*, pp. 168–169.

87. Moore, *Archbold*, pp. 73–74. For a slightly different version, see Maybee, *Railroad Competition*, pp. 324–325.

88. *Titusville Morning Herald*, March 6, 1872.

89. *Ibid.*, March 9, 1872.

90. *Ibid.*

91. *Ibid.*, March 11, 1872; *Derrick's Hand-Book*, I, 173.

92. *Titusville Morning Herald*, March 11, 1872.

93. Emery testimony, *Industrial Commission Report*, I, 605. A pipeline connection with the Baltimore and Ohio had been planned by the producers (Maybee, *Railroad Competition*, p. 354, n. 40, citing *Pittsburgh Commercial*, March 7, 1872).

94. *Penna. Laws, 1872*, pp. 22–23.

95. *The Legislative Journal, Containing the Debates and Proceedings of the Pennsylvania Legislature, for the Session of 1872* (Harrisburg, 1872), p. 740. Volumes in this series, also titled *The Legislative Record . . .* , hereafter are cited by short title and date.

96. *Penna. Laws, 1872*, pp. 22–23, 26.

97. The article was reprinted in the *Titusville Morning Herald*, March 19, 1872.

98. *Cleveland Leader*, March 13, 1872.

99. *Ibid.*, March 30 and April 6, 1872.

100. The contract is in Tarbell, *Standard Oil Co.*, I, 327–328.

101. *Derrick's Hand-Book*, I, 177.

102. *Cleveland Leader*, April 16, 1872.

103. *The State of Ohio, General and Local Laws and Joint Resolutions Passed by the Sixtieth General Assembly . . .* (Columbus, 1872), p. 194.

104. *Titusville Morning Herald*, March 19, 1872; *Penna. Laws, 1872*, p. 446.

105. New York *Sun*, March 9, 1872.

Chapter II. Pipeline Combination and Public Policy

1. See *A History of the Rise and Fall of the South Improvement Company* (Lancaster, Penna., [1872]), pp. 76–96, reprinted in Tarbell, *Standard Oil Co.*, I, 309–326.

2. Blanchard testimony, *Hepburn Proceedings,* III, 3394. Although the Empire owned other pipelines at this time, it did not acquire the Union until 1873.

3. *Ibid.*

4. Testimony of Henry M. Flagler before a committee of the Ohio legislature, March, 1879, in Tarbell, *Standard Oil Co.,* I, 329–335.

5. Blanchard testimony, *Hepburn Proceedings,* III, 3395.

6. Henry, *Early Hist. Petroleum,* pp. 284–285.

7. *Ibid.*

8. Nevins, *Rockefeller,* I, 443.

9. *Ibid.;* "Producers' Appeal of 1878 to Governor John F. Hartranft of Pennsylvania," in *House Trust Investigation, 1888,* pp. 351–356.

10. Vanderbilt testimony, *Hepburn Proceedings,* II, 1574.

11. Although Bostwick & Co. may have constructed a pipeline earlier than 1873, this is apparently the year that a line was first constructed in the interest of Standard Oil. Compare the *Oil and Gas Journal–Oil City Derrick,* Diamond Jubilee Number, p. 23, with *Derrick's Hand-Book,* I, 925.

12. A sketch of O'Day's life is in *Derrick's Hand-Book,* I, 920–927.

13. Certificates filed with the Secretary of the Commonwealth of Pennsylvania, December 9, 1873; Nevins, *Rockefeller,* I, 443.

14. Rutter testimony, *Hepburn Proceedings,* III, 2544.

15. Nevins, *Rockefeller,* I, 415, citing *Titusville Courier,* August 26, 1872.

16. Quoted in *Derrick's Hand-Book,* I, 201.

17. Commonwealth of Pennsylvania, *First Annual Report of the Bureau of Statistics of Labor and Agriculture, for the Years 1872–1873* (Harrisburg, 1874), p. 257.

18. *Derrick's Hand-Book,* I, 710–711.

19. Letter reprinted in *Pittsburgh Commercial,* March 31, 1874.

20. *Penna. Leg. Jour., 1874,* pp. 1147, 1450, 1973, 2072.

21. *Penna. Laws, 1874,* pp. 172–175.

22. *Ibid.,* pp. 73–107.

23. *Pittsburgh Commercial,* July 7, 1874.

24. *Pittsburgh Daily Dispatch,* September 8, 1874.

25. *Ibid.,* July 11, 1874; *Pittsburgh Commercial,* August 12, 1874.

26. *Pittsburgh Commercial,* August 12, 1874.

27. *Ibid.,* August 21, 24, 1874.

28. *Pittsburgh Daily Dispatch,* September 4, 1874. In the light of this argument it is interesting to note that attorneys for the Conduit, seeking to avoid payment of taxes, later argued that it was not a transportation company. See *Columbia Conduit Co.* v. *Commonwealth,* 90 Pa. St. 307 (1879).

29. According to the agreement among the pipelines to participate in

this pool, these practices included rebates, special rates, and selling oil for less than its cost and full pipage charges.

30. Blanchard testimony, *Hepburn Proceedings,* III, 3438–3443.

31. *Ibid.*

32. The pipelines' agreement is in Tarbell, *Standard Oil Co.,* I, 354–358.

33. Blanchard testimony, *Hepburn Proceedings,* III, 3424, 3445.

34. The Rutter circular is in Tarbell, *Standard Oil Co.,* I, 359–360.

35. *Derrick's Hand-Book,* I, 234–236; *Pittsburgh Gazette,* October 24, 1874.

36. *Pittsburgh Daily Dispatch,* September 29, 1874.

37. *Pittsburgh Commercial,* September 3, 1874.

38. *Pittsburgh Daily Dispatch,* September 19, 1874.

39. *Pittsburgh Gazette,* October 3, 1874.

40. *Ibid.,* November 25, 1874; *Pittsburgh Daily Dispatch,* October 22, 1874.

41. *Pittsburgh Daily Dispatch,* October 15, 27, 1874; November 2, 1874.

42. *Ibid.,* November 30, 1874; December 3, 1874.

43. *Ibid.,* December 5, 7, 1874. See also issues of February 5, 8, 1875.

44. *Derrick's Hand-Book,* I, 236–238; *Penna. Leg. Rec., 1875,* p. 1044; Tarbell, *Standard Oil Co.,* I, 217–218.

45. *Derrick's Hand-Book,* I, 711.

46. *Pittsburgh Gazette,* January 30, 1875.

47. *Pittsburgh Daily Dispatch,* January 30, 1875.

48. *New York Tribune,* January 30, 1875.

49. *Pittsburgh Gazette,* February 15, 17, 1875.

50. *New York Tribune,* February 6, 1875.

51. When the refined oil pipeline was under consideration, President Garrett of the Baltimore and Ohio promised to deliver Pittsburgh oil to Philadelphia for 60 cents a barrel. Apparently the rate actually turned out to be 80 cents, but this was approximately half the pool's $1.50 charge for the same service (*Pittsburgh Daily Dispatch,* September 29, 1874; *Penna. Leg. Rec., 1875,* p. 1047).

52. *Penna. Leg. Rec., 1875,* pp. 638–639, 1047–1049, 1051.

53. *Ibid.,* pp. 1047–1049.

54. *Ibid.,* p. 875.

55. *Ibid.,* pp. 638–639, 1045.

56. *New York Tribune,* February 6, 1875.

57. The Pennsylvania Transportation Company was granted a charter for a seaboard pipeline in 1875. In debate on the pipeline legislation it was charged that Cleveland and New York interests were paying Harley (whose name was reported as "Hooley") and others $10,000 a month not to construct a pipeline to Pittsburgh or Philadelphia. When Harley sub-

sequently undertook to build a seaboard line, he accused Pennsylvania Railroad officials of opposing a project for which they had secured the charter (McLaurin, *Sketches in Crude-Oil*, p. 270; *Penna. Leg. Rec., 1875*, pp. 638–639; New York *Daily Graphic*, October 12, 1876).

58. *Penna. Leg. Rec., 1875*, p. 639.

59. Quoted in *Pittsburgh Daily Dispatch*, March 12, 1875.

60. *Penna. Leg. Rec., 1875*, p. 1054.

61. *Ibid.*, p. 878.

62. *Ibid.*, p. 1113.

63. It was charged in House debate that the difference between the price of oil "in the woods" and in pipelines ranged from 12.5 to 15 cents a barrel (*ibid.*, p. 1044).

64. According to the producers' representatives, the requirement of members of the pipeline pool that producers pay pipage charges on oil in storage on the first of each month forced sale of oil at a sacrifice (*ibid.*, p. 1051).

65. *Ibid.*, p. 970.

66. Pittsburgh refiners termed the bill "extremely burdensome and obnoxious" (*Pittsburgh Daily Dispatch*, March 2, 1875).

67. For a description of export operations at Baltimore, see Baltimore *Sun*, March 27, 1875.

Chapter III. Pipelines as Competitive Weapons

1. Blanchard testimony, *Hepburn Proceedings*, III, 3446.

2. Details are in Blanchard's testimony before the Hepburn Committee and can be most conveniently found in Tarbell, *Standard Oil Co.*, I, 365–368.

3. Shipments of oil from Baltimore since January 1, 1875, totaled more than 83,000 barrels. The Pennsylvania reportedly cut its rates on March 17 (Baltimore *Sun*, March 27, 1875).

4. *New York Tribune*, May 10, 1875.

5. See *Pittsburgh Daily Dispatch*, May 7, 1875 and *Titusville Courier*, June 21, 1875.

6. *Pittsburgh Daily Dispatch*, July 20, 1875.

7. *Ibid.*, May 8, 1875.

8. *Derrick's Hand-Book*, I, 245.

9. *Pittsburgh Daily Dispatch*, May 22, 1875.

10. *Ibid.*, July 31, 1875.

11. *Ibid.*, July 26, 1875.

12. In Titusville, for example, the large firms of Porter, Moreland & Company and Bennett, Warner & Company had joined the Standard alliance. Smaller refiners soon followed in their wake.

13. See Festus P. Summers, *Johnson Newlon Camden: A Study in Individualism* (New York and London, 1937), pp. 172 ff.

14. *New York Tribune,* March 26, 1875.

15. *Ibid.*

16. *Pittsburgh Daily Dispatch,* June 21, 1875.

17. Cassatt testimony, *The Commonwealth v. The Pennsylvania Railroad Company,* in *House Trust Investigation, 1888,* pp. 196, 199.

18. Blanchard testimony, *Hepburn Proceedings,* III, 3451.

19. The contract is in *House Trust Investigation, 1888,* pp. 210–212.

20. Nevins, *Rockefeller,* I, 515.

21. *Derrick's Hand-Book,* I, 261.

22. James F. Hudson, *The Railways and the Republic* (New York, 1886), p. 79.

23. New York *Daily Graphic,* October 12, 1876.

24. *Ibid.* The *Cleveland Leader,* September 15, 1876, declared: "To show that this project is practical it is only necessary to state that pipes on a similar plan have already been laid from the wells to Pittsburgh, and would doubtless have been laid also to this city were it not for the greedy selfishness of the Pennamites in refusing to allow their Legislature to grant a charter for the purpose, merely because Cleveland is not located in the State owned by Tom Scott."

25. New York *Daily Graphic,* October 12, 1876. The relationship between the Pennsylvania Railroad and the Pennsylvania Transportation Company at this time is not clear. A witness before the House Committee on Manufactures in 1888 indicated that the seaboard pipeline project was undertaken in co-operation with the railroad (*House Trust Investigation, 1888,* p. 82).

26. *Pittsburgh Daily Dispatch,* July 3, 1876.

27. *Ibid.,* July 18, 1876.

28. Quoted in *Pittsburgh Daily Dispatch,* September 5, 1876. The *Oil City Derrick* declared that Standard Oil was using its steadily growing power against exporters and was thus responsible for the increase in crude oil prices. See *Derrick's Hand-Book,* I, 266–267.

29. *Derrick's Hand-Book,* I, 262 ff.

30. *Ibid.,* p. 271.

31. *Ibid.*

32. *Ibid.,* pp. 272–273.

33. Tarbell, *Standard Oil Co.,* I, 178.

34. Archbold and Vandergrift had been successful in their efforts to purchase or lease refineries in the Oil Regions. Lockhart and Frew had been less successful in Pittsburgh, where the Columbia Conduit kept some independent refineries alive. In the Parkersburg, Philadelphia, and Baltimore areas Standard's representatives were active in neutralizing and purchasing competitors. By the end of 1877 New York was the only major

refining center where Standard was not dominant (Hidy and Hidy, *Pioneering*, pp. 18–20).

35. Potts's testimony, *House Trust Investigation, 1888*, pp. 259–260.
36. See *House Trust Investigation, 1888*, p. 54.
37. Blanchard testimony, *Hepburn Proceedings*, III, 3472–3475.
38. The contract is in *ibid.*, II, 1468–1469.
39. Jewett testimony, *ibid.*, p. 1470.
40. For a description of the Empire's resources, see Nevins, *Rockefeller*, I, 522–525.
41. The contract is quoted, *ibid.*, pp. 520–521.
42. Jewett testimony, *Hepburn Proceedings*, II, 1463.
43. Vanderbilt testimony, *ibid.*, p. 1575.
44. Cassatt testimony, *loc. cit.*, pp. 175, 182–183.
45. Flagler testimony, *House Trust Investigation, 1888*, p. 772.
46. Cassatt testimony, *loc. cit.*, pp. 182–183.
47. Jewett testimony, *Hepburn Proceedings*, II, 1466.
48. Cassatt testimony, *loc. cit.*, p. 178.
49. Enrolled in Charter Book no. 9, pp. 674–676, Commonwealth of Pennsylvania.
50. *Penna. Leg. Rec., 1881*, p. 746.
51. *Derrick's Hand-Book*, I, 278, 280.
52. *Ibid.*, pp. 283–284.
53. Benjamin B. Campbell's testimony, *The Commonwealth v. Pennsylvania Railroad Company*, in *House Trust Investigation, 1888*, pp. 134–135.
54. Tarbell, *Standard Oil Co.*, I, 188–189.
55. Cassatt testimony, *loc. cit.*, p. 176.
56. Blanchard testimony, *Hepburn Proceedings*, III, 3462.
57. *Philadelphia Record*, September 28, 1877.
58. *Ibid.*, September 15, 1877.
59. Cassatt testimony, *loc. cit.*, p. 178.
60. *Ibid.*, pp. 202, 205, 207. When asked whether the railroads feared that Standard Oil would seek another outlet to tidewater, Cassatt replied: "That was generally the idea, that the Standard Oil Company would have it in its power, through arrangements for the transportation of its oil, to take this business off the trunk lines in a body; and there was a good deal of force in what they said."
61. *Ibid.*; Jewett testimony, *Hepburn Proceedings*, II, 1514.
62. Cassatt testimony, *loc. cit.*, p. 179.
63. Flagler testimony, *House Trust Investigation, 1888*, p. 772.
64. *Ibid.*
65. Moore, *Archbold*, p. 132.
66. The letters are in Tarbell, *Standard Oil Co.*, I, 371–373.
67. Vanderbilt testimony, *Hepburn Proceedings*, II, 1575.
68. Blanchard testimony, *ibid.*, III, 3452.

69. Tarbell, *Standard Oil Co.*, I, 194–195.

70. Nevins, *Rockefeller*, I, 545.

71. *New York Tribune*, October 26, 1877.

72. *Derrick's Hand-Book*, p. 291.

73. *Industrial Commission Report*, I, 795.

74. O'Day to Cassatt, February 15, 1878, exhibit in connection with Cassatt testimony, *loc. cit.*, p. 209.

75. John C. Welch, "The Standard Oil Company," *North American Review*, CXXXVI (February, 1883), 374–375.

76. The letter is most readily found in Tarbell, *Standard Oil Co.*, I, 374.

77. Cassatt testimony, *loc. cit.*, p. 205. Cassatt said: "They could have opened those pipe lines to shipments at very low rates by water and to rival roads, and could have diverted a large quantity of oil from our lines if they had chosen to do so."

78. In December, 1879, the West Penn delivered 12,756 barrels of crude to Pittsburgh, and the Allegheny Valley delivered 44,852 barrels. Only 12,464 barrels arrived by pipeline (*Annual Report of the Secretary of Internal Affairs of the Commonwealth of Pennsylvania, 1878–1879*, Part III, p. 282).

79. Cassatt to Comptroller, Pennsylvania Railroad Company, May 15, 1878, exhibit in connection with Cassatt testimony, *loc. cit.*, p. 210.

80. Jewett testimony, *Hepburn Proceedings*, II, 1474.

81. Blanchard testimony, *ibid.*, III, 3472–3473.

82. *Ibid.*, p. 3475.

83. *Ibid.*

84. Rutter testimony, *ibid.*, pp. 2540–2541.

85. Vanderbilt testimony, *ibid.*, II, 1577.

86. *Ibid.*, p. 1581.

87. Cassatt to Comptroller of the Pennsylvania Railroad, May 15, 1878, *loc. cit.*

Chapter IV. Pipelines and the Producers' Attack on Standard Oil

1. *Derrick's Hand-Book*, II, 255.

2. Allan Nevins, *Study in Power: John D. Rockefeller, Industrialist and Philanthropist* (2 vols.; New York and London, 1953), I, 291; Tarbell, *Standard Oil Co.*, I, 216–218. "Immediate shipment" was no new practice. J. A. Bostwick, Standard Oil's crude oil buyer, simply took advantage of United Pipe Lines' virtual monopoly in the Bradford field to make discount buying a regular practice.

3. *New York Tribune*, December 28, 1877.

4. *Derrick's Hand-Book*, I, 294.

5. *Ibid.*, pp. 289–290.

6. *Ibid.*, II, 260.

7. Camden was instructed to purchase a Maryland pipeline charter if that were necessary to thwart the producers' line. See Nevins, *Study in Power*, I, 298–299.

8. A sketch of Emery's life is in *Derrick's Hand-Book*, I, 659–660. See also his obituary notice in the Philadelphia *Public Ledger*, November 20, 1924.

9. Tarbell, *Standard Oil Co.*, I, 214; *Derrick's Hand-Book*, II, 263.

10. *Derrick's Hand-Book*, II, 267.

11. *Ibid.*, p. 274. The *Oil City Derrick* accused the Equitable of opposing the P.P.U.'s plans for a Buffalo pipeline.

12. By July, 1878, the Bradford field was producing over 18,000 barrels a day. Over 500,000 barrels were in storage, tanks were running over, and pipelines were overwhelmed.

13. *Derrick's Hand-Book*, II, 271.

14. Cassatt testimony, *The Commonwealth v. The Pennsylvania Railroad Company*, in *House Trust Investigation, 1888*, pp. 204–205; George Rice testimony, *Industrial Commission Report*, I, 698.

15. *Derrick's Hand-Book*, II, 269–270.

16. *New York Tribune*, August 8, 1878.

17. Interview with New York refiner, reported in *ibid.*, July 22, 1878.

18. *New York Tribune*, August 8, 1878.

19. The letter is in *Hepburn Proceedings*, II, 1570–1571. James H. Rutter of the New York Central handled the matter, but the policy was clearly Vanderbilt's (*ibid.*, p. 1572).

20. *New York Tribune*, August 8, 1878.

21. Blanchard testimony, *Hepburn Proceedings*, III, 3470.

22. Cassatt testimony, *loc. cit.*, pp. 190–191.

23. *Ibid.*, p. 201.

24. In June, 1878, Benson was reported seeking funds in Philadelphia for a pipeline between Parker City and Columbia, where it was to connect with the Philadelphia and Reading, which was to complete the connection to Philadelphia (*New York Tribune*, June 10, 1878).

25. The Tide-Water's articles of incorporation are in Tarbell, *Standard Oil Co.*, II, 295–297.

26. Nevins, *Rockefeller*, I, 576, citing Benson, *Short History of the Tidewater*.

27. R. J. Andrews, "Development of the Pipe Line Industry," in Paul J. Graber (ed.), *Common Carrier Pipe Line Operations and Accounting* (Tulsa, 1951), p. 4.

28. *Derrick's Hand-Book*, II, 291, 293.

29. Nevins, *Rockefeller*, I, 577, citing Benson, *Short History of the Tidewater*.

30. A. R. Crum and A. S. Dungan (eds.), *Romance of American Petroleum and Gas* (New York, 1911), p. 244.

31. *Pittsburgh Daily Dispatch,* April 1, 22, 1879.

32. *Railway World,* June 7, 1879.

33. *Ibid.*

34. *Ibid.*

35. Nevins, *Rockefeller,* I, 580, 586; Crum, *Romance Amer. Petroleum,* pp. 244–246.

36. *Derrick's Hand-Book,* II, 297.

37. *Ibid.,* pp. 275–278.

38. *Oil City Derrick,* October 18, 1890. Zane joined the Producers' Union in July, 1878, after failing to gain acceptance for his plan (*Derrick's Hand-Book,* II, 276).

39. *Derrick's Hand-Book,* I, 294.

40. *Ibid.,* p. 295.

41. *Railway World,* January 19, 1878.

42. *Ibid.,* January 12, 1878.

43. *Ibid.,* February 2, 1878.

44. *Ibid.,* January 12, 1878.

45. Cited in *Pittsburgh Daily Dispatch,* January 17, 1878.

46. *Ibid.,* January 15, 1878.

47. Quoted, *ibid.*

48. *Derrick's Hand-Book,* II, 259.

49. *Pittsburgh Daily Dispatch,* January 19, 1878.

50. *Derrick's Hand-Book,* I, 295.

51. *New York Tribune,* January 25, 1878.

52. See notice in *Pittsburgh Daily Dispatch,* January 24, 1878. Some grounds for Warden's statement can be found in *ibid.,* January 5, 1878.

53. *Derrick's Hand-Book,* I, 295.

54. *New York Tribune,* January 29, 1878.

55. *Penna. Leg. Rec., 1878,* p. 404.

56. *Ibid.,* pp. 402–403.

57. *Derrick's Hand-Book,* I, 295.

58. *Penna. Leg. Rec., 1878,* p. 1716.

59. Campbell testimony, *The Commonwealth* v. *The Pennsylvania Railroad Company,* in *House Trust Investigation, 1888,* p. 151.

60. Quoted in Tarbell, *Standard Oil Co.,* I, 215.

61. *Derrick's Hand-Book,* I, 297.

62. *Railway World,* May 4, 1878.

63. The legal opinion of the New York Attorney General is quoted in *ibid.*

64. *Pittsburgh Daily Dispatch,* May 23, 1878.

65. *Cong. Rec. Appendix,* 44th Cong., 1 sess., pp. 111–114.

66. Interview with Hopkins in *New York Herald,* January 19, 1884.

67. *Cong. Rec.,* 44th Cong., 1 sess. (May 22, 1876), p. 3264.

68. Tarbell, *Standard Oil Co.,* I, 168–171.

69. New York *Sun,* November 23, 1878.

70. Interview with Hopkins, *New York Herald,* January 19, 1884.

71. Tarbell, *Standard Oil Co.,* I, 214.

72. *Cong. Rec.,* 45th Cong., 2 sess. (January 21, 1878), p. 442.

73. *Ibid.* (May 8, 1878), p. 3280.

74. *Ibid.* (May 9, 1878), p. 3325.

75. *Ibid.,* p. 3326.

76. *Ibid.* (May 8, 1878), pp. 3275–3276.

77. Campbell testimony, *loc. cit.,* p. 159.

78. *Ibid.*

79. The document is reprinted in Tarbell, *Standard Oil Co.,* I, 381–390.

80. *Derrick's Hand-Book,* I, 303.

81. *Ibid.,* p. 302.

82. Quoted, *ibid.,* p. 303.

83. *New York Tribune,* July 15, 1878.

84. *Derrick's Hand-Book,* II, 271.

85. *New York Tribune,* July 16, 1878.

86. *Derrick's Hand-Book,* I, 304; New York *Sun,* November 13, 1878.

87. New York *Sun,* November 13, 1878.

88. "A History of the Organization, Purposes, and Transactions of the General Council of Petroleum Producers' Unions . . . from 1878 to 1880," in *House Trust Investigation,* 1888, pp. 690–716. Hereafter cited as *History, P.P.U.*

89. *The Commonwealth* v. *The Pennsylvania Railroad Company, loc. cit.,* pp. 158–159.

90. *History, P.P.U.,* pp. 697–699.

91. *Ibid.,* pp. 700–701.

92. *Ibid.,* p. 702.

93. *Ibid.,* p. 705.

94. *Ibid.,* p. 707.

95. *Railway World,* April 26, 1879.

96. George R. Blanchard, *Politico-Railway Problems and Theorists* (New York, 1880), p. 23.

97. Moore, *Archbold,* p. 118.

98. Ida M. Tarbell, *All in the Day's Work* (New York, 1939), p. 209.

99. *New York Tribune,* December 13, 1878.

100. Flagler had earlier contemplated a test of the New York pipeline law, but he doubted apparently that the statute would be used (Nevins, *Study in Power,* I, 298). A case did arise, however, and Judge Barker in Supreme Court, Special Term, of Orleans County, upheld the law, declaring, "the encouragement of cheap methods of transportation falls

within the class of things which Government may aid" (*New York Tribune*, December 30, 1878).

101. Quoted in *Pittsburgh Daily Dispatch*, January 9, 1879.

102. *Ibid.*, February 3, April 14, 1879.

103. *Ibid.*, May 2, 1879.

104. *Penna. Leg. Rec., 1879*, I, 175.

105. *Pittsburgh Daily Dispatch*, May 2, 1879.

106. See A. K. McClure, *Old Time Notes of Pennsylvania* (2 vols.; Philadelphia, 1905), II, 500–502.

107. *Penna. Leg. Rec., 1879*, II, 1646.

108. *Railway World*, May 17, 1879.

109. *Pittsburgh Daily Dispatch*, March 22, 1879.

110. *Acts of the Legislature of West Virginia at Its Fourteenth Session* (Wheeling, 1879), pp. 35–36.

111. In debate over federal pipeline regulation in 1906, Senator Stephen B. Elkins of West Virginia pointed out that since 1879 producers in his state had had no occasion to invoke the pipeline law against Standard Oil (*Cong. Rec.*, 59th Cong., 1 sess. [June 26, 1906], p. 9251).

112. Nevins, *Study in Power*, I, 348.

113. *Hepburn Proceedings*, I, 45.

114. Flagler testimony, *House Trust Investigation, 1888*, p. 783.

115. *Ibid.*, p. 783.

116. Blanchard testimony, *Hepburn Proceedings*, III, 3498.

117. *Ibid.*, p. 3481.

118. *New York Tribune*, June 25, 1879.

119. *Hepburn Proceedings*, I, 45.

120. *New York Tribune*, June 25, 1879.

121. Archbold testimony, *Hepburn Proceedings*, III, 2670.

122. Quoted in testimony of George Rice, *Industrial Commission Report*, I, 697.

123. *Hepburn Proceedings*, I, 46.

124. Vanderbilt testimony, *Hepburn Proceedings*, II, 1596.

125. *Railroad Gazette*, November 7, 1879.

126. *History, P.P.U.*, pp. 710–711.

127. The agreement is in *ibid.*, pp. 711–713.

128. *Ibid.*, p. 715.

129. *Ibid.*, pp. 713–714.

Chapter V. Standard Oil's Pipeline Empire and Pipeline Legislation

1. *Derrick's Hand-Book*, I, 318.

2. Flagler testimony, *House Trust Investigation, 1888*, p. 305.

3. Rockefeller affidavit, *Standard Oil Co.* v. *William C. Scofield et al.*, Court of Common Pleas, Cuyahoga County, Ohio.

4. See Nevins, *Rockefeller*, I, 562.

5. Samuel F. Peckham, *Production, Technology, and Uses of Petroleum and Its Products* (47th Cong., 2 sess., Misc. Doc. 42, pt. 10, Washington, 1884), p. 102.

6. Tarbell, *Standard Oil Co.*, II, 25.

7. An excellent account of Standard Oil's pipeline system at this time is in Hidy and Hidy, *Pioneering*, pp. 77–89.

8. *Derrick's Hand-Book*, I, 310, 323.

9. Nevins, *Study in Power*, I, 366.

10. *New York Times*, March 4, 1880.

11. *Derrick's Hand-Book*, I, 330.

12. Moore, *Archbold*, p. 167; C. B. Matthews' affidavit, *Industrial Commission Report*, XIII, 647.

13. Matthews' testimony, *House Trust Investigation, 1888*, pp. 424–425.

14. *Ibid.*

15. *New York Tribune*, September 23, 1880.

16. *Ibid.*

17. *Derrick's Hand-Book*, I, 327.

18. *Oil Paint & Drug Reporter*, January 17, 1883, cited in Nevins, *Study in Power*, I, 371.

19. O'Day testimony, *House Trust Investigation, 1888*, pp. 276–277. See map and account of Standard Oil trunk lines in *Scientific American*, LXVI (February 27, 1892), 1, 134–135.

20. *Industrial Commission Report*, I, 760–763; Gilbert H. Montague, *The Rise and Progress of the Standard Oil Company* (New York and London, 1903), pp. 84–87.

21. Archbold testimony, *House Trust Investigation, 1888*, pp. 325–326, 328.

22. Nevins, *Study in Power*, I, 367–369.

23. Emery testimony, *Industrial Commission Report*, I, 104.

24. A detailed account of these developments, citing the documents concerned, is in *Petroleum Age*, VI (March, 1887), 1569–1570.

25. *Ibid.*, III (May, 1884), 709–710.

26. Hidy and Hidy, *Pioneering*, ch. iv, contains interesting data on the key figures of National Transit and their *modus operandi*.

27. *Dictionary of American Biography* (New York, 1930–1944), V, 341–342.

28. Nevins, *Rockefeller*, I, 606.

29. A list of the stocks contributed by these investors is in Hidy and Hidy, *Pioneering*, p. 47.

30. E. Benjamin Andrews, "Trusts according to Official Investigations," *Quarterly Journal of Economics*, III (January, 1889), 133.

31. *Ibid.*, p. 130.

32. Dodd statement, *Industrial Commission Report*, I, 799.

33. Rockefeller affidavit, *ibid.*, p. 797.

34. This was the Solar Oil Company, which became inactive by 1882.

35. Crum, *Romance Amer. Petroleum*, p. 244.

36. *Ibid.*, p. 246.

37. Archbold to Potts, November 25, 1881, quoted in Nevins, *Study in Power*, I, 378. Rockefeller testified in 1888 that Standard Oil owned a 5 to 10 per cent interest in Tide-Water.

38. *Ibid.*, p. 376.

39. Nevins, *Rockefeller*, I, 591–592.

40. Lewis Emery, Jr., had pressed for the tax investigation and had authorized Patterson to draw on him for his expenses up to $6,000. See Philadelphia *Press*, March 3, 1883.

41. Tarbell, *Standard Oil Co.*, II, 18; Moore, *Archbold*, pp. 151–152; Nevins, *Study in Power*, I, 438, n. 28; II, 148.

42. Philadelphia *Press*, March 3, 1883.

43. Tarbell, *Standard Oil Co.*, II, 18. See *Patterson v. Tidewater Pipe Company, Limited*, Court of Common Pleas, Crawford County, Pennsylvania, December, 1882,

44. Lloyd, *Wealth against Commonwealth*, p. 111.

45. *Pittsburgh Daily Dispatch*, January 19, 1883; Tarbell, *Standard Oil Co.*, II, 19.

46. *Pittsburgh Daily Dispatch*, January 4, 1883. In the newspaper attack on Standard Oil two events in its history were generally highlighted —the South Improvement Company and the absorption of pipelines after the Rutter circular of 1874.

47. *Ibid.*, January 8, 1883.

48. *Ibid.*, January 9, 1883.

49. *Ibid.*, January 12, 1883.

50. *Ibid.*, January 27, 1883.

51. Tarbell, *Standard Oil Co.*, II, 20.

52. Standard Oil purchased the tanks, lines, and associated equipment of the Union Oil Company in September, 1882, but its Tide-Water stock was apparently acquired later (Hidy and Hidy, *Pioneering*, p. 84; Nevins, *Study in Power*, I, 376).

53. *Pittsburgh Daily Dispatch*, January 19, 1883.

54. Tarbell, *Standard Oil Co.*, II, 21.

55. *Pittsburgh Daily Dispatch*, February 22, 1883.

56. *Ibid.*, February 21, 1883.

57. *Ibid.* See also Nevins, *Study in Power*, I, 352–353, 361–362.

58. Philadelphia *Press*, March 17, 1883.

59. Henry D. Lloyd, "Story of a Great Monopoly," *Atlantic Monthly*, XLVII (March, 1881), 321.

60. *Ibid.*, pp. 333–334.

61. John C. Welch, "The Standard Oil Company," *North American Review*, CXXXVI (February, 1883), 191–200.

62. See Summers, *Camden*, p. 211.

63. Nevins, *Study in Power*, II, 472.

64. Johnson N. Camden, "The Standard Oil Company," *North American Review*, CXXXVI (February, 1883), 183.

65. *Ibid.*, pp. 186–187.

66. *Ibid.*, p. 189.

67. *Pittsburgh Daily Dispatch*, January 17, 1883.

68. *Industrial Commission Report*, I, 660.

69. Quoted in *Pittsburgh Daily Dispatch*, March 16, 1883.

70. *Railway World*, March 3, 1883.

71. In January, 1883, 300,000 barrels of crude and crude equivalent went by pipe to Cleveland, 105,716 to Buffalo. In addition, 206,600 barrels were moved by the Tide-Water and 376,574 by Standard Oil's seaboard lines. Only 304,837 barrels of crude moved out of the producing region by rail (*ibid.*, citing *Stowell's Petroleum Reporter*, February 26, 1883).

72. Quoted in Philadelphia *Press*, April 6, 1883.

73. Nevins believes that Cooper was definitely a Standard spokesman. See *Study in Power*, II, 473.

74. Philadelphia *Press*, April 6, 1883.

75. *Ibid.*

76. *Ibid.*

77. *Ibid.*

78. *Ibid.*, April 7, 1883. The *Press* correspondent at Harrisburg termed the pipeline and antidiscrimination measures "anti-corporation bills which for fourteen years have knocked vainly at the legislature doors for passage" (*ibid.*, June 2, 1883).

79. *Ibid.*, May 17, 1883.

80. *Ibid.*, May 11, 1883.

81. *Ibid.*, May 14, 1883.

82. The bill passed its third reading in the House on May 22 but got no farther.

83. Philadelphia *Press*, June 1, 1883.

84. *Ibid.*, June 2, 1883.

85. *Ibid.*

86. *Ibid.*

87. *Ibid.*

88. See *Penna. Laws, 1883*, pp. 186–189.

89. See *ibid.*, pp. 92–95.

90. Commonwealth of Pennsylvania, "Papers of the Governors," *Pennsylvania Archives Fourth Series,* ed. by George E. Reed (Harrisburg, 1900–1902), XI, 339.

91. The contracts are in Tarbell, *Standard Oil Co.*, II, 300–308.

Chapter VI. The Place of Pipelines in Petroleum Transportation and Public Policy

1. "Report of Committee upon the Pipe Line Transfer," quoted in *Petroleum Age,* III (May, 1884), 709–711.

2. *Ibid.*

3. *Petroleum Age,* III (April, 1884), 681–682.

4. *Ibid.*, 683.

5. See *Industrial Commission Report,* I, 700–703.

6. Samuel Dodd maintained that the contract had been misconstrued by those who claimed the railroads paid Standard Oil a rebate. See *ibid.*, pp. 760–762.

7. The Erie received $126,908.63 during the first half of 1884 as rebates on crude oil shipped to "Standard Oil Co. and interests" at New York, Philadelphia, and Baltimore (Hidy and Hidy, *Pioneering,* p. 726 n. 18).

8. *Industrial Commission Report,* I, 665–666.

9. *Ibid.*, pp. 761–762.

10. *Report of the Commissioner of Corporations on the Transportation of Petroleum, May 2, 1906* (Washington, 1906), p. 90.

11. Rice testimony, *House Trust Investigation, 1888,* p. 574. O'Day's action may have been in retaliation for Rice's alleged attempt to prevent National Transit from getting a right of way for a Macksburg to Parkersburg pipeline in 1884. See Boyle testimony, *Industrial Commission Report,* I, 486.

12. Testimony of Van H. Bukey, superintendent of the West Virginia Transportation Company, *House Trust Investigation, 1888,* pp. 557–559.

13. See report of Special Master George K. Nash, in the case of *Parker Handy and John Paton, Trustees* v. *The Cleveland and Marietta Railroad Company et al.*, in Tarbell, *Standard Oil Co.*, II, 348–354.

14. *Ibid.*

15. *Ibid.; House Trust Investigation, 1888,* pp. 273–275.

16. Testimony of F. G. Carrel, freight agent of the Cleveland and Marietta, *ibid.*, pp. 346–347.

17. Quoted in Rice testimony, *House Trust Investigation, 1888,* p. 578.

18. *Ibid.*, p. 577.

19. See report of Special Master George K. Nash, *loc. cit.*

20. O'Day's version is in *House Trust Investigation, 1888,* pp. 273–276.

21. New York *World,* March 29, 1890.

22. See table in *House Trust Investigation, 1888,* p. 115.

23. See month by month quotations on crude at Bradford, Oil City, New York, and Pittsburgh in *Petroleum Age,* VI (1887).

24. The message was quoted in full by the *Pittsburgh Daily Dispatch,* January 5, 1887.

25. The text of this bill is in Tarbell, *Standard Oil Co.,* II, 357–360.

26. See above, pp. 126–127.

27. *Titusville Morning Herald,* February 11, 1887.

28. *Petroleum Age,* VI (February, 1887), 1551.

29. *Ibid.*

30. "Heydrich's Argument," *Petroleum Age,* VI (March, 1887), 1576.

31. Philadelphia *Press,* April 29, 1887.

32. *Petroleum Age,* VI (March, 1887), 1575; "Thomas W. Phillips' Arraignment," *ibid.* (April, 1887), 1597.

33. Philadelphia *Press,* April 29, 1887.

34. A. Leo Weil, "The Billingsley Bill," *Petroleum Age,* VI (March, 1887), 1570.

35. The cases cited included: *Railroad Commission Cases,* 116 U.S. 307 (1886); *Munn v. Illinois,* 94 U.S. 113 (1876); *Wabash, St. Louis and Pacific Railway Co. v. Illinois,* 118 U.S. 557 (1886). Note, however, that the latter case could more properly be cited as justification for federal rather than state regulation.

36. See New York *World,* May 19, 1887.

37. Philadelphia *Press,* April 28, 1887.

38. See memorials submitted by local assemblies in *Penna. Leg. Rec., 1887,* pp. 561, 800–801.

39. Philadelphia *Press,* April 29, 1887.

40. Emery testimony, *House Trust Investigation, 1888,* pp. 236, 239.

41. *Ibid.,* p. 239.

42. "Senator Emery's Vindication," *Petroleum Age,* VI (May, 1887), 1630.

43. Philadelphia *Press,* April 29, 1887.

44. *Oil City Derrick,* October 10, 1890.

45. *Ibid.,* October 25, 1890.

46. "Heydrich's Argument," *Petroleum Age,* VI (March, 1887), 1577.

47. Weil, "The Billingsley Bill," *ibid.,* 1573.

48. See Nevins, *Study in Power,* II, 473–474.

49. *New York Tribune,* March 18, 1887; *Petroleum Age,* VI (May, 1887), 1625–1626; Hidy and Hidy, *Pioneering,* p. 179.

50. New York *World,* May 19, 1887.

51. "The Death of the Billingsley Bill," *Petroleum Age,* VI (May, 1887), 1633.

52. The Constitution of the General and Local Assemblies of the

Producers' Protective Association is in *House Trust Investigation, 1888,* pp. 47–52.

53. Philadelphia *Press,* August 4, 1887.

54. *Ibid.*

55. Archbold testimony, New York State Senate, *Report of the Committee on General Laws on the Investigation Relative to Trusts* (Albany, 1888), p. 449. Hereafter this work is cited as *New York Trust Investigation, 1888.*

56. *Ibid.*

57. The agreement is in *House Trust Investigation, 1888,* pp. 69–70.

58. *Derrick's Hand-Book,* I, 466.

59. *Ibid.,* p. 472.

60. Letter of Thomas W. Phillips to Chairman, Committee on Manufactures, United States House of Representatives, April 18, 1888, in *House Trust Investigation, 1888,* pp. 110–112.

61. Archbold testimony, *New York Trust Investigation, 1888,* p. 449. The Standard Oil Trust had been profitable in this period. It paid a 20 per cent stock dividend early in 1887, and this was followed by a 10 per cent cash dividend, which was also paid on this stock.

62. Rockefeller testimony, *ibid.,* p. 430. A list of outside refiners as of January 1, 1888, can be found in *ibid.,* pp. 401–405.

63. It is virtually impossible to make even a rough estimate of pipeline profits for this period. However, in every instance where opponents of Standard Oil made a public estimate of trunk pipeline costs to the seaboard, the figure was placed at less than 10 cents per barrel. Even with a high allowance for depreciation, the open rate of 45 cents and upward must have left a wide margin of profit. Standard Oil officials refused to make public estimates of cost, but Nevins (*Study in Power,* I, 381) indicates that pipeline revenues were a bulwark of the Trust. Hidy and Hidy (*Pioneering,* pp. 628–629) do not give specific pipeline revenues but show that earnings from transportation activities formed 41.6 per cent of all earnings of the Trust for the period 1891–1911. This figure, however, is subject to many qualifications and explanations as are all accounting figures for this period and especially those for National Transit, which engaged in numerous activities.

64. *Cong. Rec.,* 48th Cong., 2 sess. (December 8, 1884), p. 97.

65. William Z. Ripley, *Railroads: Rates and Regulation* (New York, 1912), p. 446.

66. Arthur T. Hadley, *Railroad Transportation: Its History and Its Laws* (New York and London, 1886), p. 67.

67. James F. Hudson, *The Railways and the Republic* (New York, 1886), pp. 67 ff.

68. Lewis H. Haney, *A Congressional History of Railways in the United States* (2 vols.; Madison, Wis., 1908–1910), II, 301.

69. *Petroleum Age,* VI (April, 1887), 1593–1594.

70. *Ibid.*

71. *Cleveland Plain-Dealer,* March 22, 1887.

72. Dean testimony, *House Trust Investigation, 1888,* pp. 84, 90–91.

73. Kirk testimony, *ibid.,* p. 72.

74. *Petroleum Age,* VI (November, 1887), p. 1784.

75. Emery's version of the events leading up to the sale is in *House Trust Investigation, 1888,* pp. 236–239.

76. *Derrick's Hand-Book,* I, 467.

77. See *Rice* v. *Louisville & Nashville Railroad Co.,* 1 I.C.C. Rep. 503 (1888).

78. *Rice, Robinson and Witherop* v. *The Western New York and Pennsylvania Railroad Company,* 4 I.C.C. Rep. 131 (1890), pp. 145–146.

79. *Ibid.,* p. 134.

80. Testimony of George Rice, citing record of the hearings at Titusville, May 15, 1889, *Trust Investigation of Ohio Senate* ([Columbus ?], 1898), Appendix, pp. 41–42.

81. *Ibid.; Independent Producers' Association of Titusville and Oil City* v. *The Western New York and Pennsylvania Railroad Co. et al.* 5 I.C.C. Rep. 415 (1892); *Penna. Leg. Rec., 1891,* p. 566.

82. *Ibid.,* p. 458.

83. *Ibid.,* p. 460.

84. *Ibid.*

Chapter VII. Pipelines as an Issue in the Antitrust Movement and the Petroleum Industry

1. Jeremiah W. Jenks and Walter E. Clark, *The Trust Problem* (New York, 1929), p. 212.

2. *New York Tribune,* February 17, 1888.

3. *Ibid.,* February 28, 1888.

4. *New York Trust Investigation, 1888,* pp. 398, 422, 429–431, 441, 444.

5. *Ibid.,* pp. 421–422, 429.

6. *Ibid.,* p. 445.

7. Quoted in New York *World,* May 11, 1887.

8. John C. Welch, "The Standard Oil Company," *North American Review,* CXXXVI (February, 1883), 191.

9. *New York Trust Investigation, 1888,* p. 388.

10. *Ibid.,* pp. 389–390, 399.

11. *Ibid.,* p. 13.

12. *Ibid.,* p. 10.

13. *New York Tribune,* March 10, 1888.

14. *House Trust Investigation, 1888,* p. 333.

15. *Ibid.,* pp. 322–323.

16. *Ibid.,* p. 324.

17. When questioned on the cost of moving oil 500 miles by pipeline, Archbold replied: "I do not regard the business as having come to a point to give an intelligent answer to that question." He pointed out the risks of pipeline construction. "We have spent in one year several hundred thousands of dollars, and within that year it was an abandoned investment," he said. He did not specify when or where this occurred (*ibid.,* p. 325).

18. *Ibid.,* p. 283.

19. Emery testimony, *ibid.,* p. 239.

20. Kirk testimony, *ibid.,* pp. 71–72.

21. *Ibid.,* p. 46.

22. Archbold testimony, *ibid.,* pp. 340–342.

23. Emery testimony, *ibid.,* p. 239.

24. Kirk testimony, *ibid.,* p. 47.

25. I. E. Dean testimony, *ibid.,* p. 91.

26. *Ibid.,* p. 84.

27. *House Trust Investigation, 1888,* pp. ii–iii.

28. Marvin W. Schlegel, *Ruler of the Reading: The Life of Franklin B. Gowen, 1836–1889* (Harrisburg, 1947), p. 284.

29. Samuel C. T. Dodd, *Combinations: Their Uses and Abuses; with a History of the Standard Oil Trust. An Argument relative to bills pending before the New York Legislature, based upon testimony given before the Senate Committee on General Laws* (New York, 1888), p. 13.

30. *Ibid.,* p. 23.

31. *Ibid.,* p. 35.

32. *Ibid.,* pp. 27–33 *passim.*

33. *Ibid.,* p. 39.

34. *Ibid.,* p. 33.

35. George Gunton, "The Economic and Social Aspect of Trusts," *Political Science Quarterly,* III (September, 1888), 393. Gunton was later employed by Standard Oil to refute charges against it made by Dr. Washington Gladden at Chautauqua.

36. The railroad-pipeline rate parity on seaboard oil shipments remained in effect at least until 1899. See Howard Page testimony, *Industrial Commission Report,* I, 763.

37. Gunton, *loc. cit.,* 394–395.

38. See table of prices in Tarbell, *Standard Oil Co.,* II, 383.

39. Richard T. Ely, *Problems of Today: A Discussion of Protective Tariffs, Taxation, and Monopolies* (New York, 1888), p. 144.

40. E. Benjamin Andrews, "Trusts according to Official Investigations," *Quarterly Journal of Economics,* III (January, 1889), 146.

41. *Boston Herald,* January 9, 1889, cited in *Oil City Derrick,* January 17, 1889.

42. New York *World,* March 29, 1890.

43. *Ibid.*

44. Samuel C. T. Dodd, "Ten Years of the Standard Oil Trust," *Forum,* XIII (May, 1892), 301.

45. Roger Sherman, "The Standard Oil Trust: The Gospel of Greed," *ibid.* (July, 1892), 611–613.

46. *Nation,* LIX (November 8, 1894), 348.

47. Lloyd, *Wealth against Commonwealth,* p. 116.

48. *Ibid.,* p. 127.

49. *Ibid.,* p. 126. Actually the Columbia Conduit was purchased by Standard Oil in 1877; Cassatt made his famous statement to independent refiners in 1878. Transportation rates did not go up. Instead Standard Oil collected drawbacks on all crude oil shipped via the trunk lines. See above, pp. 66–67.

50. *Ibid.,* p. 463.

51. *Ibid.,* p. 117. The Conduit, of course, was the first trunk pipeline, though it was a short one compared to the Tide-Water.

52. *Nation,* LIX (November 8, 1894), 348.

53. Quoted in Alvred B. Nettleton (ed.), *Trusts or Competition?* (Chicago, 1900), p. 202.

54. Louis Filler, *Crusaders for American Liberalism* (Yellow Springs, Ohio, 1950), p. 26.

55. John M. Bonham, *Railway Secrecy and Trusts* (New York, 1890), pp. 22–23.

56. *Ibid.,* p. 126.

57. *Petroleum Age,* VI (April, 1887), 1593.

58. *Derrick's Hand-Book,* I, 499; Nevins, *Rockefeller,* II, 307.

59. For a detailed account of the venture in Lima oil, see Hidy and Hidy, *Pioneering,* ch. vi.

60. Archbold testimony, *Industrial Commission Report,* I, 561.

61. Nevins, *Study in Power,* II, 105; Hidy and Hidy, *Pioneering,* pp. 166–167.

62. Nevins, *Rockefeller,* II, 308–309.

63. Quoted in *Oil City Derrick,* January 23, 1891.

64. *Penna. Leg. Rec., 1891,* I, 539–540.

65. *Ibid.,* pp. 554–556.

66. *Ibid.,* pp. 565–566.

67. Hidy and Hidy, *Pioneering,* pp. 22, 33, 87–89.

68. See *ibid.,* ch. xxi. Representatives of National Transit told the House Committee considering the Burdick bill that pipeline profits were 10 per cent. Burdick pointed out that bookkeeping transactions could make the lines show a profit or a loss. Balance sheets and profit and loss

statements of Standard Oil pipelines for 1899–1906 can be found in petitioners' exhibits, *The United States of America, petitioner v. The Standard
Oil Company of New Jersey et al., defendants* [*Record*] (23 vols.; Washington, 1908–1910), VII, VIII, *passim.*

69. This was the first time that representatives of Standard Oil had
been invited to give their views on a pipeline bill before it was reported
to the House.

70. *Penna. Leg. Rec., 1891,* I, 568–569.

71. *Ibid.,* p. 570.

72. *Ibid.,* p. 571.

73. *Ibid.,* p. 573.

74. *Ibid.,* pp. 574–575.

75. *Ibid.*

76. Quoted in *Oil City Derrick,* February 20, 1891.

77. *Ibid.*

78. Nevins, *Rockefeller,* II, 304–305.

79. Philadelphia *Press,* February 26, 1891.

80. Quoted in *Oil City Derrick,* February 19, 1891.

81. *Ibid.,* February 20, 1891.

82. Quoted, *ibid.,* February 28, 1891.

Chapter VIII. *Pipeline Enterprise and Intra-industry Controversy*

1. James W. Lee testimony, *Industrial Commission Report,* I, 270.

2. M. L. Lockwood testimony, *ibid.,* p. 397.

3. See above, pp. 144–145.

4. Tarbell, *Standard Oil Co.,* II, 167.

5. Patrick Boyle testimony, *Industrial Commission Report,* I, 413.

6. Emery testimony, *ibid.,* p. 650.

7. *Ibid.,* pp. 651–653.

8. *Ibid.*

9. *Ibid.*

10. Tarbell, *Standard Oil Co.,* II, 170.

11. See William L. Mellon, *Judge Mellon's Sons* ([Pittsburgh ?], 1948),
pp. 154–182.

12. *Derrick's Hand-Book,* I, 855.

13. The division of opinion between the adherents of public policy
and private enterprise among Standard Oil's opponents was apparent in
this instance. The Producers' Protective Association opposed repeal of the
1883 law while members of the United States Pipe Line favored such a
step (*Penna. Leg. Rec., 1893,* II, 1548, 2728).

14. Hidy and Hidy, *Pioneering,* p. 281.

15. Lee testimony, *Industrial Commission Report*, I, 293.

16. Pennsylvania General Assembly, *House Journal, 1895*, pp. 1011–1013.

17. Lee testimony, *Industrial Commission Report*, I, 270.

18. Tarbell, *Standard Oil Co.*, II, 178.

19. *Derrick's Hand-Book*, I, 575.

20. Nevins, *Rockefeller*, II, 320.

21. Westgate testimony, *Industrial Commission Report*, I, 370.

22. New York *World*, May 24, 1894. Although many factors entered into the determination of the price of oil, Nevins points out that Standard Oil's position as manufacturer of more than 82 per cent of petroleum products in the United States "did permit price-fixing for considerable periods, and the charge of manipulation seems justified" (*Rockefeller*, II, 318).

23. Hidy and Hidy, *Pioneering*, pp. 279–281.

24. Quoted in *Pure Oil Trust vs. Standard Oil Company, Being the Report of an Investigation by the United States Industrial Commission Compiled from Private and Official Sources by the Oil City Derrick* (Oil City, Pa., 1901), p. 52.

25. Quoted, *ibid.*, p. 54.

26. Archbold testimony, *Industrial Commission Report*, I, 577.

27. Lee testimony, *ibid.*, p. 267.

28. *New York Tribune*, October 29, 1895.

29. Emery testimony, *Industrial Commission Report*, I, 654.

30. *Ibid.*, pp. 654–655.

31. *New York Tribune*, October 30, 1895.

32. Tarbell, *Standard Oil Co.*, II, 183, 186.

33. *Ibid.*, p. 187.

34. *Ibid.*, p. 179.

35. Carter's testimony in *John J. Carter v. The Producers' Company, Limited*, cited, *ibid.*, pp. 179–180. Archbold told the Industrial Commission that "we generally work in harmony with him [Carter]" (*Industrial Commission Report*, I, 577).

36. Hidy and Hidy, *Pioneering*, pp. 281–282.

37. Tarbell, *Standard Oil Co.*, II, 180–181.

38. Lee testimony, *Industrial Commission Report*, I, 261.

39. Emery testimony, *ibid.*, pp. 656–657.

40. Tarbell, *Standard Oil Co.*, II, 187.

41. See Hidy and Hidy, *Pioneering*, p. 227.

42. Nevins, *Study in Power*, II, 237–238.

43. *In the Supreme Court of Ohio. [Record,] The State of Ohio Ex. Rel. F. S. Monnett, Attorney-General, Plaintiff, vs. The Buckeye Pipe Line Company, Defendant* . . . (Columbus, Ohio, 1899), p. 26; Monnett testimony, *Industrial Commission Report*, I, 298.

44. Deposition of Henry Roeser, [*Record,*] *The State of Ohio* . . . *vs. The Buckeye Pipe Line Company* . . . , p. 264.

45. Deposition of Daniel O'Day, *ibid.*, pp. 167–168.

46. New York *World*, March 21, 1899.

47. *Ibid.*, March 18, 1899.

48. Deposition of Malcolm Jennings, [*Record,*] *The State of Ohio* . . . *vs. The Buckeye Pipe Line Company* . . . , pp. 312–322.

49. *Cong. Rec.*, 53rd Cong., 2 sess. (July 18, 1894), p. 7663.

50. Lee testimony, *Industrial Commission Report*, I, 293.

51. *Ibid.*, p. 296.

52. Monnett testimony, *ibid.*, p. 299.

53. *Ibid.*, p. 310.

54. *Ibid.*, pp. 310–311.

55. Boyle testimony, *ibid.*, p. 404.

56. *Ibid.*, pp. 471–474.

57. *Ibid.* While Boyle's comment had a solid foundation in fact, it was subject to qualification. The assertion that no pipeline had made money before 1877 was untrue. The Columbia Conduit during ten months of 1876, prior to its acquisition by Standard Oil, realized net profits of $110,570.42 (*Columbia Conduit* v. *Commonwealth*, 90 Pa. St. 307 [1879], p. 310).

58. Boyle testimony, *Industrial Commission Report*, I, 486.

59. *Ibid.*, p. 489.

60. *Ibid.*, p. 490.

61. *Ibid.*

62. Archbold testimony, *ibid.*, p. 507.

63. *Ibid.*, p. 513.

64. *Ibid.*, p. 529.

65. *Ibid.*, pp. 526–529.

66. *Ibid.*, pp. 530–531.

67. *Ibid.*, p. 559.

68. *Ibid.*, p. 569.

69. Rogers testimony, *ibid.*, pp. 583, 588.

70. *Ibid.*, p. 582.

71. *Ibid.*, p. 581. Rogers declared that the fact the 20 cents gathering charge had not been lowered for two decades was due to the policy of connecting to wells without extra charges and transporting oil at the same rate regardless of distance. According to James W. Lee, however, the Producers' Pipe Line charged 15 cents for this service (*ibid.*, p. 271).

72. Rogers testimony, *ibid.*, p. 588.

73. Phillips testimony, *ibid.*, p. 591.

74. *Ibid.*, p. 593.

75. *Ibid.*

76. *Ibid.*, p. 599.

77. *Ibid.,* p. 594. Phillips did not state the basis for these calculations. Presumably they referred only to "operating costs" and did not include a return on the investment.

78. *Ibid.,* pp. 598, 601.

79. Lewis Emery, Jr., testimony, *ibid.,* p. 603.

80. *Ibid.,* p. 605.

81. *Ibid.,* p. 609.

82. *Ibid.,* p. 610.

83. *Ibid.,* p. 615.

84. *Ibid.,* pp. 616–618.

85. *Ibid.,* p. 633.

86. *Ibid.,* pp. 635–636.

87. *Ibid.,* pp. 653–654, 659–660.

88. *Ibid.,* p. 662.

89. *Ibid.,* p. 667.

90. Howard Page testimony, *ibid.,* p. 763.

91. Emery testimony, *ibid.,* p. 671.

92. Rice testimony, *ibid.,* p. 754.

93. *Ibid.*

94. Page testimony, *ibid.,* p. 786. In a letter, December 11, 1899, Archbold thanked Penrose for his "effort with the Industrial Commission with reference to Mr. Page's appearance." Archbold told Penrose that Rice was "so erratic and ridiculous as to defeat himself with anybody who would give his testimony careful consideration, but I think, aside from its unfairness to us, there is a possible political point in having it answered."

95. John D. Rockefeller, answer to interrogatories, *Industrial Commission Report,* I, 795.

96. *Ibid.,* p. 796.

97. *Ibid.,* p. 797.

98. *Ibid.*

99. Archbold to Penrose, January 5, 1900, quoted in "Campaign Contributions," *Testimony before a Subcommittee of the Committee on Privileges and Elections, United States Senate, Sixty-Second Congress, Second Session, pursuant to S. Res. 79* . . . (2 vols.; Washington, 1912–1913), I, 151. This document hereafter is cited as *Clapp Investigation.*

100. Rogers testimony, *Industrial Commission Report,* I, 585.

101. See Hidy and Hidy, *Pioneering,* pp. 310–311.

102. Rogers testimony, *Industrial Commission Report,* I, 586.

103. Archbold to Penrose, February 21, 1900, quoted in *Clapp Investigation,* I, 151.

104. Archbold to Penrose, July 3, 1901, quoted, *ibid.,* p. 152.

105. Archbold to Quay, July 3, 1901, quoted, *ibid.,* p. 153.

106. *Pure Oil Trust vs. Standard Oil Company,* p. 501.

107. *Ibid.,* p. 575.

108. *Ibid.*, p. 558.
109. *Ibid.*, p. 560.

Chapter IX. *Politics, Pipelines, and the Mounting Attack on Standard Oil*

1. Quoted in Nevins, *Rockefeller*, II, 516.
2. Roosevelt testimony, *Clapp Investigation*, I, 187.
3. *Ibid.*, p. 119.
4. *Ibid.*, p. 123.
5. *Ibid.*, p. 131. Archbold felt that the administration's subsequent attack on Standard Oil could be traced to this occurrence (*ibid.*, p. 134).
6. See Elting E. Morison (ed.), *The Letters of Theodore Roosevelt* (8 vols.; Cambridge, Mass., 1951–1954), IV, 883–884.
7. New York *World*, October 26, 1904.
8. Roosevelt to Cortelyou, October 27, 1904, in *Clapp Investigation*, I, 178.
9. *Ibid.*, p. 133.
10. *Ibid.*
11. Roosevelt testimony, *ibid.*, pp. 192–193.
12. Tarbell, *All in Day's Work*, p. 242.
13. *Ibid.*, p. 206.
14. *Ibid.*, p. 214.
15. See Hidy and Hidy, *Pioneering*, pp. 662–663.
16. Tarbell, *Standard Oil Co.*, II, 276–277.
17. *Ibid.*, p. 292.
18. *Nation*, LXXX (January 5, 1905), 15–16.
19. Filler, *Crusaders for American Liberalism*, p. 105; Hidy and Hidy, *Pioneering*, p. 663.
20. Montague, *Rise Standard Oil Co.*, pp. 63–65.
21. *Ibid.*
22. *Ibid.*, pp. 49–50.
23. *Ibid.*, p. 143.
24. *Ibid.*
25. Hidy and Hidy, *Pioneering*, p. 663.
26. *Ibid.*, p. 467; United States Bureau of Corporations, *Report of the Commissioner of Corporations on the Petroleum Industry* (3 vols.; Washington, 1907–1909), I, 140–142. Cited hereafter as Bureau of Corporations, *Report on Petroleum Industry*.
27. Bureau of Corporations, *Report on Petroleum Industry*, I, 143–145.
28. The Bureau of Corporations included in its figures for Standard Oil the runs of lines in which the combination held any interest. On this basis,

Standard Oil's pipeline runs only decreased from 94.8 per cent of total runs in the Appalachian field in 1900 to 91.5 per cent in 1905.

29. *Ibid.*, p. 133.

30. *Ibid.*, pp. 194–195.

31. *Ibid.*, p. 168. See also Hidy and Hidy, *Pioneering*, p. 404.

32. Bureau of Corporations, *Report on Petroleum Industry*, I, 167.

33. A full description of the steps taken by Standard Oil management to protect its share of declining Appalachian production is in Hidy and Hidy, *Pioneering*, pp. 373–383.

34. Bureau of Corporations, *Report on Petroleum Industry*, I, 168.

35. See *ibid.*, p. 99.

36. Hidy and Hidy, *Pioneering*, p. 394.

37. Crum, *Romance Amer. Petroleum*, p. 53.

38. Hidy and Hidy, *Pioneering*, p. 394.

39. *Ibid.*, p. 397.

40. Philip Eastman, "The Kansas State Refinery Bill and Its Significance," *Arena*, XXXIII (May, 1905), 503.

41. See Hidy and Hidy, *Pioneering*, p. 397; also Isaac F. Marcosson, "The Kansas Oil Fight," *World's Work*, X (May, 1905), 6160.

42. F. S. Barde, "The Oil Fields and Pipe Lines of Kansas," *Outlook*, LXXX (May 6, 1905), 23.

43. Eastman, *loc. cit.*, p. 500.

44. Quoted by Ida M. Tarbell, "Kansas and the Standard Oil Company," II, *McClure's Magazine*, XXV (October, 1905), 614.

45. William E. Connelley claimed credit for these bills. See his "The Kansas Oil Producers against the Standard Oil Company," Kansas State Historical Society, *Transactions, 1905–1906*, IX (Topeka, 1906), 94–101.

46. *Atchison Daily Globe*, February 7, 1905.

47. *Ibid.*, February 8, 1905.

48. Tarbell, "Kansas and the Standard Oil Company," II, *loc. cit.*, p. 617; Eastman, *loc. cit.*, p. 502.

49. Barde, *loc. cit.*, p. 25.

50. Quoted in *Literary Digest*, XXX (February 25, 1905), 272. The Kansas refinery law was declared unconstitutional on July 7, 1905. See *State* v. *Kelly*, 71 Kans. 811 (1905).

51. *Independent*, LVIII (March 2, 1905), 453.

52. *Cong. Rec.*, 58th Cong., 3 sess. (February 15, 1905), 2666.

53. *Independent*, LVIII (March 2, 1905), 453.

54. Quoted by Joseph B. Bishop, *Theodore Roosevelt and His Time Shown in His Own Letters* (2 vols.; New York, 1920), I, 428.

55. *Cong. Rec.*, 59th Cong., 1 sess. (December 5, 1905), p. 92.

56. See John M. Blum, "Theodore Roosevelt and the Hepburn Act: Toward an Orderly System of Control," in Morison (ed.), *Letters T. Roosevelt*, VI, 1558–1571.

Chapter X. The Pipeline Amendment to the Hepburn Act

1. Roosevelt to Knapp, March 19, 1906; Knapp to Roosevelt, March 22, 1906; Roosevelt to Knapp, April 21, 1906 (Roosevelt MSS, Library of Congress).

2. *New York Tribune,* May 4, 5, 1906.

3. *Report of the Commissioner of Corporations on the Transportation of Petroleum May 2, 1906* (Washington, 1906), p. xx.

4. *Ibid.,* p. 90.

5. *Ibid.,* p. 60.

6. *Cong. Rec.,* 59th Cong., 1 sess. (May 4, 1906), p. 6358.

7. *Ibid.,* p. 6361.

8. *Ibid.,* pp. 6365–6366.

9. *Ibid.,* p. 6368.

10. See above, pp. 209–210.

11. *Cong. Rec.,* 59th Cong., 1 sess. (May 4, 1906), p. 6366.

12. *Report of the Commissioner of Corporations on the Transportation of Petroleum May 2, 1906,* p. 23. This question was discussed in some detail by Howard Page during his appearance before the Industrial Commission. See *Industrial Commission Report,* I, 770–777.

13. *Cong. Rec.,* 59th Cong., 1 sess. (May 4, 1906), pp. 6368–6369.

14. *Ibid.,* p. 6373.

15. *New York Tribune,* May 5, 1906.

16. New York *Sun,* May 5, 1906.

17. *Pittsburgh Daily Dispatch,* May 5, 1906.

18. *Boston Evening Transcript,* May 5, 1906.

19. Washington *Evening Star,* May 4, 1906.

20. New York *World,* May 5, 1906.

21. Philadelphia *Press,* May 8, 1906.

22. The statement is in the *New York Tribune,* May 5, 1906. A dispatch published by the Philadelphia *Press,* May 13, 1906, said that Standard Oil had a copy of Roosevelt's message of May 4 at least a day in advance.

23. *Pittsburgh Daily Dispatch,* May 7, 1906.

24. Quoted in the *New York Tribune,* May 5, 1906.

25. Philadelphia *Press,* May 11, 1906.

26. *New York Tribune,* May 12, 1906.

27. *Railroad Gazette,* XL (May 11, 1906), 480.

28. The statement is given in full in *ibid.* (May 25, 1906), pp. 528–530.

29. Philadelphia *Press,* May 10, 1906.

30. On May 17 Senator Stone proposed excluding pipelines from the operation of the commodities clause, but he found little support for the

step and withdrew his proposed amendment (*Cong. Rec.,* 59th Cong., 1 sess. [May 17, 1906], p. 7016).

31. Lodge to Roosevelt, May 29, 1906, Roosevelt MSS, Library of Congress.

32. Roosevelt to Hepburn, May 29, 1906, *ibid.*

33. *Clapp Investigation,* II, 1575.

34. *Pittsburgh Daily Dispatch,* June 23, 1906.

35. *Ibid.*

36. *Ibid.*

37. Lodge to Roosevelt, June 22, 1906. Roosevelt MSS, Library of Congress.

38. New York *Sun,* June 28, 1906.

39. Philadelphia *Press,* June 27, 1906.

40. *Cong. Rec.,* 59th Cong., 1 sess. (June 25, 1906), p. 9103.

41. *Ibid.,* p. 9105.

42. *Ibid.,* pp. 9108–9109.

43. *Ibid.* (June 26, 1906), pp. 9250–9252.

44. *Ibid.,* pp. 9252–9253.

45. *Ibid.,* p. 9254.

46. *Ibid.,* pp. 9256, 9257.

47. *Ibid.,* p. 9337.

48. *Ibid.* (June 28, 1906), p. 9584.

49. *Ibid.* (June 29, 1906), p. 9641.

50. *Ibid.*

51. *Ibid.,* p. 9644.

52. *Ibid.,* pp. 9645–9646.

53. *Ibid.,* p. 9647.

54. *Ibid.,* p. 9650.

55. 34 U.S. Stat. at L. 584.

56. *New York Tribune,* June 30, 1906.

57. *Cong. Rec.,* 59th Cong., 1 sess. (May 17, 1906), p. 7000.

58. *Railroad Discriminations and Monopolies in Coal and Oil,* 59th Cong., 2 sess., House Doc. 606 (Washington, 1907), p. 5.

59. *Ibid.,* p. 14.

60. See *Report of the Commissioner of Corporations on the Petroleum Industry* (3 vols.; Washington, 1907–1909).

61. *In the Matter of Pipe Lines,* 24 I.C.C. Rep. 1 (1912), p. 10.

62. *Ibid.,* p. 6.

63. Lodge said that one of the counsel of Standard Oil had informed him that Standard Oil pipelines east of the Mississippi were common carriers (*Cong. Rec.,* 59th Cong., 1 sess. [May 4, 1906], p. 6365; see also, above, pp. 124–125, 154–155).

64. *Prairie Oil & Gas Co.* v. *United States,* 204 Fed. Reporter 798 (1913), p. 820.

65. The Pennsylvania decisions were: *National Transit Company* v. *Weston et al.,* 121 Pa. 485 (1888); *Boyle* v. *Smithman,* 146 Pa. St. 255 (1892); *Giffin* v. *South West Pennsylvania Pipe Lines,* 172 Pa. 580 (1895). By 1913 sixteen states had pipeline legislation conferring eminent domain or common carrier status or both. These laws are quoted in the appendix of *The Pipe Line Cases, Brief for the United States, in the Supreme Court of the United States, October Term, 1913* (Washington, 1913).

66. *Prairie Oil & Gas Co.* v. *United States, loc. cit.,* pp. 803, 821.

67. *Ibid.,* p. 819.

68. *In the Matter of Pipe Lines, loc. cit.*

69. *Prairie Oil & Gas Co.* v. *United States, loc. cit.,* pp. 803–804.

70. *Ibid.,* p. 812.

71. *Ibid.,* p. 808.

72. *Ibid.,* p. 815.

73. *Ibid.,* p. 819.

74. *Ibid.,* p. 825.

75. *The Pipe Line Cases,* 234 U.S. 548 (1914), p. 554.

76. *Ibid.,* p. 550.

77. *Ibid.,* p. 552.

78. *Ibid.,* pp. 552–553.

79. *Ibid.,* p. 548.

80. *Ibid.,* p. 560.

81. *Ibid.,* pp. 562–563.

82. *Ibid.,* pp. 571–573.

83. Federal Trade Commission, *Report on Pipe-Line Transportation of Petroleum* (Washington, 1916), pp. 4, 441.

84. I. L. Sharfman, *The Interstate Commerce Commission: A Study in Administrative Law and Procedure* (5 vols.; New York, 1931–1937), II, 98.

85. *Reduced Pipe Line Charges and Gathering Rates,* 243 I.C.C. Rep. 115 (1940), pp. 138–139.

Bibliography

MANUSCRIPTS

Library of Congress

Theodore Roosevelt Papers, Division of Manuscripts, Library of Congress. The following papers proved useful: correspondence with Henry Cabot Lodge, 1901–1906; personal letter books, December 5, 1905–August 10, 1906; materials relating to the Interstate Commerce Commission, 1904–1906.

PUBLIC DOCUMENTS

United States

Bureau of Corporations. *Report of the Commissioner of Corporations on the Petroleum Industry.* 3 vols. Washington, 1907–1909.

——. *Report of the Commissioner of Corporations on the Transportation of Petroleum May 2, 1906.* Washington, 1906.

Congress. *Congressional Record,* 44th Cong., 1 sess.–59th Cong. 1 sess. Washington, 1876–1906.

——. House of Representatives, Committee on Interstate and Foreign Commerce. *Railroad Discriminations and Monopolies in Coal and Oil.* 59th Cong., 2 sess., House Doc. 606. Washington, 1907.

——. House of Representatives, Committee on Manufactures. *Report on*

Investigation of Trusts. 50th Cong., 1 sess., House Report No. 3112. Washington, 1888.

——. Miscellaneous Documents. Peckham, Samuel F. *Production, Technology, and Uses of Petroleum and Its Products.* 47th Cong., 2 sess., Misc. Doc. 42, pt. 10. Washington, 1884.

——. Senate, Committee on Privileges and Elections. *Testimony before a Subcommittee of the Committee on Privileges and Elections, United States Senate, Sixty-Second Congress, Second Session, Pursuant to S. Res. 79. . . .* 2 vols. Washington, 1912–1913.

Federal Trade Commission. *Report on Pipe-Line Transportation of Petroleum.* Washington, 1916.

Industrial Commission. *Reports of the Industrial Commission. . . .* 19 vols. Washington, 1900–1902.

States

NEW YORK

Assembly. *Proceedings of the Special Committee on Railroads, Appointed Under a Resolution of the Assembly to Investigate Alleged Abuses in the Management of Railroads Chartered by the State of New York.* 8 vols. New York, 1879–1880.

Senate. *Report of the Committee on General Laws on the Investigation Relative to Trusts.* Albany, 1888.

OHIO

General Assembly. *General and Local Laws and Joint Resolutions, Passed by the Sixtieth General Assembly. . . .* Columbus, 1872.

Senate. Trust Investigation Committee. *Trust Investigation of Ohio Senate. . . .* Columbus [?], Ohio, 1898. Record of proceedings before a committee appointed by the President of the Ohio Senate.

PENNSYLVANIA

Bureau of Statistics of Labor and Agriculture. *First Annual Report of the Bureau of Statistics of Labor and Agriculture for the Years 1872–1873.* Harrisburg, 1874.

General Assembly. *Journal of the House of Representatives of the Commonwealth of Pennsylvania . . . 1878–1895.* Harrisburg, 1878–1895.

——. *Journal of the Senate of the Commonwealth of Pennsylvania . . . 1878–1895.* Harrisburg, 1878–1895.

——. *Laws of the General Assembly of the State of Pennsylvania . . . 1862–1883.* Harrisburg, 1862–1883.

——. *The Legislative Journal, Containing the Debates and Proceedings of the Pennsylvania Legislature . . . 1872–1874.* Harrisburg, 1872–1874.

——. *The Legislative Record . . . with Index, 1875–1893.* Harrisburg, 1875–1893.

Secretary of Internal Affairs. *Annual Report of the Secretary of Internal Affairs . . . 1874/1875–1878/1879.* Part III, "Industrial Statistics." 3 vols. Harrisburg, 1875–1880.

Secretary of the Commonwealth. "Papers of the Governors," *Pennsylvania Archives Fourth Series.* Ed. by George E. Reed. 12 vols. Harrisburg, 1900–1902.

WEST VIRGINIA

Acts of the Legislature of West Virginia at Its Fourteenth Session. Wheeling, 1879.

Court and Interstate Commerce Commission Cases

Boyle v. Smithman, 146 Pa. St. 255 (1892).
Columbia Conduit Co. v. Commonwealth, 90 Pa. St. 307 (1879).
Giffin v. South West Pennsylvania Pipe Lines, 172 Pa. 580 (1895).
Independent Producers' Association of Titusville and Oil City v. The Western New York and Pennsylvania Railroad Company et al., 5 I.C.C. Rep. 415 (1892).
In the Matter of Pipe Lines, 24 I.C.C. Rep. 1 (1912).
In the Supreme Court of Ohio. [Record.] The State of Ohio Ex. Rel. F. S. Monnett, Attorney General, Plaintiff, vs. The Buckeye Pipe Line Company, Defendant. . . . Columbus, 1899.
Munn v. Illinois, 94 U.S. 113 (1876).
National Transit Co. v. Weston et al., 121 Pa. 485 (1888).
Prairie Oil & Gas Co. v. United States, 204 Fed. Rep. 798 (1913).
Railroad Commission Cases, 116 U.S. 307 (1886).
Reduced Pipe Line Charges and Gathering Rates, 243 I.C.C. Rep. 115 (1940).
Rice v. Louisville & Nashville Railroad Co., 1 I.C.C. Rep. 503 (1888).
Rice, Robinson and Witherop v. The Western New York and Pennsylvania Railroad Company, IV I.C.C. Rep. 131 (1890).
The Pipe Line Cases, Brief for the United States in the Supreme Court of the United States, October Term, 1913. Washington, 1913.
The Pipe Line Cases, 234 U.S. 548 (1914).
The United States of America, petitioner, v. The Standard Oil Company

of New Jersey, et al., defendants. [*Record.*] 23 vols. Washington, 1908–1910.

Wabash, St. Louis and Pacific Railway Co. v. Illinois, 118 U.S. 557 (1886).

BOOKS AND PAMPHLETS

Bishop, Joseph B. *Theodore Roosevelt and His Time Shown in His Own Letters.* 2 vols. New York, 1920.

Blanchard, George R. *Politico-Railway Problems and Theorists.* New York, 1880.

Bonham, John M. *Railway Secrecy and Trusts.* New York, 1890.

Cochran, Thomas C. *Railroad Leaders, 1845–1890: The Business Mind in Action.* Cambridge, 1953.

Cone, Andrew, and Johns, Walter R. *Petrolia: A Brief History of the Pennsylvania Petroleum Region, Its Development, Growth, Resources, etc., from 1859 to 1869.* New York, 1870.

Crum, A. R., and Dungan, A. S. (eds.). *Romance of American Petroleum and Gas.* New York, 1911.

The Derrick's Hand-Book of Petroleum: A Complete Chronological and Statistical Review of Petroleum Developments from 1859 to 1899 [*1898*]. 2 vols. Oil City, 1898–1900.

Dodd, Samuel C. T. *Combinations: Their Uses and Abuses; with a History of the Standard Oil Trust. An Argument relative to bills pending before the New York Legislature, based upon testimony given before the Senate Committee on General Laws.* New York, 1888.

Ely, Richard T. *Problems of Today: A Discussion of Protective Tariffs, Taxation, and Monopolies.* New York, 1888.

Filler, Louis. *Crusaders for American Liberalism.* [New ed.] Yellow Springs, Ohio, 1950.

Giddens, Paul H. *The Birth of the Oil Industry.* New York, 1938.

Graber, Paul J. (ed). *Common Carrier Pipe Line Operations and Accounting.* Tulsa, 1951.

Hadley, Arthur T. *Railroad Transportation: Its History and Its Laws.* New York and London, 1886.

Haney, Lewis H. *A Congressional History of Railways in the United States.* 2 vols. Madison, 1908–1910.

Henry, J. T. *The Early and Later History of Petroleum with Authentic Facts in Regard to Its Development in Western Pennsylvania.* Philadelphia, 1873.

Hidy, Ralph W. and Muriel E. *Pioneering in Big Business, 1882–1911.* New York, 1955.

Hudson, James F. *The Railways and the Republic.* New York, 1886.

Jenks, Jeremiah W., and Clark, Walter E. *The Trust Problem.* New York, 1929.

Johnson, Allen, Malone, Dumas, and Starr, Harris E. (eds.). *Dictionary of American Biography.* 21 vols. New York, 1930–1944.

Lloyd, Henry D. *Wealth against Commonwealth.* New York, 1894.

McClure, A. K. *Old Time Notes of Pennsylvania.* 2 vols. Philadelphia, 1905.

McLaurin, John J. *Sketches in Crude-Oil.* Harrisburg, 1896.

Maybee, Rolland H. *Railroad Competition and the Oil Trade, 1855–1873.* New York, 1940.

Mellon, William L. *Judge Mellon's Sons.* [Pittsburgh ?], 1948.

Millern, Alexander von. *All about Petroleum and the Great Oil Districts of Pennsylvania, West Virginia, Ohio, etc.* New York, 1864.

Montague, Gilbert H. *The Rise and Progress of the Standard Oil Company.* New York and London, 1903.

Moore, Austin L. *John D. Archbold and the Early Development of Standard Oil.* New York, [193?].

Morison, Elting E. (ed). *The Letters of Theodore Roosevelt.* 8 vols. Cambridge, 1951–1954.

Morris, Edmund. *Derrick and Drill.* New York, 1865.

Nettleton, Alvred B. (ed). *Trusts or Competition?* Chicago, 1900.

Nevins, Allan. *John D. Rockefeller: The Heroic Age of American Enterprise.* 2 vols. New York, 1940.

——. *Study in Power: John D. Rockefeller, Industrialist and Philanthropist.* 2 vols. New York and London, 1953.

Peto, Sir Samuel M. *The Resources and Prospects of America Ascertained during a Visit to the States in the Autumn of 1865.* London and New York, 1866.

Pure Oil Trust vs. Standard Oil Company, Being the Report of an Investigation by the United States Industrial Commission, Compiled from Private and Official Sources by the Oil City Derrick. Oil City, 1901.

Ripley, Willam Z. *Railroads: Rates and Regulation.* New York, 1912.

Schlegel, Marvin W. *Ruler of the Reading: The Life of Franklin B. Gowen, 1836–1889.* Harrisburg, 1947.

Sharfman I. L. *The Interstate Commerce Commission: A Study in Administrative Law and Procedure.* 5 vols. New York, 1931–1937.

Smiley, Alfred W. *A Few Scraps, Oily and Otherwise.* Oil City, Penna., 1907.

Summers, Festus P. *Johnson Newlon Camden: A Study in Individualism.* New York and London, 1937.

Tarbell, Ida M. *All in the Day's Work.* New York, 1939.

——. *The History of the Standard Oil Company.* 2 vols. New York, 1904.

PERIODICALS

Articles

Andrews, E. Benjamin. "Trusts according to Official Investigations," *Quarterly Journal of Economics,* III (January, 1889), 117–152.

Barde, F. S. "The Oil Fields and Pipe Lines of Kansas," *Outlook,* LXXX (May 6, 1905), 19–32.

Camden, Johnson N. "The Standard Oil Company," *North American Review,* CXXXVI (February, 1883), 181–190.

Connelley, William E. "The Kansas Oil Producers against the Standard Oil Company," Kansas State Historical Society, *Transactions 1905–1906,* IX (Topeka, 1906), 94–101.

Destler, Chester McA. "The Standard Oil, Child of the Erie Ring, 1868–1872," *Mississippi Valley Historical Review,* XXXIII (June, 1946), 89–114. For criticism of this article by Julius Grodinsky and the reply by Destler, see "A Variance of Views on the Standard Oil Company," *ibid.* (March, 1947), 617–628.

Dodd, Samuel C. T. "Ten Years of the Standard Oil Trust," *Forum,* XIII (May, 1892), 300–310.

Eastman, Philip. "The Kansas State Refinery Bill and Its Significance," *Arena,* XXXIII (May, 1905), 500–505.

Gunton, George. "The Economic and Social Aspect of Trusts," *Political Science Quarterly,* III (September, 1888), 385–408.

Lloyd, Henry D. "Story of a Great Monopoly," *Atlantic Monthly,* XLVII (March, 1881), 317–334.

Marcosson, Isaac F. "The Kansas Oil Fight," *World's Work,* X (May, 1905), 6155–6166.

Seely, Charles A. "A Week on Oil Creek," *Scientific American,* XV (September 1, 1866), 144.

Sherman, Roger. "The Standard Oil Trust: The Gospel of Greed," *Forum,* XIII (July, 1892), 602–615.

Tarbell, Ida M. "Kansas and the Standard Oil Company," *McClure's Magazine,* XXV (September–October, 1905), 469–481, 608–622.

Welch, John C. "The Standard Oil Company," *North American Review,* CXXXVI (February, 1883), 191–200.

Magazines

The Independent, LVIII (1905).
The Literary Digest, XXX (1905).
The Nation, LIX (1894), LXXX (1905).
Petroleum Age, III (1884); VI (1887).
Railroad Gazette, XI (1879); XL (1906).
Railway World (January, 1878–March, 1883).

Newspapers

Atchison (Kans.) *Daily Globe.* February, 1905.
Baltimore American. January, 1878.
Baltimore *Sun.* March, 1875.
Boston Evening Transcript. May–June, 1906.
Cleveland Leader. March–April, 1872; September, 1876.
Cleveland Plain-Dealer. March, 1887.
Oil City Derrick. January, 1889; October, 1890–February, 1891.
New York *Daily Graphic.* October, 1876.
New York Herald. January, 1884.
New York *Sun.* March, 1872; November, 1878; January–June, 1906.
New York Times. March, 1880.
New York Tribune. 1875–1906, broken file.
New York *World.* 1887–1906, broken file.
Philadelphia *Press.* March–June, 1883; April–August, 1887; February, 1891; May–June, 1906.
Philadelphia *Public Ledger.* November, 1924.
Philadelphia Record. August–October, 1877.
Pittsburgh Commercial. January, 1872; March–August, 1874.
Pittsburgh (*Daily*) *Dispatch.* 1874–1906, broken file.
Pittsburgh Gazette. May, 1874–June, 1875.
Titusville (Pa.) *Morning Herald.* July, 1865–April, 1866; March, 1872; February, 1887.
Washington *Evening Star.* May, 1906.
Wheeling Daily Intelligencer. January–March, 1879.

Index

Books published for The American Historical Association from the income of the Albert J. Beveridge Memorial Fund

ORIGINS OF INTER-AMERICAN INTEREST, 1700–1812
Harry Bernstein

THE TERRITORIES AND THE UNITED STATES
Earl S. Pomeroy

FIGHTING POLITICIAN: MAJOR GENERAL N. P. BANKS
Fred Harvey Harrington

THE SPANISH STRUGGLE FOR JUSTICE IN THE CONQUEST OF AMERICA
Lewis Hanke

JOHN WILLIAM DRAPER AND THE RELIGION OF SCIENCE
Donald Fleming

MEXICAN SILVER AND THE ENLIGHTENMENT
Clement G. Motten

THE AGRICULTURAL HISTORY OF THE GENESEE VALLEY
Neil A. McNall

STEAM POWER ON THE AMERICAN FARM
Reynold M. Wik

HORACE GREELEY: NINETEENTH-CENTURY CRUSADER
Glyndon G. Van Deusen

ERA OF THE OATH: NORTHERN LOYALTY TESTS DURING THE
CIVIL WAR AND RECONSTRUCTION
Harold M. Hyman

HISTORY OF MARSHALL FIELD & CO.
Robert W. Twyman

ROBERT MORRIS: REVOLUTIONARY FINANCIER
Clarence L. Ver Steeg

A HISTORY OF THE FREEDMEN'S BUREAU
George R. Bentley

THE FIRST RAPPROCHEMENT: ENGLAND AND THE
UNITED STATES, 1795–1805
Bradford Perkins

MIDDLE-CLASS DEMOCRACY AND THE REVOLUTION IN MASSACHUSETTS,
1691–1780
Robert E. Brown

THE DEVELOPMENT OF AMERICAN PETROLEUM PIPELINES:
A STUDY IN PRIVATE ENTERPRISE AND PUBLIC POLICY, 1862–1906
Arthur Menzies Johnson